Lawyers Practice & Procedure Series

Executorship & Administration Practice & Procedure

by Michael WA Ryan
Senior Probate Executive

Third edition

Tolley Publishing Company Limited

A United News & Media publication

ISBN 1 86012 049-0

Third edition published September 1995

Published by
Tolley Publishing Company Limited
Tolley House
2 Addiscombe Road
Croydon
Surrey
CR9 5AF
0181 686 9141

© Tolley Publishing Company Limited 1995

Typeset in Great Britain by
Action Typesetting Limited, Northgate Street, Gloucester

Printed and bound in Great Britain by
BPC Books & Journals Limited

Preface

The last edition of this book gave details of the then proposed changes for dealing in shares which were to be called TAURUS. Those proposed changes failed and CREST, which is being developed by the Bank of England will take its place. CREST is a rolling settlement. Other major international equity markets already operate such a system.

Formerly the UK market operated a two-week settlement which was proving to be detrimental to the stockmarket. At present, companies have to issue share certificates (Companies Act 1985) and they are unable to register sales and purchases (transfers) without the relevant certificate. Crest will allow for transfers to be actioned electronically, and holdings will be registered on a computer, without the requirement for a certificate to be issued. However, shareholders will still be able to have a share certificate issued to them if they wish.

The two-week settlement was reduced to a ten-day settlement in July 1994, and it is expected that this will be reduced to five days during 1995. Then CREST will be introduced, and the current 'Talisman' share transfer system will be incorporated in CREST. It is planned that eventually settlement will be three days after a transaction. Those shareholders who still deal in share certificates will have to deliver the certificates and signed transfer forms to the brokers promptly when selling shares. For share purchases, the brokers will have to hold 'cleared funds' to enable them to deal.

The last edition also mentioned the Courts and Legal Services Act 1990, and the proposals which will affect probate and the administration of estates. These details have been repeated in this edition.

Because of their importance, The Solicitors' Practice Rules 1990, rule 15 – client care, are also repeated in this edition.

A new chapter (11) dealing more fully with taxes (income tax, CGT, and IHT) has been added, but references to the various taxes throughout the book have been retained.

Law Reform (Succession) Bill

This Bill will give effect to some of the Law Commission's recommendations on Family Law – distribution on intestacy and the effect of divorce on wills.

Clause 1   Intestacy or partial intestacy – distribution of estates.

Subs 1   Introduces a survivorship provision between spouses on

Subs 2 | intestacy so that the spouse of the deceased will only benefit if he or she survives the deceased for 14 days.

Subs 2   Abolishes the 'hotchpot' rule.

Clause 2   Amends the provision for family and dependants and provides for a co-habitant to make application for provision from the estate.

The Solicitors' Practice Rules 1990, rule 15 – client care

This rule came into force on 1 May 1991, and provides:

(1) Every principal in private practice shall operate a complaints handling procedure which shall, *inter alia*, ensure that clients are informed whom to approach in the event of any problems with the service provided.

(2) Every solicitor in private practice shall, unless it is inappropriate to the circumstance:

(A) ensure that clients know the name and status of the person responsible for the day-to-day conduct of the matter and the principal responsible for its overall supervision;

(B) ensure that clients know whom to approach in the event of any problem with the service provided;

(C) ensure that clients are at all relevant times given any appropriate information as to the issues raised and the progress of the matter.

Courts and Legal Services Act 1990

[Please note that, at the time of writing, this Act was not yet in force.]

Insurance companies, banks and building societies are now able to apply for grants of representation. The Lord Chancellor may authorise other bodies to apply. The Act shows that the following may prepare papers for probate:

- a qualified solicitor;
- a barrister;
- a duly certificated Notary Public;
- the Public Trustee;
- the Official Solicitor.

Subject to the conditions set out below, the following institutions may also carry out probate business:

- banks duly authorised by the Bank of England under the Banking Act 1987;
- building societies which are duly authorised under s 9 Building Societies Act 1986;
- insurance companies duly authorised under s 3 or 4 Insurance Companies Act 1982;

- subsidiaries of authorised banks, building societies or insurance companies whose business (or part of whose business) consists of acting as executor or trustee.

The Conditions: banks, building societies, insurance companies or subsidiaries of any of them must be members of or otherwise subject to a scheme established for the purpose of dealing with complaints about the provision of probate services and must comply with such regulations as the Lord Chancellor may prescribe relating to complaints.

Supreme Court Act 1981, s 115 – grants to trust corporations

This section provides that it is an offence for any person applying for a grant to make a false or misleading statement in his application or to support the application with a document which he knows to be false or misleading; or to recklessly make a statement or support his application with a document which is false or misleading. Such a person is liable on conviction on indictment to imprisonment for a term not exceeding two years or to a fine, or to both; and on summary conviction, such a person is liable to imprisonment for a term not exceeding six months or to a fine not exceeding the statutory maximum, or to both.

The Act also mentions that oaths or affidavits required on applications for a grant of representation in any non-contentious or common form probate business can be administered by 'every justice' (i.e. justice of the peace). The justice administering the oath must state in the *jurat* or attestation the place and the date of the event. If any justice is interested in any proceedings, he cannot exercise the powers conferred by s 115. All documents puporting to be signed by a justice will be admitted in evidence: no proof is required of the signature or of the fact that he is a justice.

Commissioner for Oaths

Every solicitor holding a current practising certificate, general notaries, and members of the Incorporated Company of Scriveners who have been admitted to practise as public notaries within the jurisdiction of the company have the right to use the title 'Commissioner for Oaths'.

The Act also provides for 'authorised persons' (to be designated in the future) who will also be recognised as Commissioners for Oaths.

Contents

Chapter 1

Introduction

The purpose of this book is to guide practitioners step by step through the administration of estates of persons dying testate, intestate and partially intestate, from the time of receiving initial instructions from the client, to preparing final accounts, and distributing the net estate.

Chapter 2 explains the procedure for taking instructions, and lists the details to be obtained from clients, and the advice and warnings to be given to personal representatives, i.e. executors where the deceased left a will, and administrators where the deceased died intestate. It details the important steps to be taken to safeguard the deceased's assets.

Chapter 3 concentrates on wills, and suggests how a search can be made for missing documents; what the practitioner should look for when reading the will, and how to advise the executors.

Many complications may arise when dealing with wills and the executor's duties, and Chapter 4 seeks to call the practitioner's attention to the problems that may be encountered, and how they may be dealt with. Although intestacy can also bring its own problems, these are not usually so varied as in estates of persons dying testate, possibly because intestacy is not subject to the errors that can arise when preparing and later interpreting a will, particularly if of the 'home made' variety.

Chapter 5 deals with letters of administration (with the will) in cases where there is a will but for various reasons, for example where the will does not appoint executors, probate cannot be applied for. Chapter 6 deals with the letters of administration following death intestate. The order of priority of entitlement to apply for a grant is shown, and the requirements for the application are explained.

The assets and liabilities must be identified and their values obtained, and this information is then used to prepare the application for a grant of representation, whether it is a grant of probate applied for by the executors, or a grant of letters of administration to the administrators. Chapters 7 and 8 detail all the information to be collected together, and cover both real and personal property, taking into account the various taxes to which the estate may be subject.

Once the extent of the estate has been ascertained, the application for a grant of representation must be prepared. This involves drawing up the Oath for Executors or Oath for Administrators, and the Inland Revenue Account, if appropriate, for inheritance tax calculations.

1

Chapter 9 deals with these matters, and also covers small estates where an Inland Revenue Account is not required, and estates where a grant of representation may be dispensed with.

Throughout the book, references to inheritance tax should be taken as references to capital transfer tax if the death occurred before 18 March 1986, unless otherwise stated.

Clearly not all estates are liable to inheritance tax: either because the value of the estate is too small or the estate passes to certain classes of beneficiary, e.g. a spouse or a charity. Therefore not all estates require the completion of an Inland Revenue Account. In other cases one of a variety of different accounts may be required, even where no tax is due. These variations are explained in Chapter 10, and ways of raising immediate funds to pay the tax, while the assets of the estate are not available for this purpose are suggested.

Chapter 11 deals entirely with income tax, capital gains tax and inheritance tax.

Several types of special grant are mentioned in Chapter 12. Examples of applications for some of these are given in Appendix 5, but this book does not pretend to cover every variation.

Once the grant has been obtained, the calling in and conversion of the assets must be dealt with as expeditiously as possible. There are various considerations connected with the priority of claims and liabilities, and the timing of encashment, which are explained in Chapter 13.

In Chapter 14 there are details of some of the methods of modifying a person's entitlement under a will or intestacy, and some of the more usual ways of doing so are explained briefly.

Chapter 15 deals with the distribution of the estate once it is in the hands of the personal representatives. Particular problems such as missing beneficiaries are covered; and the preparation of the estate accounts is discussed.

Beneficiaries have remedies against the personal representatives if there has been any maladministration of the estate, and Chapter 16 deals with this, and with trustees.

This book deals mainly with non-contentious probate but Chapter 17 deals with caveats, warnings, service of and appearance to warnings. It has been included to guide practitioners through the first stages of contentious matters and does not deal comprehensively with contentious probate.

New chapters on enduring powers of attorney (18) and the Court of Protection (19) have been included in this edition. It is hoped that the information in these two chapters will be of assistance in those cases where the subject matter is relevant.

The Appendices contain a number of specimen forms; and a checklist for use when taking initial instructions, which can later be used to prepare the application for a grant, and then transformed into a working account for use when calling in the assets and settling the debts. The value of such a form is that, if used methodically, it provides immediate up-to-date information on the progress of the administration. Suggested standard probate letters are given in Appendix 2.

The Administration of Estates Act 1925 governs much of what is said in this book. Briefly, ss 1 to 3 of the Act deal with the devolution of the realty and chattels to the personal representatives. Sections 5 to 21 contain general provisions relating to:

(a) *executors* – the cessation of their right to prove a will, the withdrawing of a renunciation, change of representation, and the rights of executors who prove a will;

(b) *administrators* – the vesting of an intestate estate before a grant has been issued, and the rights and liabilities of an administrator.

Sections 22 to 24 are special provisions relating to settled land – special executors, their power to dispose of settled land, and the position where the trustees do not obtain representation.

The rights and obligations of the personal representatives are dealt with by ss 25 to 31, including their duty as to the inventory, actions by and against personal representatives, their protection, the power to make rules, and the situation where a nominee of the Crown takes a grant.

Administration of the assets is covered by ss 32 to 44, and ss 45 to 52 deal with the distribution of the residuary estate. Sections 53 to 58 are supplemental covering matters such as definitions and the application of the Act.

Chapter 2

Taking instructions

1. First instructions

Notification of a death is often received from a member of the deceased's family, either by telephone, in writing or by personal attendance. Unless that person has been involved in the administration of an estate on a previous occasion, he will need advice and guidance on the steps to be taken. At this stage it is important to ascertain if there is a will or other testamentary document. The full names, addresses, and if possible the telephone numbers of the executors should be noted, and the executors should be notified of the death, and advised to safeguard the deceased's assets. Where the deceased died intestate the full details of the proposed personal representatives should be noted, and they should be contacted as above.

Any will or a copy or the will should be read immediately it is available to ascertain whether it contains any specific requests concerning burial in a particular cemetery or in a numbered or family plot, or a request for cremation and any instructions regarding the disposal of the ashes. The deceased might have donated his body for medical research, or organs for transplant. In either case it is extremely important to notify the appropriate authority at once, since deterioration might defeat the purpose of the gift. Information is usually available from the local hospital, and funeral directors can be very helpful.

Upon death, the deceased's property vests in the executor(s) if there is a valid will appointing executors. If there is no will, the Law of Property (Miscellaneous Provisions) Act 1994 vests the estate of an intestate in the Public Trustee, instead of the President of the Family Division, as was the case previously, until such time as a grant of administration is issued. The Act also extends to estates where there is a will but no executor at the date of death or later. The practitioner's first task is to ensure the client has authority to deal with the estate; after that, the practitioner should begin the process of identifying the property of the deceased. In a short initial interview, it is usually sufficient to ask the client to collect together and bring in everything in the name of the deceased, and anything held in the joint names of the deceased and another. Any missing details can be sorted out later, and the schedule of assets and liabilities set out at page 233 can be utilised. It may be of help to the client if he is given a list or a questionnaire to assist him in identifying the deceased's assets and liabilities.

2. Personal representatives

If the person giving the initial instructions is not an executor named in the will, or the person entitled to apply for letters of administration on an intestacy (see page 42), the full names, addresses and descriptions of the proposed personal representative(s) must be obtained, and they should be contacted. The person giving the initial instructions should be warned against intermeddling (see page 26). An executor takes his appointment from the will, whereas a proposed personal representative of an intestate is not constituted as personal representative until the grant of letters of administration is issued. Instructions to deal in the estate should of course be accepted only from a person who has the legal authority to do so.

3. Initial interview

It is not usually absolutely necessary for the proposed personal representative to attend at the solicitor's office immediately, and in any event, this is not always possible. If the personal representative is the next of kin of the deceased, he may be fully occupied in making the funeral arrangements, contacting relatives etc., and may not be in a position to give precise instructions concerning the estate immediately. An appointment should be made for him to bring in details of the estate as soon as is convenient, possibly the day after the funeral. In most cases, the personal representatives wish to discuss matters as soon as possible, and they should therefore be given an appointment at the earliest possible date.

If the intended personal representative is a member of the deceased's family there may be a problem of shock and distress, which may make it difficult to assimilate the advice and information being given. It can therefore be helpful to give him a list of the details which are required, or to ask him to take notes during the interview. It is easy to lose sight of the fact that many clients may not have dealt with an estate before, and may be unused to attending a solicitor's office; they may be nervous, and this does not help their concentration. The notes taken by the client can be taken away, and the client can then collect together all the details of assets and liabilities needed to commence administering the deceased's estate, and deliver these back to the solicitor's office. The details mentioned in the remaining parts of this chapter should be obtained from the proposed personal representative.

(a) Testate or intestate?

Upon receipt of notification of a death, the office records should be checked; if there is a will it should be extracted immediately, and photocopies given or posted to each named executor. If the will is not immediately available, the client's full names, address, post code, and telephone number, if any, should be noted so that he can be contacted as soon as a search for a will (see page 11) has been made. Instructions may be taken, and details of assets and liabilities noted, even if a will has not yet been found, but clients should be warned that if the will names others as executor(s), the client will be responsible for any fees incurred if the executors decide to instruct another solicitor.

Sometimes the person giving initial instructions will produce a copy of a will; great care must be taken to check that it is a copy of the last will. A later will or codicil might appoint different executors or vary the disposal of the estate.

The executor(s) may be given a copy of the will, but it is not a public document until it has been proved by the issue of a grant. Therefore any attempt by other persons to obtain a copy of the will should be strongly resisted unless the executors agree that a copy or copies may be released. See also Chapter 3 as to wills.

(b) Details of the deceased

A note should be made of the deceased's full name and address, regardless of whether there is a will or not. If there is a will, any previous address at which the deceased lived when the will was prepared should also be noted. The client should give the deceased's date of birth and the date of death, and his occupation, or last occupation if the deceased was retired, plus his income tax district and reference. The age of the deceased should then be calculated and noted. All this information will be required if and when an application for a grant is made (see Chapter 12).

(c) Beneficiaries

When taking first instructions, the full names and addresses and post codes of beneficiaries should be listed and, in the case of any minor beneficiaries, their dates of birth can be noted in the file for use when the estate is ready to be distributed (see Chapter 14). Notes may also be taken as to whether any beneficiary may wish to accept any items from the estate (not specifically dealt with in the will if there is one), as part payment, or in consideration of their entitlement under the will or intestacy.

(d) Personal effects

The proposed personal representative may enter the testator's house for the purpose of removing the deceased's personal effects, provided this can be carried out without any difficulty. If there is a surviving spouse and the deceased died intestate, there should normally be no reason to remove the personal effects. If the deceased lived alone, it is advisable for the personal representative as soon as possible to remove any valuables for safekeeping (see page 62).

(e) Death certificate and DSS benefits

A death certificate should be obtained from the proposed personal representative as soon as possible. There is a limited time in which to register deaths, usually seven to ten days. The cost is £2.50 for each certificate.

If there is to be an inquest, and this is adjourned, a certificate should be obtained from the Coroner, and this can be used until the death certificate is available. The Coroner can issue a certificate enabling the body to be buried before the death is registered.

Copies of certificates of deaths which have already been registered (and copies of birth and marriage certificates) may be obtained by applying in person at St Catherines House, 10 Kingsway, London WC2B 6JP. If making a postal application, this should be addressed to OPCS (Office of Population Censuses and Surveys) General Register Office, Smedley Hydro, Trafalgar Road, Birkdale, Southport PR8 2HH (tel: 0151 471 4200 or 01704 569824). The fee for a standard certificate is £12.00 if the exact PSR (Public Search Room at St Catherines) index reference is given with the application. Otherwise the fee is £15.00. Cheques should be made payable to 'OPCS'.

When registering the death at the office of the Registrar of Births, Deaths and Marriages, the personal representative will be given a certificate of registration of death – Form BD8. This form should be completed and signed by the person who has paid, or intends to pay, the funeral account, or by the personal representative.

Only one person need sign the BD8 (even though there may be several personal representatives); it can then be sent to the local office of the DSS. The form BD8 asks if the declarant wishes to claim any arrears of benefits due to the deceased; where this has been confirmed, a claim form will be issued to the declarant by the DSS.

If the deceased was receiving retirement pension the pension book should be returned to the DSS with the form BD8. If the pension was being paid quarterly the death should also be registered with the DSS quarterly payments section in Newcastle upon Tyne (DSS, CPB, Newcastle upon Tyne NE98 1YX), and the local DSS office should be advised that this has been done.

Where a pension is payable to a widow aged between 45 and 60 years, an increased 'widow's allowance' is paid to the widow for the six months following the death of her spouse. Thereafter the pension will be reduced to the standard rate of single person's pension plus any additions according to the widow's circumstances.

Widow's Payment. A lawful widow can claim a lump sum payment from the DSS which currently amounts to £1,000. This is a single payment and is tax free. The rules explaining who is entitled are found in DSS booklet NP45 'A guide to Widows' Benefits'. A widow may be entitled to a Widowed Mother's Allowance if she is not entitled to a Widow's Pension.

(f) Funeral expenses from the Social Fund

Section 32 Social Security Act 1986 abolished the 'death grant' in 1987 and introduced a scheme to assist with funeral expenses, which replaced the single payment from supplementary benefits. These payments are made from the Social Fund and may be available to persons who are receiving family credit, income support or housing benefit from the DSS. Capital exceeding £500 (£1,000 for persons over 60), and lump sums payable from insurance policies and other sources are taken into account, in calculating the amount of assistance available. Leaflets SF200 and D49, issued by the DSS, give detailed information of this scheme. Where assistance with funeral costs is available under the scheme, the funeral arrangements are made by the claimant.

Form SF200 states that the Social Fund will help towards the cost of a simple funeral within the United Kingdom, including:

- bringing the body home if the person died away from home but in the United Kingdom;
- travel to arrange the funeral or to go to the funeral (one return journey only);
- the death certificate;
- an ordinary coffin;
- a car for the coffin and bearers, and one other car;
- flowers from the claimant;
- fees for the undertaker, minister and organist for a simple funeral;
- cemetery or crematorium fees;
- up to £75 extra costs because of the religion of the person who has died.

The claimant must apply within three months of the date of the funeral; the claim must be made on form SF200 (available from the DSS). The DSS now take into account not only the finances of the deceased, but also of the person applying for assistance towards the costs of the funeral.

If the person who died was a war pensioner, assistance may be available if the person died of a disablement for which he or she was entitled to a pension, or died in hospital while having treatment for that disablement, or was entitled to a constant attendance allowance. The application for war pensioners is made to:

War Pensions Directorate
Norcross
Blackpool FY5 3TA
Tel. 01253 858858

Section 32(4) of the Act also provides for recovery of the payment from the deceased's estate, and the claim takes priority as payment of funeral expenses. The executor or administrator is liable to repay it whether he arranged the funeral or not.

Where there is no suitable applicant, local authorities continue to provide funerals in cases of hardship under the Public Health (Control of Disease) Act 1984, the funeral arrangements being entirely under the control of the relevant local authority which has the right to reclaim the cost of providing the funeral from the deceased's estate (information is available from council offices). Where a person dies in a hospital and relatives cannot be traced, the health authority may arrange the funeral and claim against the deceased's estate, if any. This usually occurs when, for example, the deceased was a person of no fixed abode.

(g) Tracing the assets and liabilities

Whether or not the deceased left a will, the details of assets and liabilities which form the estate, and which may be required to obtain a grant of representation, must be traced in the same way. The proposed personal representative should be asked to collect the details of all assets and debts in the sole name of the deceased or in the joint names of the deceased and another or others.

The checklist set out in Appendix 1 may be used to ensure all the necessary information is collected; and, in appropriate circumstances, a copy may be given to the client to help him or her to gather together the necessary details and documents. Chapters 7 and 8 deal in detail with each of the items mentioned in the checklist.

(h) Medical cards

The deceased's medical card should be returned to the National Health Service:

NHS Central Register
Smedley Hydro
Southport
Merseyside PR8 1BR

Summary

- Is there a will?
- Is it valid?
- Is it dated?
- Is it signed and witnessed?
- Does it name executors?
- Are there any funeral wishes in the will?
- Does the will allow the executors to spend only a limited sum for the headstone or are they free to decide?
- Has the body been donated for organ transplants or medical research? Is there a donor's card among the personal papers?
- Check that the names and addresses of the deceased and the executors in the will are complete and correct, and note their descriptions and occupations.

- Check that the names and addresses of beneficiaries are complete and correct.

- Note full names and dates of birth of minor beneficiaries and keep a record on file.

- Ascertain the deceased's tax district and reference and the details of any accountants who normally dealt with the tax affairs.

- Will all executors/administrators agree to accept the appointment?

- Prepare a full list of all assets and liabilities including joint assets and joint liabilities.

- Keep full details (a photocopy if possible) of all insurance documents, especially policies which do not form part of the estate but on which the deceased paid the premiums. These might have to be produced to the CTO.

- Obtain a death certificate. A copy which has been certified is usually acceptable, but insurance companies invariably require sight of the certificate issued by the registrar of deaths.
  Remember that the deceased's birth and marriage certificates may be required, especially if there is an annuity.

- Advise the personal representatives that they must do everything in their power to safeguard the estate assets, possibly by having valuables removed, to a secure insured situation until they are either transferred or sold.

- Check as early as possible that there are sufficient assets to cover the cost of the funeral and professional charges.

Chapter 3

Wills

1. Search for wills

Since 1987 many firms have started to use the Law Society's 'personal assets log' which gives, *inter alia*, a client's personal details, the name and address of his solicitors, and the whereabouts of the client's will. It is hoped that this system will greatly reduce the incidence of missing wills.

(a) General enquiries

Where it is believed that the deceased made a will but it cannot be found, a thorough search must be made. Enquiries can be made of other solicitors and banks in the area. It is general practice to send out a circular letter simply asking for anyone with knowledge of a will to send details, and if nothing is heard within seven days to assume there is no trace. This is not entirely satisfactory and it is preferable to send letters addressed to the senior partner of a firm of solicitors, or the manager of a bank, requesting them to reply specifically 'yes' or 'no'. A checklist should be maintained, and anyone failing to reply within a short period should be contacted again.

Consideration should also be given to placing an advertisement in the *Law Society's Gazette* and the local newspaper(s), although again this can be unsatisfactory in that it relies on the chance of someone reading it and following it up.

Where the deceased travelled widely, or where it is believed that he might have instructed a solicitor or bank in another part of the country, enquiries should, if it is practicable to do so, be made in the appropriate area or areas. Obviously, each case must be considered on its own merits and from the information available the appropriate search can be made.

(b) The Court of Protection

If the deceased was a patient whose affairs were administered by the Court of Protection before his death that court might have knowledge of a will. The court would have obtained a certificate of the safe custody of any will which was in existence at the time of the appointment of a receiver by that court, which should prevent the release of the will without the written authority of the court.

In certain circumstances it is possible for the Court of Protection to prepare a will, in which case it is usually held by that court.

Enquiries of the Court of Protection should be addressed to The Public Trust Office, Protection Division, Stewart House, 24 Kingsway, London WC2B 6JX.

(See chapter 19)

(c) Deposited wills

Under the Wills (Deposit for Safe Custody) Regulations 1978, the deceased's will may have been deposited at the Principal Registry of the Family Division, in which case a 'Certificate of deposit of a will' would have been issued to the depositor as a receipt for the will. The procedure for obtaining release of wills so deposited is:

   (i) production of the certificate of deposit;

   (ii) production of proof of the testator's death;

   (iii) an undertaking by the person receiving the will to lodge the same on any application for a grant.

(d) Affidavit of search

In certain circumstances, an affidavit of search (see Appendix 5 for a form) may be required where, for example, a will is undated, where a codicil misquotes the date of the will, or where it appears that another document might have been attached to the will. The affidavit must show that the testator has made all possible enquiries to trace any other testamentary document and that the search has been unsuccessful. An affidavit of plight and condition may also be required (see Appendix 5). These affidavits should be submitted to the Probate Registry with the application for the grant (see Appendix 5). Where there is no trace of any testamentary document, or if the testamentary document found is not acceptable for a grant of probate, the case proceeds as an intestacy and the application will be for a grant of letters of administration or for a grant of letters of administration (with the will) (see Chapters 5 and 6).

2. Validity of will

Once the will is obtained it, or if there is some delay in receiving it, a copy, must be checked at once to make certain it is valid. There is little point in carrying out the other tasks if the will later proves to be invalid, because an executor named in an invalid will has no authority to deal with the estate. If an executor has commenced dealing with the estate and the will is subsequently found to be invalid, he has intermeddled (see page 26) and should be advised immediately to cease all dealings with the estate and to surrender up to the proposed personal representative any items held, and to account fully for all dealings in which he has been involved.

To be valid, a will (other than a privileged will) must:

(a) be in writing; and

(b) deal with property in England and Wales or appoint executors; and

(c) be dated and signed by the testator or someone on his behalf, or bear the mark of the testator;

(d) be witnessed. It is not necessary that the will bears an attestation clause but it must have been signed by the testator in the presence of two witnesses present at the same time who attested or signed the will thereafter. If there is no attestation clause, evidence of due execution (see Appendix 5) will be required to prove the will. Someone else may sign on behalf of a testator on his instruction, e.g. in the case of a blind testator; and

(e) the testator must have attained 18 years at the time he made the will (or 21 years if he made the will before 1 January 1970).

(Wills Act 1837 as amended by the Administration of Justice Act 1982)

In due course, the will is 'proved' by the granting of probate or letters of administration (with will annexed) (see Chapter 12). If the will is not valid, the administration proceeds as on intestacy.

An application to a Probate Registry should be made if the validity of the will is in doubt. The Registry may require an affidavit from a witness but, initially, the relevant facts should be set out in a letter, with the original will or a copy.

3. Lost will

If it is certain that a will was made but that it has been lost, for example by the bank or the solicitors who drafted it, an application must be made for an order to prove a copy of the completed draft will (or codicil) (r 54 Non-Contentious Probate Rules 1987). The application is made to a district judge or a registrar who may require some or all of the following:

(a) an affidavit of due execution (see Appendix 5) sworn by one of the attesting witnesses exhibiting the draft document;

(b) a sworn statement by the appropriate person, who may be a bank official or one of the partners of the firm of solicitors, setting out the precise facts leading to the realisation that the document has been lost, and exhibiting the copy draft to be proved;

(c) an affidavit from the applicant reciting all the relevant facts of the loss and showing who, if anyone, would be prejudiced by the proof of a copy of the document, and showing the efforts that have been made to trace the original document. See Appendix 5 for the appropriate form.

The executor's oath is not submitted to the Probate Registry until after the other three documents mentioned above have been produced to the registry, and an order for proof of the copy has been made. The oath will recite the district judge's or registrar's order.

Occasionally it may be necessary under r 54 Non-Contentious Probate Rules 1987 to file consents to the admission of the will by persons prejudiced, and if consents are required the Probate Registry will advise accordingly. The effect of a consent is that the person giving it agrees to the admission of the will even though his position may be prejudiced by the will being proved (see Appendix 5 for a form of consent). If the district judge or registrar is satisfied, he will issue an order that the copy, or the reconstructed will, be admitted. When the grant is later issued, it will be limited until the original will or a more authentic copy is proved. If the original will is subsequently found, a *Cessate* grant (see page 119) may be obtained if necessary.

In certain circumstances the fact that a will has been lost may raise the presumption that the deceased died intestate. If this results in the same distribution of the estate as was provided for in the missing will, it will usually be simpler to assume that there is an intestacy.

4. Copies of wills

The contents of a will should not be revealed to anyone, even after the death of the testator, until the will has been proved, and requests to supply copies of the will should be refused. However, the executor(s) named in the will should see the will, or be given a copy, to enable them to decide whether or not to accept the appointment. After a grant of probate has been issued, copies of the will may be given to the residuary beneficiaries, but it is not normal practice to provide full copies to other legatees, although they can be given a copy of that part which relates to their legacy.

After being proved, copies of a will may be purchased by anyone who wishes to obtain a copy, by applying to any Probate Registry.

5. Joint wills and mutual wills

Where two testators make their wills in one instrument the document is known as a joint will. On the death of the first testator the whole will is proved, and when the survivor dies the whole will is again proved.

The common practice of a husband and wife both making wills leaving all their estate to each other is often described as the making of joint wills; these are in fact separate wills and each is proved separately.

6. Two testamentary documents

Where there are two testamentary documents, and the second or later document does not revoke the earlier, and does not dispose of all of the estate, both should be submitted for probate. But if it is not known which of the two documents was executed first, both are to be admitted to probate if they both appear to form the testator's wishes when read together. If they do not, then neither will be admitted to probate (*Townsend* v *Moore* [1905] AC 66).

If the documents are admitted, and if different executors are appointed in each document, probate may be granted to both (or all) executors jointly.

A district judge's or registrar's directions must be sought where there is any doubt.

7. Testator's name

The spelling of the testator's name and his signature in the will should be checked in case of a typographical error, and because many people are accustomed to using only one first name, a shortened version of it, a nickname, or they sign using only one initial. The name should also be checked with the executor(s) or the deceased's family and against the death certificate. If names have been omitted from the will or an error has been made, the executor's oath (see Appendix 5) will have to include an explanation (e.g. that the name of the deceased was John Stewart Bloggs but that he held premium savings bonds in the name John Bloggs). If he held several assets in the different name or shortened version of his name, only one asset need be mentioned in the oath.

If the testator has changed his name since making the will, the oath should state when the name was changed and how it was changed (e.g. by deed poll, or by use and repute). If the change was by use and repute the oath should show the testator's total abandonment of his previous name. If there is doubt of complete abandonment, the changed name will be shown as an alias in the oath and in the grant of representation. When the change was by deed poll the oath should describe the testator as 'formerly ....'; the date of the deed poll should be stated and the deed poll produced.

There are cases where the testator holds assets in a number of different names, and an affidavit of alias may be necessary, or details may be included in the executor's oath (r 9 Non-Contentious Probate Rules 1987). The Probate Registry will advise the requirements when the facts have been made known. If the testator's name differs from the name in the will, again an affidavit of alias may be required. This type of problem should be discussed with the Probate Registry in the first instance before the oath is prepared for swearing by the personal representative.

8. Change of address of testator

It is often found that the testator has changed his address since making the will. Most printed forms of oath contain the words 'formerly of ....'. When completing the oath (see page 122), the testator's address at the date of his death will be included, and the address shown in the will or last codicil is inserted in the oath after the words 'formerly of'. Any other addresses the deceased had between the date of the will and the date of his death are not normally entered in the oath. If more addresses than the address in the will and the last residential address are required by the applicant to be shown in the grant, a written request for additional addresses to be shown in the grant must be made, but no more than four addresses will be allowed.

If the testator has changed his domicile since making the will, the change of domicile does not alter the validity or interpretation of the will.

9. Attesting witnesses

An affidavit of due execution is an affidavit by one of the attesting witnesses to the testator's signature (see Appendix 5 for a form). Should such an affidavit be necessary (see paras 2 and 3 above and r 16 Non-Contentious Probate Rules 1987) but the witnesses have died, cannot be traced or for any other valid reason cannot execute an affidavit, it may still be possible to prove the will by submitting an affidavit of handwriting of the testator (see Appendix 5 for a form) together with the consent to the will being proved by all the people who would otherwise be prejudiced, i.e. those entitled to benefit on an intestacy.

10. Damage to will

Great care should be taken when handling wills, and at no time should other papers, e.g. a letter, be attached to a will except on the testator's instructions. When a will is received with other documents attached to it, the additional documents should not be removed and the will and attachments should be forwarded to the Probate Registry intact when applying for a grant.

If a will is posted to an executor in another part of the country for swearing, the covering letter should quite clearly warn him against inadvertently allowing the will to become marked in any way by writing (apart from the executor's signature and marking of the commissioner for oaths). Neither should the will be marked by pins, staples, paper clips, or other methods of joining papers together.

When the will, oath and other papers are posted, they should be placed loose in an envelope large enough to contain them, and a pre-addressed envelope for return of the documents could be included to avoid having them returned in an unsuitable package.

Far more serious is the damage to wills caused by lack of care by the executor, his solicitors, or the bank holding the will. It is unwise to keep an original will in the estate file while preliminary work prior to the application for a grant is being conducted; a copy should be made for the file and the original returned to safe keeping, to be removed only when it is required to be exhibited with the oath.

If the will is marked the district judge or registrar may, under r 14 Non-Contentious Probate Rules 1987, require a written explanation for the marking, and may require an affidavit of plight and condition to be sworn (see Appendix 5 for a form). All marks which might indicate the addition of other testamentary documents must be accounted for, although there is no longer any requirement for an affidavit (r 14).

Where a will or codicil has been damaged or partially destroyed by accidental means, e.g. by burning, water or other mishap, whereby part or all of the document is unreadable, the Probate Registry should be consulted in the first instance for guidance on how the document should be dealt with.

An affidavit of plight and condition will probably be necessary to explain the condition of the document. The affidavit is submitted to the Probate Registry with the application for the grant, and should include details of the condition of the document when it was executed, its condition after the death of the testator, and where it was kept. The affidavit will have to show that the damage was not caused by the testator attempting to revoke the document or partially revoke it. See Appendix 5 for a form.

If it appears that there has been an attempt to revoke the will by destruction, deletion or other means, the registrar will require evidence to show why it should not be considered to have been revoked by the testator, again by means of an affidavit of plight and condition.

11. Alterations to the will

Any alterations in a will or codicil which have not been duly attested, and cannot be shown to have been made before the testamentary document was executed should be considered carefully. If the testator was of foreign nationality, domicile or residence, the alterations may be acceptable because of the foreign connection. The district judge or registrar should be asked to consider the document before it is submitted for probate, and he may direct that a fiat copy of the will should be proved. The copy is prepared by the solicitor acting for the applicant, and it should ignore any writing which has been added to the will after it was executed, and should include any writing that has been crossed out or otherwise deleted in the original, as far as this is possible. Where it is not possible to decipher any part of the original will, the fiat copy should show blanks. The copy is then submitted for probate and will be endorsed by the district judge or registrar.

12. Testator under 18

No will is valid if made by a person domiciled in England and Wales who was under the age of 18 years at the time of making the will (Wills Act 1837, as amended by the Family Law Reform Act 1969). Although the Family Law Reform Act 1969, which came into force on 1 January 1970, reduced the age of majority from 21 to 18 years, the age limit for a will made before 1 January 1970 remains 21 years. There are exceptions to the age limit in the case of privileged wills – see below.

13. Privileged wills

Section 11 Wills Act 1837, as extended by the Wills (Soldiers and Sailors) Act 1918, states that any soldier or member of the air force in actual military service or any sailor at sea may dispose of his estate without the formalities required by s 9 Wills Act 1837. The serviceman does not have to have attained the age of 18 years, and the privileged will does not have to be signed by the testator or to be witnessed.

A noncupative will is an oral testamentary disposition by a soldier, sailor or airman which must be made to a credible witness, and is valid. An order by a district judge or registrar is required to prove such a will, and an affidavit is required in support of an application for a grant.

14. Refusal to release a will

If another solicitor or a bank holds the will they normally release it when a death certificate and a letter of authority signed by all the executors is produced. If for any reason a person holding the will refuses to release it a subpoena should be issued for that person to bring the will into the Probate Registry. If the person still refuses to release it, the subpoena may be enforced by committal of that person. See r 50 Non-Contentious Probate Rules 1987.

15. Property abroad

Where a will is made dealing only with property abroad the court has power to issue a grant, but normally refuses to do so because the object of a grant of probate is to enable a personal representative to administer the estate in England and Wales.

16. Admission of codicil

Where a will has been revoked, a codicil may nevertheless be admitted to probate even if the codicil is unintelligible without the will (*Re Turner's Goods* (1872) LR 2 P&D 403).

17. Partial intestacy

Where the will of the deceased does not dispose of the entire estate a partial intestacy occurs. If there is a surviving spouse he or she is entitled to the statutory legacy under intestacy (see Chapter 6) but the value of any benefit received by the spouse under the will is taken into account in calculating the statutory legacy. If the benefit under the will exceeds the statutory legacy the Act is construed as though there were no reference in it to the statutory legacy or interest thereon. Thus, if under the terms of the will the surviving spouse receives more than the value of the statutory legacy (£125,000, or £200,000 for deaths on or after 1 December 1993) (see Chapter 6), he or she has no entitlement under the partial intestacy.

But if the spouse receives less than the statutory legacy under the will he or she may receive the balance from the amount in the partial intestacy.

18. Conditions in the will

When it has been ascertained that the will is valid, the contents of the will should be checked to make certain that any conditions have been fulfilled. If there are any unfulfilled conditions, the will cannot be proved. Conditions may be, for example, the appointment of a person as executor 'if he survives me for the period of one calendar month', in which case a grant of probate will not be issued until one calendar month has elapsed since the date of death.

Where there are conditions the executor's oath (see Chapter 7) should not be sworn until after the conditions have been met. If a condition has not been met, and an application for a grant is made, probate will not be granted until such time as the condition is fulfilled. If there is a condition that the executor must survive the testator for a given period and the oath is sworn before that period has expired, the district judge or registrar will require a letter from the solicitor, dated after the end of the period, confirming that the executor is alive at that time.

19. Effects of divorce

Where the testator was divorced since making his will, and named a former spouse in the will as executor and/or beneficiary, the will takes effect as if the former spouse were not named in it, and any benefit under the will lapses unless it appears from the will that the testator had a contrary intent (see s 18A Wills Act 1837). This does not affect any claim under the Inheritance (Provision for Family and Dependants) Act 1975 (see page 167).

In its 22nd Report (Cmnd 7902, 1980) the Law Reform Committee recommended that on divorce a will should remain valid but any gift to a divorced spouse should be interpreted as if the divorced spouse had predeceased the testator. The recommendations were incorporated in the new s 18a Wills Act 1837, enacted by s 18(2) Administration of Justice Act 1982. However, in *Re Sinclair (deceased)* [1984] 3 All ER 362 it was held that 'lapse' should mean 'failure' and divorce should not suggest death. Whenever the entitlement to a grant depends upon the interpretation of the word 'lapse', an order under s 116 Supreme Court Act 1981 should be sought. The application is *ex parte* to a district judge.

Summary

- Is there a missing will?

- Make a thorough search of strong-room and will files if the deceased was your client.

- Write to all firms of solicitors and all banks in the vicinity.

- Has a will been deposited at the Probate Registry?

- If the deceased was a patient under the Court of Protection does the court have knowledge of a will?

- If necessary, advertise in the *Law Society Gazette* or other appropriate medium.

- Is there a copy will?

- If sufficient evidence is available it will be possible to prove a copy will or a reconstruction of a will.

- Is there more than one testamentary document? If so check all documents carefully to make certain that the correct executors act.

- Are the names and addresses of the testator and the executors complete and correct?

- If the deceased's names differ in any way from the names in the will or if he held assets in a shortened version of his name, in a *nom de plume*, or, if a testatrix holds an asset in her former name, this should be included as an alias in the oath. If there is any doubt at all an affidavit of alias may be required.

- If the testator's address at the date of death differs from the address in the will the oath must state the address at the date of death preceded by the words 'formerly of'.

- Protect the will from accidental damage by placing it separately in a secure place away from the day-to-day estate file.

- If the will is marked or damaged in any way find out, if possible, how the mark was caused, because an affidavit of plight and condition may be required by the Probate Registry.

- In the case of a young testator, make certain that he was of age when he executed the will unless it is a privileged will.

- If the testator left no estate in England and Wales there is no need for a grant. However, a grant might be required to enable the executors to deal with assets abroad. If so, an explanatory letter should be sent to the district registrar with a request for a grant to be issued and giving the relevant details.

- Even if a will is not valid for any one of a number of reasons, an accompanying codicil might be a valid testamentary document which can be proved.

- If a will fails to dispose of all the residuary estate there may be a partial intestacy. If there is, full details of the deceased kin will have to be obtained to enable the residue to be distributed.

- If there are any conditions in the will, for example, if a gift is given only if the recipient survives by a certain period or attains a certain age, then the gift does not become due until the condition has been fulfilled.

- If the testator has divorced since making the will, and the will names the former spouse as executor and/or beneficiary, the will is construed as if the former spouse had predeceased the testator.

Chapter 4

Executors

Executors are appointed by the will. One executor or up to a maximum of four may prove the will at any one time (s 114(1) Supreme Court Act 1981). If more than four are named in the will, power may be reserved to the non-proving executors (r 27 (1)–(3) Non-Contentious Probate Rules 1987) (see page 28) until such time as they are able to apply for probate; this may be, for example, if one or more of the proving executors dies. Alternatively, one or more of the executors may renounce their right to apply for a grant (see page 25).

There is no restriction on the choice of executors but if a minor is appointed he cannot act in the administration of the estate or prove the will until he attains his majority (see page 23). Probate will not be granted to a mentally incapable person during the period of incapacity (see page 24).

1. Duties

The duties of personal representatives, both executors and administrators, are set out in s 25 Administration of Estates Act 1925 and are:

'(a) to collect and get in the real and personal estate of the deceased and administer the estate according to law;

(b) when required to do so by the Court exhibit on oath in the Court a full inventory of the estate and when required to do so render an account of the administration of the estate to the Court;

(c) when required to do so by the High Court deliver up the grant to that Court.'

A personal representative may be called upon by any person interested in the estate to exhibit an inventory of the estate and to render an account of his administration. An inventory may be called for before the end of six months after the final distribution of the estate, but there does not appear to be any time limit set down in the Administration of Estates Act 1925 regarding the rendering of an account.

An application for an order to exhibit an inventory and account is made by summons to a district judge of the Principal Probate Registry or a District Probate Registrar, and the application should be supported by affidavit. An order to file an inventory and an account may be enforced by committal.

2. Executors' authority

An executor's authority is derived from the testator's will, while that of an administrator derives from the grant of letters of administration (see Chapter 9). The estate of the deceased vests in his executor at the date of death, and the executor may commence identifying and safeguarding the estate assets before probate has been granted provided he intends to take the grant. His appointment may be unrestricted, which is the usual type of appointment, when he is known as the general executor, sometimes called the universal executor; or his appointment may be limited or conditional and he is known as a special executor. An executor is correctly described either as the executor of the will of the testator, or as the executor of the testator; he is not the executor of the estate of the testator.

No-one may prove the will in priority to the executor(s).

An executor cannot act while temporary administration (a grant *ad colligenda bona*) is in force, until that grant has been revoked or recalled. This type of grant is usually limited to allow such acts to be done as are necessary to safeguard the estate until further representation is granted. They are always grants of letters of administration and cease when a general grant is obtained. See also page 119.

3. Limited or conditional appointment

The appointment may be limited to part of the estate, for example the deceased's business affairs only, or to specific property. The testator may appoint different executors to deal with his property in England, and others to deal with his property abroad. Executors appointed to deal only with the property abroad are not entitled to a grant in England.

4. Minors

Commonly, where the testator has minor children at the date of making the will, executors are appointed unless or until the child or children attain the age specified in the will, whereupon the child(ren) are to become executors. The executor's oath must state whether or not the child or children have attained that age.

A minor cannot prove the will or act in the administration of the estate until he attains his majority or any later age mentioned in the will.

A distinction is drawn between a minor executor who has no interest in the residuary estate, and one who has such an interest. Where he has no such interest and is the sole executor appointed, it is normal to issue a grant of letters of administration (with the will) to the residuary beneficiary (although a district judge or registrar may direct otherwise). The grant will be limited for the use and benefit of the minor and until he attains the age of 18, or the later age specified in the will. On attaining that age, he may apply for a grant if he wishes to do so, but this is not obligatory. The grant of letters of administration (with the will) is granted to two grantees if there is a minority interest, or to a trust corporation with or without such other person as the court thinks fit (see ss 114(2) and 118 Supreme Court Act 1981).

Where a sole minor executor has an interest in the residuary estate, a minority interest arises and a grant of letters of administration (with the will) will be issued for his use and benefit under the normal priorities of r 32 Non-Contentious Probate Rules 1987 (see page 39). The person with a first right to such a grant is the parent of the minor who has, or is deemed to have, parental responsibility for the minor in accordance with:

- s 2(1), 2(2) or 4 Children Act 1989; or

- para 4 or 6 of Sch 14 to that Act; or

- an adoption order within the meaning of s 12(1) Adoption Act 1976; or

the guardian of the minor who is appointed, or deemed to have been appointed, in accordance with s 5 Children Act 1989 or in accordance with para 12, 13 or 14 of Sch 14 to that Act.

A district judge or a registrar may appoint a person to obtain a grant for the use and benefit of a minor jointly with a person mentioned above, or to the exclusion of or in default of such a person.

Two applicants are always required where a minority interest arises.

If only one of the executors is a minor, power may be reserved to him (see page 28), and on attaining his age of majority, or any later age specified in the will, he may apply for a grant of double probate (see page 119). In the meantime, the other executors may prove the will and administer the estate.

Where all the executors are minors, administration (with the will) will be granted to the person who has, or is deemed to have, parental responsibility until one of the minors attains his majority or the later age specified in the will, whereupon the administration ceases and the executor who has attained the requisite age will be entitled to a grant of probate.

No-one may renounce a minor's right to probate on his behalf, and power should be reserved for the minor until he attains his majority or the later age mentioned in the will.

5. Executor mentally incapable

Where the sole executor cannot take out a grant because he is incapable of managing his affairs, and where he has no beneficial interest in the estate, the grant may be made to a residuary beneficiary named in the will. The grant will be limited for the use and benefit of the executor and during his incapacity.

If the incapable sole executor has an interest in the estate, the grant for his use and benefit is made under the provisions of r 35 Non-Contentious Probate Rules 1987. A person who has been authorised by the Court of Protection in the matter of the executor has priority to take a grant on his behalf. The Court of Protection order must give the appointed receiver power to take a grant, otherwise his application will not be accepted by the Probate Registry. The sealed order of the Court of Protection must be produced with the application for a grant.

If there is a minority or life interest arising under the will, the order will contain provision for another person to be nominated as co-administrator.

Where no one has been appointed by the Court of Protection, the next person in priority is the lawful attorney acting under an enduring power of attorney which has been registered at the Court of Protection. Notice must be given to that court, by the solicitor acting, of the intention to apply for a grant. Such notice must be accompanied by a certificate from the responsible medical officer in charge of the patient. The certificate must state that the patient is incapable of managing his affairs, and that he is unlikely to recover within a period of three months. Applicants must check that the three-month period has not expired at the date of applying to the Probate Registry. If it has, a new medical certificate will be required. A formal acknowledgement must be obtained from the Court of Protection and this should be forwarded together with the doctor's certificate, and the application for a grant, to the Probate Registry. The application will be for a grant for the use and benefit of the incapable person during his incapacity.

Where the incapable executor is not a beneficiary under the will the notice to the Court of Protection is not needed.

If no-one has been appointed by the Court of Protection and all other persons entitled to a grant have renounced, the Probate Court may issue a grant for the use and benefit of the incapable personal representative to another, as provided in r 35 Non-Contentious Probate Rules 1987.

If the incapable executor is one of several executors appointed, power will be reserved to him until he recovers. Where an incapable person recovers he may apply for a *Cessate* grant (see page 119).

6. Renunciation

An executor is not obliged to accept the appointment as long as he has not intermeddled in the deceased's estate (see below). Where an executor does not wish to prove the will he may renounce probate thereof, whereupon all his rights and obligations as an executor cease. Renunciation of probate only does not act as renunciation of letters of administration in another capacity. If the executor is also entitled to apply for a grant in a lower capacity and wishes to renounce that right also, his renunciation must be of probate and of letters of administration (with the will). By contrast, if an administrator renounces, he may not apply for a grant in another capacity except with the leave of a district judge or registrar (r 37(2) Non-Contentious Probate Rules 1987).

The renunciation may be made by signing a form of renunciation, which should be witnessed, but does not need to be under seal. It is then submitted with the application for the grant sworn by the other executor(s). The renunciant may apply to retract his renunciation at a later date, but the retraction is only allowed in special circumstances by leave of the court. The application for leave to retract must be supported by an affidavit. If allowed, a note of the retraction is made on the original grant of probate by the Probate Registry.

In an estate where all the executors or the surviving executors have renounced probate of the will (and where applicable, letters of administration (with the will)), a grant of letters of administration (with the will) may be obtained, in the first instance by one or more of the residuary legatees and devisees in trust named in the will. In the absence of such beneficiaries, the order of priority given in r 20 Non-Contentious Probate Rules 1987 (see page 40) should be followed.

Where a trust corporation is appointed executor by the will, they should be advised of the death and asked if they intend to accept the appointment. Where the estate is small, or where the surviving spouse is the sole beneficiary, trust corporations will often agree to renounce.

Where the partners in a firm (solicitors or accountants) are named as executors, and they all wish to renounce, and there are numerous partners, it would be unreasonable for all of them to renounce individually. This could be unacceptably expensive. In such circumstances, one of the partners could apply for an order under s 116 Supreme Court Act 1981 for the residuary legatee and devisee to be granted letters of administration (with the will).

(See Appendix 5 for forms).

7. Intermeddling

If one of the executors appointed in the will is contemplating renouncing or otherwise not accepting his appointment, he should not interfere in the estate in any way whatsoever. Any executor who has intermeddled and who has not taken out probate within six months of the death can be cited under r 46(3) by any person with an interest in the estate, to take out a grant. An executor who has intermeddled can be cited to take out a grant only; he cannot be cited to 'accept or refuse'. In a citation against an executor who has intermeddled, the affidavit must state the instances of intermeddling, that the deceased has been dead for six months, and state the date of death. An executor who has simply neglected to apply for a grant may be cited to 'accept or refuse' probate.

8. Executor de son tort

If a person not named as an executor intermeddles in any way which denotes he has assumed authority or intends to exercise an executor's functions, his acts may make him an *Executor de son tort* to the extent of the deceased's estate coming into his possession; he becomes liable for payment of capital transfer tax or inheritance tax, and is liable to be sued by the rightful personal representative, a beneficiary or a creditor. However, if a person arranges for the deceased's funeral out of necessity, he may appropriate sufficient money from the deceased's estate to settle the account. He may also safeguard the deceased's goods, and do other acts of a charitable nature or of necessity, and by so doing he does not make himself liable as an *executor de son tort*.

9. Chain of executorship

In an estate where the executor has obtained a grant of probate, and he dies before having completed the administration of the estate, the surviving executors can continue to administer the estate. If power has been reserved to any named executor he may now apply to take double probate as long as no more than four executors are acting at any one time (s 114(2) Supreme Court Act 1981). If any executor has renounced he may apply to have his renunciation set aside (particularly where there are no surviving executors) and if the renunciation is set aside, he may obtain a grant, and complete the administration of the estate.

If the sole or last surviving executor appointed dies, and there are no other executors, the executors of the deceased executor's will can continue with the administration of the estate. This chain of representation can continue through any number of executors. It must be emphasised however that a chain can only pass through each surviving proving executor. If the now deceased executor died intestate, or without leaving a proving executor no chain exists, and a *de bonis non* grant (see below) must be taken out by a person entitled under r 20 Non-Contentious Probate Rules 1987.

10. De bonis non

If a sole or last surviving executor obtains a grant of probate and dies leaving the testator's estate unadministered or partly unadministered, and he dies intestate or without leaving any executor(s) who prove his will, a grant of letters of administration *de bonis non* in respect of the unadministered estate should be applied for in order to complete the administration. The administrator's oath must clear off all executors (i.e. by renunciation or death) including those to whom power is reserved, and must show the way in which the chain of representation has been broken. The oath must also clear off all persons with a prior right to the grant. Where an Inland Revenue Account is required in such a case, it will be in Form A5c.

The order of priority for this type of grant is the same as for a normal case of administration (with the will) (see page 40), the first persons in priority being:

(i) any residuary legatee or devisee in trust;

(ii) any beneficial residuary legatee or devisee including one for life, or any person sharing in the undisposed of estate.

11. Power reserved

A reluctant executor or one who finds it inconvenient to apply for a grant at the time of the application may have power reserved to him instead of renouncing all his right and title to a grant, thereby allowing a grant to be issued to the other executors (r 27(1) Non-Contentious Probate Rules 1987), and thereafter, he may renounce, if he wishes, after his co-executors have obtained the grant.

Power is reserved by inserting the executor's name in full in the box which is usually provided for this purpose on most standard forms of oath. If no such box appears on a form, the following words will effect reservation of power: 'Power reserved to .... the other executor(s)'. The oath must state that notice of the application for a grant has been given to the executor(s) to whom power is to be reserved. The registrar is given power to dispense with the giving of such notice if he is satisfied that it is not practicable to do so, or if it would result in unreasonable expense or delay (r 27(3)). An example of the form to be used to apply to dispense with the giving of a notice has been included in Appendix 5. The executor to whom power has been reserved may accept the appointment at a later date, if this proves necessary, by applying for a grant of double probate (see page 119).

Where the will has already been proved, the application for a grant of double probate must recite that an official copy of the true last will and testament is produced. This official copy is obtained from the probate registry. The fee includes an additional small charge for each additional page of the will, but the cover (or back page) of the will is not counted and is not reproduced in the grant unless it contains a testamentary disposition.

12. Solicitor executors

If a testator has appointed 'the partners of X and Co, Solicitors', to be the executors, the appointment relates to the partners of that firm at the date of the will, and not at the date of death, unless a contrary intention is expressed. Where a firm of solicitors is appointed executors without actually naming the individual partners, and where all of the partners do not or cannot apply (a maximum of four executors may prove at any one time (s 114(1) Supreme Court Act 1981)), the oath must state that those partners applying are (or were) partners in that firm at the date of the will unless a contrary instruction is given in the will. The oath must state 'power is reserved to the remaining partners at the date of death in the firm of .... the other executors'. Where one or more of the partners in the firm applies for probate, notice need not be given to the partners to whom power has been reserved.

It should be noted that if the solicitors are appointed as executors only, and the estate is disposed of in the will direct to the beneficiaries, then any renunciation relates only to the named executors' right to a grant of probate of the will. On the other hand, if the will gives the estate in the first instance to the executors and trustees, then any renunciations must also relate to a grant of letters of administration (with the will) (see, page 25, 6. Renunciation).

13. Description of executors in the oath

After the name and address of each executor in the oath (see Chapter 12) his description should be inserted. If the executor is retired, his former occupation should be annotated followed by the word 'retired'. Any executor who has had no occupation should be described as 'of no occupation'. Descriptions which are not acceptable include 'gentleman', 'esquire', 'of independent means', and other descriptions which are too vague. 'Knight' or 'peer' is an acceptable description provided the deponent's full title is given (see RSC O 41(1),(4)).

Where a female deponent has no occupation and no previous occupation she should be described by her status, e.g. 'single woman' if divorced, 'married woman', 'widow' or 'spinster' as appropriate, 'Lady' if the wife or widow of a Baronet; or if the woman has a higher title of her own, then her own title. If the oath shows the marital status of a woman it will also appear in the grant.

If an executor has changed his name since the date of the will he should be described in the oath as '......... formerly and in the will called ....', and evidence of the change should be produced. This evidence may take the form of recitation of a change of name deed or the recitation of the adoption of a new name by common usage (see also page 15, 7. Testator's name).

When an executrix has married since the date of the will she should be described as '.......... formerly .... spinster'. If a widow has remarried she should be described as '......... formerly ...., widow'. If the executrix has divorced, her description will be '..........., single woman' (or, if she has remarried, 'married woman'). In the latter case the oath should include a statement of the divorce and that she has since intermarried with X. The Probate Registry will advise if full details of the divorce are required.

The applicant's relationship to the testator (if any) does not appear in the grant except where he is appointed by his relationship to the testator and not named in the will; e.g. where the will provided 'I appoint my wife to be the sole executrix'. In such a case the oath should include that, at the date of the will, the deponent was the lawful wife of the testator. This also applies, of course, where a wife appoints her husband and does not name him.

If the description of the executor named in the will is incorrect, or it is not sufficient, evidence will have to be given as to who the testator intended to appoint, and the grant will be issued according to the evidence, to the person entitled, and his correct description will be inserted in the grant together with the description given in the will.

Where a divorced executrix has reverted to her maiden name, but is referred to in the will by her married name, the oath should describe her as, for example 'Mary Jones single woman, previously Mary Brown married woman'.

14. Executor witness

There is much confusion about the ruling that a witness may not benefit from the will, and about executors acting as a witness to the testator's signature.

The executor or executors may witness the testator's signature and this does not invalidate the appointment as an executor. But any person who is a witness to the signature of the testator and that witness's spouse may not benefit from the will. If there are such witness/beneficiaries it does not invalidate the will, but the will is dealt with as if the gift to the witness had not been inserted (s 15 Wills Act 1837).

15. Executor in prison

The fact that an executor is in prison does not deprive him of his right to accept the appointment, and obtain a grant of representation. He may apply personally, or he may appoint an attorney (see below) to obtain a grant on his behalf. However, the court has statutory powers to pass over such an executor, and make the grant to another person. The statutory powers are given under s 116 Supreme Court Act 1981. This section applies as from 1 January 1982 irrespective of the date on which the deceased died.

16. Bankrupt executor

An executor who is bankrupt, insolvent or a felon is not refused a grant of probate on these grounds alone. However, under s 116 Supreme Court Act 1981 the court may pass over the executor and order any other person to take a grant. If there is a solvent executor who is willing to act, the court may refrain from appointing a receiver. See page 140 for insolvent estates.

17. Executor abroad

When an executor is abroad and wishes to accept the appointment he should be asked to arrange to swear the executor's oath before a consular official at the nearest British Embassy or Consulate. As there is always the danger of documents being lost in the post, it is advisable to forward the will, oath and any other documents required to be signed and sworn by the executor, direct to the Embassy or Consulate via the Foreign and Commonwealth Office in London in the diplomatic bag, with the request that they be returned in the same way. In the first instance, a request should be made to the Consular Department of the Foreign and Commonwealth Office in London. The executor may live a long distance away from the nearest British Consulate, and he may therefore swear the documents before a notary. Probate registrars have a discretion to accept an oath sworn abroad before any person professing to have powers to administer such oaths in that country. In such circumstances application may be made for leave to mark a copy will rather than the original.

When the personal representative is a member of HM Armed Forces serving abroad (or a member of a family of such a serving member), he may swear the oath before an officer of the rank of major or above, or the equivalent in other branches of the Armed Forces (Army Act 1955).

18. Grant to an attorney

The law relating to the grant to an attorney is contained in r 31 Non-Contentious Probate Rules 1987.

An attorney of one executor may not join in an application for a grant of probate with other executors.

A sole executor may appoint an attorney to take out a grant of letters of administration (with the will) for the use and benefit of that executor and until the executor shall obtain probate of the will. The executor appoints his attorney by way of a power of attorney. If the executor subsequently wishes to apply for probate, he must apply for a *Cessate* grant (see page 119).

In the event of the donor of a power of attorney dying, the attorney may not continue to act, and a *de bonis non* grant (see page 27) will be required if part of the estate remains unadministered. Where the attorney is acting under an enduring power of attorney, and the donor is mentally incapable, r 35 applies.

19. Debtors

If a debtor of the testator is appointed as an executor in the will, the debt is released (in law) because the executor must account for the debt as an asset of the estate, and he must be taken as having the amount of the debt in his possession at the date of death as one of the assets. He is liable for interest on the debt from the date of death. However, if he does not take out a grant, the debt cannot be released.

20. Missing executors

Every effort must be made to trace a missing executor, but when this is unsuccessful the registrar should be advised of the situation and the will should be lodged in the Probate Registry. The registrar will then indicate whether or not he requires a citation (see Appendix 5) to be advertised. If so, the missing executor should be cited, in an advertisement, to accept or refuse probate. If the missing executor fails to make an appearance the district judge or registrar may make an order passing him over, and direct that the grant be issued to a person entitled in a lower degree. An executor must accept or refuse all of the estate; he cannot accept or refuse part only.

A letter bearing the full names of a missing executor (or any missing person) may be sent to Special Section A, Room 101B, DSS Records Branch, Newcastle-upon-Tyne, with an explanatory covering letter, which should give the date of birth of the missing person. If Special Section can trace the person in its records, it will forward the letter to him.

21. Executor dies before probate

In an estate where an executor has survived the testator but he dies before taking out a grant of probate, all his rights as an executor cease. There will be no chain of executorship. If there are other executors they will take out a grant of probate and the oath must clear off the executor who has died, e.g. 'that .... mentioned in the will survived the within-named testator but has since died without taking upon himself probate of the will and that [we are the surviving] [I am one of the surviving] executor[s]'. If there are no other executors, an application for a grant of letters of administration (with the will) may be made by one of the residuary legatees and devisees mentioned in the will.

22. Capacity of the executors

The capacity in which executors claim the grant is as follows:

1.	One executor appointed	The sole executor
2.	One executrix appointed	The sole executrix
3.	Executors are all males	The executors
4.	Executors are all females	The executrices
5.	Executors are males and females	The executors
6.	One or more executor has died	The surviving executor(s)
7.	One or more renounces	One (or two etc.) of the executors
8.	Power reserved to any executors	One (or two etc.) of the executors
9.	Executors appointed on attaining 18 years	'The executors (or the sole executor) the said ...... having attained the age of 18 years'
10.	Executors appointed during life or widowhood plus a general executor	'The executors (or the sole executor), plus a general executor but as to the said .... during life or widowhood'
11.	Executor appointed with power limited to English property	The executor for England
12.	Executor appointed for life, another appointed on his death, the latter is	The executor appointed
13.	No limitation for life or otherwise but others substituted on death, the first named executor if he applies is described as	The (sole) executor(s) named in the said will
14.	No limitation in actual appointment but there is also a substitution of executors on certain events	The executors named in the said will as therein mentioned
15.	When a codicil cancels an appointment in the will, or when it cites the death of an executor	The executors named in the said codicil

23. Executors' names

The names of all the executors in a will should be checked carefully and if there is any error or omission this should be dealt with in the executor's oath (e.g. 'Robert Mark Smith in the will called Robert Smith'). If an error is quite pronounced it might be necessary to swear an affidavit of identity, for example the wrong christian names or surname might have been inserted as 'Bill Arthur Brown' where the applicant is properly called William Arthur Brown. Where the will appoints a spouse as executor without naming him or her, the oath must show that the applicant was the deceased's husband or wife at the date of making the will, or as appropriate if the will was made in contemplation of marriage.

The names of the executors appear in the grant in the order in which they appear in the oath, which in turn, usually follows the order in the will. It might be useful to deliberately change the order in certain circumstances, for example where one of the executors has a life interest in all or part of the estate, and capital is invested in stocks or shares in the joint names of all of the executors. Many companies send dividend or interest cheques in the name of the first named holder only, and where this is the person entitled to the payment, the other joint holders do not have to continually endorse cheques for payment. However, all named holders will have to sign for any sales of investments.

24. No executor named

If the testator has failed to name an executor, a grant of probate cannot be obtained, and a grant of letters of administration (with the will) should be applied for by the residuary legatees and devisees, or other persons entitled under r 20 Non-Contentious Probate Rules 1987 (see page 40). The oath should state that no executor was named in the will, and should recite the applicant's title to the grant and clear off all persons with a prior right (see Chapter 5).

Checklist: Pre-lodgement of grant application; Wills

Extracting solicitors:	Full name, address, postcode, DX No and reference is required.
Codicil:	If there is a codicil or codicils refer to in oath.
Survival clause in the will:	Where the will contains a survival clause e.g. 'I appoint ... provided he survived me by 28 days' ensure the survival period has elapsed before the oath is sworn. If oath sworn before survival period has elapsed, confirm in covering letter when lodging papers that survival period has now elapsed and applicant still alive. The clause also applies to residuary beneficiaries applying

for letters of administration (with will annexed), where executors do not apply, but there is a survival clause relating to those receiving their beneficial interest.

Will:

1.   Check the will (and any codicils) are properly dated and the attestation clause was properly completed. If there is a defect, evidence of due execution on affidavit by a witness will be required, unless the provision of Rule 12(3) applies.

2.   Check the will has been marked by the deponent(s) and commissioner for oaths.

Name of deceased:

Check the name corresponds with the name in the will. Where the deceased was known by another name the true and proper name must be specified and the reason for the alias to be included in the oath, if necessary in a separate paragraph at the end. (An alias name will only be shown in the grant if the deceased held an asset (e.g. bank account, real property) in the alias name.)

Name(s) of executor(s):

Check the names correspond with those in the will, if any difference explain in oath (or by filing separate affidavit of identity) e.g. 'William Smith commonly known as and referred to in the will as Bill Smith'.

Clearing executors:

Where not all the executors are applying ensure the oath clears those not proving by reciting their previous death, renunciation or having power reserved. Ensure the oath states that notice has been given to the non-proving executors.

Where the appointment is of partners in the firm ensure the oath states the time the appointment is effective e.g. 'the Partners at the date of death of the deceased...'.

Substituted appointment of executors:

Where the appointment of an executor is conditional upon the failure of another appointment, the oath should show how the first appointment has failed.

Date of death:

Check date of death coincides with date of the death certificate. Where the certificate states date of death as 'on or about...', the oath must state when the deceased was 'last seen alive' or 'last known to be alive' and when the body was found.

Age of deceased: Age of deceased at death to be inserted *especially* in 'excepted estate' cases.

Domicile: Ensure domicile inserted: where the domicile is foreign and where different systems of law operate in different parts of the country, ensure that the State of domicile is inserted e.g. 'in the State of Texas, United States of America'.

Settled land: Complete settled land clause.

Attorney applications: Ensure the fact that the attorney of the person entitled is recited and that the limitation 'for the use and benefit of ...... and until further representation be granted' is included after the words 'I will collect, get in and administer', etc.

Excepted estates: Ensure the gross and net figures appropriate to the date of death and value of the estate are inserted *and* that the clause stating the case is an excepted estate is inserted.

Jurat: Ensure the jurat is completed and has been signed by the deponent(s) and the commissioner(s).

Summary

- A maximum of four executors may prove a will at any one time. Power may be reserved to non-proving executors.

- The personal representatives duties are to collect in and safeguard all of the assets, and settle, as soon as possible the estate liabilities, and when this has been done, to distribute the estate in accordance with the will or under intestacy.

- The executor derives his authority from the will, and the administrator from the grant of letters of administration.

- An executor's appointment may be limited or may be a conditional appointment, for example to deal with specific property only.

- There may be executors appointed to deal with property in England and Wales and different executors appointed to deal with property abroad.

- A minor cannot become a personal representative until he attains his majority. If a minor is appointed in the will and the appointment is conditional on him attaining an age over the age of majority, he cannot prove the will until he has attained that stated age.

- During the period of minority, a grant may be obtained limited for the use and benefit of the minor and until he attains the age stated.

- If only one of the executors is a minor, power may be reserved to him, and a grant issued to the other executors.

- If an executor is mentally incapable, he cannot take out a grant. If a receiver has been appointed under the Court of Protection that court can give the receiver power to take a grant. Where no receiver is appointed, an attorney under a registered enduring power of attorney may apply. If neither appointment has been made a grant may be made to a residuary beneficiary such grant being limited for the use and benefit of the executor and during his incapacity.

- If the incapable executor is one of several executors power can be reserved to him until he recovers.

- When an incapable executor recovers he may apply for a cessate grant.

- Any executor may renounce probate and the will should be checked to make certain that the executor is not also entitled to apply for a grant in a lower capacity. If he is, then his renunciation must be of probate and of letters of administration with the will. If there are special circumstances, the court may give leave for the executor to retract his renunciation.

- Where partners in a firm are named as executors, it would be unreasonable for all of them to renounce individually, and in those circumstances one of the partners may apply to the probate court for an order under s 116 Supreme Court Act 1981 for the residuary legatee and devisee to be granted letters of administration with the will.

- Any executor who has intermeddled in the estate cannot renounce, and can be cited under r 46(3) to take out a grant.

- Where an executor neglects to take out a grant he may be cited to accept or refuse probate.

- Any person not named as executor who intermeddles, and in so doing shows that he has assumed authority may find that his acts have made him an executor *de son tort*.

- If the last surviving executor dies leaving the estate unadministered, and dies without leaving executors, a grant of letters of administration *de bonis non* will be needed to complete the estate administration.

- An executor may have power reserved to him instead of renouncing, and he may thereafter renounce.

- If power is reserved and thereafter the executor wishes to apply for probate, and the grant has already been taken out, he must apply for a grant of double probate.

- If a firm has been named as executors, only four may apply and power should be reserved to those partners not now applying.

- An executor's description must be inserted in the oath after his name. If he is retired his former occupation should be noted followed by 'retired'.

- The descriptions 'gentleman', 'esquire' or 'of independent means' are too vague and are not acceptable.

- Where a female deponent has no occupation or previous occupation she should be described by her status, e.g. single woman, widow etc.

- Where an executrix has married since the will she should be described as Mrs A formerly Miss B spinster.

- Executors may act as witnesses to the testator's signature on the will and this does not invalidate their appointment. However, a witness to the testator's signature cannot benefit under the will.

- Where an executor is in prison he can still accept the appointment and obtain a grant personally or through an attorney. However, the court has a statutory power to pass over such an executor. A bankrupt, insolvent or a felon is not refused a grant on these grounds alone.

- An executor living abroad who wishes to accept the appointment should swear the oath before a consular official or, if he is in the armed forces, he may swear the oath before an officer of the rank of major or above, or the equivalent.

- Where there are other executors applying, the attorney of one executor may not join in the application. However, the attorney of a sole executor may take out a grant of letters of administration for the use and benefit of that executor.

- Where an executor cannot be traced a probate registrar should be advised. The registrar will then give directions. Where an executor survives the testator but dies before taking out a grant, all his rights as executor cease. There will be no chain of executorship.

- The oath should explain any correction in the executors' names between the actual name and the names in the will if these differ. If an error is quite pronounced it may be necessary to swear an affidavit of identity.

- If it is required for the names in the oath to be shown in an order different to the order in which they appear in the will, they should be placed in the order required in the oath.

- Where no executor is named a grant of probate cannot be obtained and a grant of letters of administration with the will must be applied for. This is usually applied for by the residuary legatees and devisees.

Chapter 5

Letters of administration (with the will annexed)

For the general duties of an administrator, see page 22. The administrator derives title from the grant of representation, and previously until a grant has been issued, the estate of the deceased vested in the President of the Family Division of the High Court. Now, the Law of Property (Miscellaneous Provisions) Act 1994 vests the estate of an intestate in the Public Trustee, instead of the President of the Family Division, as was the case previously, until such time as a grant is issued. The Act also extends to estates where there is a will but no executor at the date of death or later.

The proposed administrator must in normal circumstances ascertain the values of the deceased's assets and liabilities before he can apply for the grant of representation, but this does not prevent him or anyone else from dealing with parts of the estate if this is done to protect the estate.

1. When an application is made

Where any person other than the executor proves the will, the application should be as for a grant of administration (with the will). No more than four administrators may be appointed at any one time.

Some of the reasons for this type of grant are:

(i)   no executor has been named in the will (see page 33);

(ii) the appointment of the executor is void for uncertainty;

(iii) the executor has renounced probate of the will or has not appeared to a citation to accept or refuse (see page 25);

(iv) the executor has predeceased the testator, or survived him but since died without having proved the will (see page 32);

(v)   an attorney appointed by the executor applies for the grant (see page 31);

(vi) the executor is a minor or is incapable (see page 23);

(vii) the court passes over the executor and appoints someone else (see page 30).

2. Priority

Priority of right to a grant of administration (with the will) for deaths after 1 January 1988 is given in the following order (r 20 Non-Contentious Probate Rules 1987):

(i) an executor who for some reason has been unable to apply for a grant of probate;

(ii) a residuary legatee or devisee in trust for another person or persons;

(iii) a residuary legatee or devisee, whether entitled for life or otherwise, including one entitled upon a contingency, or, where the residue is not wholly disposed of by the will, any person entitled to share in the residue not wholly disposed of;

(iv) the personal representative of a residuary legatee or devisee;

(v) any other legatee or devisee;

(vi) the personal representative of any other legatee or devisee.

The residuary legatee is the person who receives the residuary personal estate remaining after all specific bequests. The residuary devisee is a person who receives the residuary real estate. Residuary legatees and devisees have an equal right to the grant and one or more of them, up to a maximum of four, may apply. Any dispute as to who should apply may be referred to a district judge or registrar on summons.

Where there is a minority or life interest (see page 49) not less than two people, or a trust corporation alone, must apply (s 114 Supreme Court Act 1981). However, the court may appoint a single individual (not being a trust corporation) as administrator even if there is a minority or life interest if 'it appears to the Court to be expedient in all the circumstances'. If there is only one residuary legatee or devisee *for life*, a grant may be made to him, and an *ultimate* residuary legatee or devisee jointly, the latter being described in the oath as the residuary legatee or devisee substituted. As can be seen, priority is given to a person who has an interest in the residue. One should therefore ascertain that the will effectively disposes of the residuary estate, and the decision of a district judge or registrar should be obtained in cases where there is doubt.

3. Requirements for grant

All persons with a prior right to a grant of administration (with the will) must be cleared off in the oath and the way in which they have been cleared off must be shown (see page 50). The capacity of the deponent must be included and he must state whether or not there is a minority or a life interest, or settled land.

4. Universal legatee and devisee renounces

If the sole residuary legatee and devisee named in the will does not wish to take out a grant of administration (with the will), the guidance of a district judge or a registrar should be sought.

Summary

- Reasons for letters of administration with or without the will may be:
  - No executor has been named or the executors' appointment is void
  - The excutor has died
  - The executor has renounced probate
  - The executor is a minor
  - An attorney of the executor applies for the grant.
- Priority of persons having a right to grant of administration (with the will):
  - An executor
  - A residuary legatee or devisee
  - A personal representative of residuary legatee or devisee
  - Any other legatee or devisee
  - Personal representative of any other legatee or devisee.
- For letters of administration (with the will) or for letters of administration all persons with a prior right to a grant must be cleared off in the oath.
- Where the universal legatee and devisee does not wish to take out a grant, the guidance of a district judge or registrar should be sought.

Chapter 6

Letters of administration

Where the deceased died wholly intestate letters of administration are granted to enable the estate to be realised and administered. Even in cases where there is no estate a grant may be necessary, for example, for the purposes of appointing a new trustee (see page 162), to conduct litigation or to deal with settled land (see page 162).

The administrator receives his authority to deal with the estate from the grant of letters of administration, and until the grant is issued. The Law of Property (Miscellaneous Provisions) Act 1994 vests the estate of an intestate in the Public Trustee, instead of the President of the Family Division, as was the case previously, until such time a grant is issued. The Act also extends to estates where there is a will but no executor at the date of death or later. However, this is only temporary until a grant has been issued, and prevents the estate from becoming *in bona vacantia* (see page 48). (For the general duties of the administrator, see page 22.)

If the client is not one of the persons entitled to a grant he cannot give instructions to deal with the estate, and the person or persons who are entitled to the grant must be found. If a solicitor has acted on the instructions of a person who later proves not to be the person entitled, the true personal representative may decline to pay the costs incurred and the solicitor will have to seek to recover them from the person who gave the instructions.

1. Priority of entitlement to grant

The order of priority for entitlement to the grant is shown below, together with the 'statutory legacies' on intestacy and the order of priority of the beneficiaries. Where more than one person is equally entitled to a grant, preference will be given to a living applicant over a representative of a deceased person who would have been entitled to the grant if still living (r 27(5) Non-Contentious Probate Rules 1987).

Diagrammatically, the order of priority may be illustrated as follows. References to paragraph numbers relate to the table on pages 44–47.

The Law Reform (Succession) Bill (which had only received a second reading in Parliament at the time of writing) recommends an amendment to the intestacy rules so that a surviving spouse will only inherit if he or she survives the intestate by 14 days.

Where the deceased died intestate after 1 June 1987

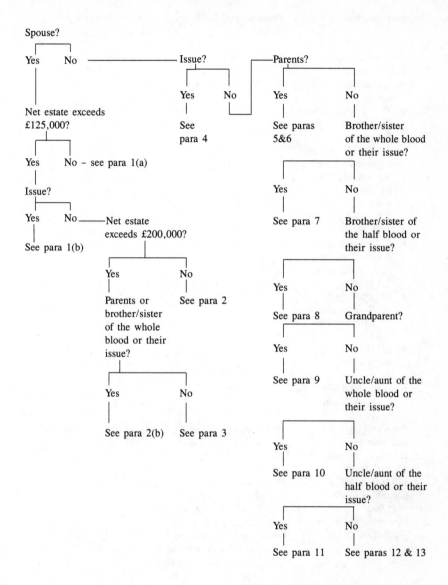

(a) Table of priority

Intestate dies leaving	Person(s) entitled to the estate	Person(s) entitled to a grant
1. (a) Surviving spouse and issue: Net estate not exceeding – • £5,000 where death on or after 1.1.53 but before 1.1.67; • £8,750 where death on or after 1.1.67 but before 1.7.72; • £15,000 where death on or after 1.7.72 but before 15.3.77; • £25,000 where death on or after 15.3.77 but before 1.3.81; • £40,000 where death on or after 1.3.81 but before 1.6.87; • £75,000 where death on or after 1.6.87; • £125,000 where death on or after 1.12.93	Surviving spouse	Surviving spouse
(b) Surviving spouse and issue: Net estate exceeding £5,000, £8,750, £15,000, £25,000, £40,000, £75,000 or £125,000 (see above for appropriate dates)	The surviving spouse receives personal chattels and £5,000, £8,750, £15,000, £25,000, £40,000, £75,000 or £125,000 as appropriate free of costs and duty/tax with interest at 6% pa together with a life interest in half of the remainder of the estate with reversion to issue. The issue receive the other half absolutely	Surviving spouse and a child*
2. (a) Surviving spouse No issue: Net estate not exceeding–	Surviving spouse	Surviving spouse

*Where a minority or life interest arises, there must be at least two applicants for the grant.

Intestate dies leaving	Person(s) entitled to the estate	Person(s) entitled to a grant
• £20,000 where death on or after 1.1.53 but before 1.1.67; • £30,000 where death on or after 1.1.67 but before 1.7.72; • £40,000 where death on or after 1.7.72 but before 15.3.77; • £55,000 where death on or after 15.3.77 but before 1.3.81; • £85,000 where death on or after 1.3.81 but before 1.6.87; • £125,000 where death on or after 1.6.87; • £200,000 where death on or after 1.12.93		
(b) Surviving spouse No issue: Net estate exceeding £20,000, £30,000, £40,000, £55,000, £85,000, £125,000 or £200,000 (see (a) above for appropriate dates)	The surviving spouse receives personal chattels and £20,000, £30,000, £40,000, £55,000, £85,000, £125,000 or £200,000 as appropriate free of costs and duty/tax with interest at 6% pa together with half of the remainder absolutely. The other half of the remainder to the parents absolutely. If no parents survive, the other half of the remainder is shared equally between brothers and sisters of the whole blood, the issue of such brothers and sisters as have predeceased the intestate receiving the share to which their parent would have been entitled	Surviving spouse*
3. Surviving spouse without issue, parent,	Surviving spouse	Surviving spouse

*Where a minority or life interest arises, there must be at least two applicants for the grant.

45

Intestate dies leaving	Person(s) entitled to the estate	Person(s) entitled to a grant
brother or sister of the whole blood or their issue, irrespective of the value of the estate		
4. No surviving spouse but issue	Issue in equal shares; lawful issue of predeceasing issue receiving the share to which their parent would have been entitled (issue includes illegitimate children if death occurred on or after 1.1.70)	Issue*
5. No surviving spouse or issue but both parents	Both parents in equal shares	Either or both parents
6. No surviving spouse or issue but a parent	The parent	The parent
7. No surviving spouse or issue but brothers and sisters of the whole blood and the issue of such brothers and sisters as have predeceased the intestate	Brothers and sisters of the whole blood in equal shares, the issue of such brothers and sisters as have predeceased the intestate receiving the share to which their parent would have been entitled	A person or persons entitled to share in the estate*
8. No surviving spouse, issue, parent or brothers and sisters of the whole blood, but brothers and sisters of the half blood and the issue of such brothers and sisters as have predeceased the intestate	Brothers and sisters of the half blood in equal shares, the issue of such brothers and sisters as have predeceased the intestate receiving the share to which their parent would have been entitled	A person or persons entitled to share in the estate*
9. No surviving spouse or issue but grandparents	The grandparents in equal shares	Either or both grandparents
10. No surviving spouse or issue but uncles and aunts of the whole blood and the issue of such uncles and aunts as have predeceased the intestate	Uncles and aunts of the whole blood in equal shares, the issue of such uncles and aunts as have predeceased the intestate receiving the share to which their parent would have been entitled	A person or persons entitled to share in the estate*
11. No surviving spouse or issue but uncles and aunts of the half blood	Uncles and aunts of the half blood in equal shares, the issue of such uncles	A person or persons entitled to share in the estate*

*Where a minority or life interest arises, there must be at least two applicants for the grant.

and the issue of such uncles and aunts as have predeceased the intestate	and aunts as have predeceased the intestate receiving the share to which their parent would have been entitled	
12. No blood relation with an interest as set out in 1 to 11 above	(i) The Crown (ii) The Duchy of Lancaster (iii) The Duchy of Cornwall	(i) Treasury Solicitor (ii) Solicitor for the Duchy of Lancaster (iii) Solicitor for the Duchy of Cornwall
13. A creditor		The creditor (upon renunciation or clearing off of all persons with a prior right to the grant)

*Where a minority or life interest arises, there must be at least two applicants for the grant.

Administration is usually granted to persons who have a beneficial interest in the estate where possible. For deaths on or after 1 January 1970 but before 4 April 1988, illegitimate children of the deceased had a right of succession on intestacy, as well as legitimate children – as also did the natural parents of an illegitimate child dying intestate.

However, an illegitimate child's rights of succession were limited and he could not take under the intestacy of his brothers and sisters, grandparents, uncles/aunts etc. Also, where an illegitimate person died intestate leaving no surviving spouse, issue or parent, his estate passed *in bona vacantia* (see paragraph (*e*) on page 48).

For deaths intestate on or after 4 April 1988, the illegitimacy of any person is not taken into consideration (s 1 Family Law Reform Act 1987). In oaths for administrators the surviving spouse continues to be described as 'lawful', but the oath does not need to describe any other relative as 'lawful' or 'natural'.

(b) Surviving spouse

A surviving spouse, when entitled to a life interest on the intestacy, has the right to redeem the life interest and accept a capital payment in its place. The amount of that payment is calculated according to the special rules contained in the Intestate Succession (Interest and Capitalisation) Order 1977. The right may not be exercised until after a personal representative has been appointed. The procedure is explained at page 170.

(c) Family tree

In cases where the person entitled to the grant or estate is more remote than the spouse or children of the deceased, it might prove helpful to prepare a family tree. At times a tree is required by the Probate Registry. The tree is very helpful in that it shows clearly the persons entitled to the grant/estate, and incidentally, is usually of great interest to the family.

An example of a family tree is given on the below:

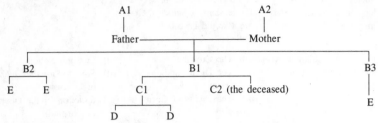

The deceased C2

A1 and A2: paternal and maternal grandparents C1: brother/sister
B1: father and mother D: nephews/nieces
B2 and B3: uncle/aunt E: cousins german

(d) Grant to creditor

If all persons entitled to share in the estate of the deceased are cleared off by death, renunciation or citation, a grant may be made to a creditor of the deceased. The creditor may be required to provide a guarantee, but no special affidavit is needed. The applicant has only to state on the oath that he is a creditor of the deceased. Any expense to which the creditor has been put in obtaining the grant may be repaid to him from the estate, before the net estate is distributed.

Administration will not be granted to a creditor of the estate who does not make a claim against the estate until after the date of death.

An undertaker may obtain the grant if he was commissioned by a person entitled to the estate. He should make an application under s 116 Supreme Court Act 1981 for an order for a grant. An undertaker is not *prima facie* a creditor of the deceased.

(e) No one entitled

Where there is nobody entitled to the estate of an intestate, the net residue passes as *in bona vacantia* to the Crown, the Duchy of Lancaster or to the Duchy of Cornwall, but may be subject to claims under the Inheritance (Provision for Family and Dependants) Act 1975 (see page 167).

Where the estate of an intestate passes *in bona vacantia*, that is where the deceased leaves no relatives who are entitled to his estate under the rules of intestacy, apart from claims under the Inheritance (Provision for Family and Dependants) Act 1975, one should consider an application for an *ex-gratia* payment:

> 'The Crown or the Duchy of Lancaster or the Duchy of Cornwall may, out of the whole or any part of the property devolving on them respectively, provide, in accordance with existing practice, for dependants, whether kindred or not of the intestate for whom the intestate might reasonably have been expected to make provision' (s 46(1) Administration of Estates Act 1925).

Any person who believes the intestate might reasonably have made provision for him/her may apply to the Treasury Solicitor, Queen Anne's Chambers, 28 Broadway, London SW1H 9JS (if the deceased lived in Cornwall, to the solicitor to the Duchy of Cornwall and if in the county Palatine of Lancaster, to the solicitor for the affairs of the Duchy of Lancaster). There is no right for anyone to receive a payment; it is discretionary. Applications should be made in the first instance by a letter setting out the facts. An additional statement for clarification may be required at a later date. Applications are not usually considered until one year after the death, and only after the administration of the estate has been completed.

If, under the Inheritance (Provision for Family and Dependants) Act 1975, a successful claim is made by relatives of the intestate, the beneficiary of a previously made *ex-gratia* payment will not, in normal circumstances, be required to repay the sum.

2. Application for grant

(a) Number of administrators

Letters of administration will be granted to one or more administrators up to a maximum of four, but if a minority or life interest arises under the intestacy there must be at least two administrators or a trust corporation alone.

(b) Minority or life interest

If there is a minority or life interest, an additional administrator may be appointed by a district judge or a registrar when one of two administrators dies after the grant has been made, but the court may appoint a single individual as administrator even if there is a minority or life interest.

(c) Description of applicants

For deaths after 4 April 1988 the applicants for a grant of letters of administration should be described in the oath as:

Applicant	Description
	Spouse The lawful husband or
	The lawful widow and relict
Issue of the marriage	The son/daughter
	The adopted son/daughter
	The legitimated son/daughter
Parent	The father/mother
	The adopter
	The father/mother by legitimation
Natural parent	The father/mother (after 1 January 1970)
Brother or sister	The brother/sister of the whole/half blood

Issue of the brother/sister	The nephew/niece (or great nephew/niece) of the whole/half blood
Grandparent	The grandfather/grandmother
Uncle or aunt	The uncle/aunt of the whole/half blood
Issue of uncle/aunt	The cousin german of the whole/half blood

(d) Contents of oath

The application for a grant of letters of administration must contain a statement clearing off, as necessary, all persons having a prior right to the grant. It must contain the name (including aliases), address, date of death, and the age of the deceased; and the name, address and description of the deponent. A statement as to whether or not there is a minority or a life interest, or settled land, must also be included. Most standard printed forms of oath contain the statement of minorities and settled land.

(e) Clearing off

For deaths after 1 January 1970 the wording for clearing off in an application for letters of administration is:

Wording	Clears
The deceased died:	
A bachelor	
A spinster	
A widow	
A widower	
A single man	
A single woman	A spouse
Without issue	Children or other issue
Without parent or any other person entitled in priority to share in the estate by virtue of any enactment	Parents
Without brother or sister of the whole or half blood or issue thereof or any other person entitled in priority to share in the estate by virtue of any enactment	Brothers and sisters and their issue
Without grandparents or any other person entitled in priority to share in the estate by virtue of any enactment	Grandparents
Without uncle or aunt of the whole blood or half blood or issue thereof or any other person entitled in priority to share in the estate by virtue of any enactment	Uncles, aunts and their issue

(f) Duplicate applications

If more than one application for a grant in the same estate is lodged by persons equally entitled, the grant will be issued to the applicant whose application is received first. However, if the second or subsequent application is received before the grant is issued, the second or subsequent application is usually allowed time to enter a caveat and the matter may be brought before the registrar by way of a summons. A caveat takes the form of a written notice to the Probate Registry that no grant is to be issued without notice being given to the person entering the caveat (the caveator). A caveat will *not* prevent the sealing of a grant *ad colligenda bona* or a grant under s 117 of the Act. Nor will it prevent the sealing of any grant on the day on which the caveat is entered, and can be extended for additional six-monthly periods (see Chapter 16).

Duplicate applications may occur due to lack of information between members of a family, and if, therefore, only one or two members of a family give instructions they should be advised to inform all other persons who are equally entitled to a grant, and to attempt to agree among themselves who is to apply and deal with the administration of the estate. This will enable the estate to be dealt with more quickly, for the benefit of all concerned.

3. Guarantees

In certain circumstances guarantees were required under r 38(1) Non-Contentious Probate Rules 1954. Under the 1987 Rules guarantees were abolished. However, the statutory provision under s 120 Supreme Court Act 1981 is still in existence and a district judge or a registrar may, therefore, still require a guarantee.

Checklist: Pre-lodgement of grant application; Letters of administration

Extracting solicitors:	Full name, address, postcode, DX No and reference.
Name of deceased:	Where the deceased was known by another name the true and proper name must be specified, and the reason for the alias to be included in the oath, if necessary in a separate paragraph at the end. (An alias name will only be shown in the grant if the deceased held an asset (e.g. bank account, real property) in the alias name.)
Letters of administration (with or without will):	Ensure that all the proper 'clearings' are recited and that the applicant's full title to apply is set out e.g. deceased died: 'A spinster without issue or parent or brother

or sister of the whole or half blood or their issue or grandparent or uncle or aunt of the whole blood or their issue or any other person entitled to share in the estate by virtue of any enactment "I am the lawful cousin german of the half blood being the (lawful) (son) (daughter) of ..... a (lawful) (uncle) (aunt) of the half blood who died in the lifetime of the said deceased and (one of) the person(s) entitled to (share) the estate".'

Life or minority interest: Where application is made for a grant of administration, check the clause relating to any life or minority interests has been completed.

Date of death: Check date of death coincides with date of the death certificate. Where the certificate states date of death as 'on or about ....' the oath must state when the deceased was 'last seen alive' or 'last known to be alive' and when the body was found.

Age of deceased: Age of deceased at death to be inserted *especially* in 'excepted estate' cases.

Domicile: Ensure domicile inserted: Where the domicile is foreign and where different systems of law operate in different parts of the country ensure that the State of domicile is inserted e.g. 'in the State of Texas, United States of America'.

Settled land: Complete settled land clause.

Attorney applications: Ensure the fact that the attorney of the person entitled is recited and that the limitation 'for the use and benefit of ...... and until further representation be granted' is included after the words 'I will collect, get in and administer' etc.

Excepted estates: Ensure the gross and net figures appropriate to the date of death and value of the estate are inserted *and* that the clause stating the case is an excepted estate is inserted.

Jurat: Ensure the jurat is completed and has been signed by the deponent(s) and the commissioner(s).

Summary

- There is a strict order of priority of persons entitled to the grant (see p. 44 *et seq.*).

- A surviving spouse is entitled to the personal chattels and the statutory legacy and a life interest in part of the remainder. When there is a life interest the surviving spouse has the right to redeem that life interest.

- In cases where the person or persons entitled to the grant and to the estate are more remote than the spouse or children of the deceased a family tree should be prepared showing the persons and their entitlement.

- Where all persons entitled in priority to a grant have been cleared off a creditor may apply for a grant.

- Undertakers are not *prima facie* creditors of the deceased.

- Where there is nobody entitled to the estate of the intestate the residue passes in *bona vacantia*. However, the Treasury Solicitor may consider claims under the Inheritance (Provision for Family and Dependants) Act 1975.

- A maximum of four administrators may apply for a grant, and there must be two administrators if a minority or life interest arises under the intestacy.

- The Administrators Oath must contain a statement clearing off all persons having a prior right to the grant, as necessary.

- Where more than one application for a grant in the same estate is lodged by persons equally entitled, a grant will be issued to the person whose application is received first. If both applications are received together or a second application is received before the grant is issued, the second or subsequent application is usually allowed time to enter a caveat and the matter brought before a registrar by way of summons.

- Under the 1987 Non-Contention Probate Rules the need for guarantees was removed. However, the statutory provision under the Supreme Court Act s 120, 1981 still exists. A district judge or registrar may still require a guarantee in certain circumstances.

Chapter 7

Identifying the estate assets

The personal representative's first duty is to ascertain the value of the assets and liabilities of the deceased's estate to see whether or not an Inland Revenue Account is needed (s 25 Administration of Estates Act 1925). The application for the grant can then be drafted and, depending on the value of the estate, the Account can be prepared. This chapter deals with the assets; Chapter 8 deals with the liabilities. In some cases a grant is not required (see page 86), or an Inland Revenue Account is not needed (see page 88). There is some overlap between this chapter and Chapter 14, which deals with the distribution of the assets after the grant has been issued.

Appendix 2 gives suggestions for standard letters which can be prepared for use in the procedures explained below.

Appendix 3 is a simple schedule of assets and liabilities.

For the authority of the executor to commence the administration see Chapter 4, and for that of an administrator, Chapter 6.

1. Cash in hand

If the deceased left any cash in hand, i.e. coins or bank notes, it should be paid into the client account, or into the personal representative's account (if such an account has been opened; see page 70) and may be used towards the payment of commissioner's fees, purchase of death certificate, Probate Registry fees and the like. This is often preferable to paying such disbursements out of office accounts and awaiting repayment from the estate at a later date. It must be remembered, however, that the funeral account is the first claim on the estate. The personal representative should give written authority that cash can be used before a grant is issued.

Where the deceased died in a hospital, the hospital authorities keep in safe custody any money and valuables given to them by the deceased until they can obtain a valid receipt for the items from the personal representative.

An elderly deceased may have held cash in the form of old bank notes which have been taken out of circulation. These should be delivered to a bank who will ascertain whether they are still legal tender. A form from the Bank of England or from a local bank may have to be completed to obtain the equivalent in current notes.

Any foreign money should be delivered to a bank and exchanged for British currency, although most banks accept notes only and not coins. The bank receipt showing the exchange rate on the date of exchange should be retained on the file.

It is usual to allow the spouse to retain the cash where:

(i) the will leaves the estate to the surviving spouse, or the spouse is entitled to the estate under intestacy;

(ii) the cash forms part of the £125,000 or £200,000 entitlement under intestacy (see Chapter 6); and

(iii) the estate is solvent.

2. Bank and building society accounts

(a) Bank account(s)

Bank accounts include current and deposit accounts, special deposits, business accounts, loan and trustee accounts, all of which may be held in the deceased's sole name or jointly with another or others.

A deceased's account(s) is frozen by the banks as soon as a death has been reported. When advising banks of the death the letter should, as appropriate:

(i) authorise and request the bank to transfer funds out of a current account into a deposit account pending production of the grant;

(ii) include an authority from the personal representative to the bank to release to safe custody items to the solicitors, plus an undertaking from the solicitors. (The *Law Society's Gazette* of 9 July 1986, pages 2139–2140, reports on the agreement to the above by certain banks.);

(iii) request a detailed schedule of those securities which will remain in the bank pending production of the grant;

(iv) request a statement of the deceased's account(s) at the date of death;

(v) if the original will (and codicil(s)) are held by the bank, authorise release;

(vi) request a list of cheques passed through an account which have not cleared due to the death. If the cheque was in payment of a debt it is an estate liability. If, however, the cheque was not for consideration or moneys worth (for example a wedding present) it will be an imperfect gift and therefore is not deducted from the account and is liable to inheritance tax (if IHT is payable on the assets).

National Savings Bank accounts are administered at the National Savings Bank in Glasgow and are dealt with as a normal bank account. Enquiries should be addressed to The Controller, National Savings Bank, Glasgow G58 1SB.

A note should be made of the bank account number, and whether it is an ordinary account or an investment account. These details will be required when completing the deceased's income tax returns.

(b) Building society account(s)

A letter should be written to any building society with which the deceased held account(s), requesting a statement of the balance in the account at the date of death, which should include interest accrued but not credited. The letter can also include a request for specimen signature forms, and withdrawal/transfer forms for completion by the personal representative. These can be signed by the personal representative in readiness for forwarding to the building society as soon as the grant is received. If the passbook/certificate is available, this should be sent to the society when making enquiries about the account balance, and is often retained by the society until the grant is produced and the account closed or transferred. A careful note should be made as to whether or not the society has retained the passbook.

If a term account is transferred to a beneficiary following the grant, the transferee agrees to the original term entered into by the deceased. If the beneficiary prefers not to be bound by the term, the account should be closed after the grant is issued, and the beneficiary can make his or her own investments.

(c) Joint accounts

Where there are accounts held in the names of the deceased and another or others, the death certificate should be produced and the account will be transferred to the surviving holder(s). Full details of joint accounts should be obtained, including interest accrued up to the date of death, together with details of the source of the funds, i.e. whether the money was provided by the deceased alone or jointly, and if the latter, in what proportion. This information may be obtained from the other joint holder(s). The details will be required when completing inheritance tax Forms 200 or 202 (see page 89), and even though the account passes by survivorship, the amount in the account which belonged to the deceased should be included in the Inland Revenue account for calculating the inheritance tax liability.

In the case of joint accounts where a joint holder was named merely to facilitate withdrawals, e.g. for an elderly or infirm person, or the joint holder was an attorney appointed by the deceased, the account must be collected in and it forms part of the estate. The bank or building society will usually transfer the account to the surviving joint holder, who should then be asked to transfer or pay it to the personal representative or his solicitor.

Note, however, that for claims under the Inheritance (Provision for Family and Dependants) Act 1975 (see page 167) one-half of joint property may be classed as part of the deceased's estate even though it has been transferred into the sole name of the surviving joint holder. If the property is subject to a mortgage secured by an endowment, half of the insurance proceeds forms part of the estate (*Powell v Osbourne* 1992).

3. Premium bonds, National Savings Certificates and Income Bonds

(a) Premium bonds

A list of all the premium savings bonds held by the deceased should be prepared and sent to the Controller, Bonds and Stock Office, Mythop Road, Marton, Blackpool FY3 9YP (telephone (01253) 66151), with the premium bonds (if available) and the bond holder's card. The office should be asked if there are unclaimed prizes or any other bonds registered in the deceased's name, and if so, a search will have to be made to find the bonds. Where bond certificates cannot be found, the Bonds and Stock Office will provide a declaration for the personal representative to complete which will enable him to encash the missing bonds. An encashment form should also be requested, which can be completed by the personal representative to encash the bonds when the grant is available. In many cases the Controller may advise that sight of the grant is not required, in which case the bonds can be dealt with immediately. In a small estate where a grant is not required (see page 86) the full names of the personal representatives must be noted on the encashment form.

Premium savings bonds may not be transferred to any other person, but they may be left in the prize draw up to the end of the month in which the first anniversary of the death falls, and they will then be removed from the draw whether or not they have been encashed.

Bonds remain eligible for prizes until the end of the first anniversary as above, or until encashed, and any prizes won after the date of death will be included in the net estate for distribution, but they do not form part of the estate for the purposes of obtaining the grant, or for calculating inheritance tax.

The Bonds and Stock Office will contact the executors after the first anniversary of the death if the premium savings bonds have not been encashed. Even if it is decided to leave the premium savings bonds in the prize draw until the first anniversary of the death it is sensible to produce the grant of representation to the Bonds and Stock Office, if required, as soon as it is available. If the administration of the estate has been completed before the first anniversary of the death, and the grant has not yet been exhibited, additional work will be created for the executors/solicitors/accountants who dealt with the administration of the estate.

(b) National Savings Certificates and Income Bonds

National Savings Certificates should be listed, and a copy of the list, together with the certificates (if available) and the holder's card should be sent to the Director of Savings, Savings Certificates and SAYE Office,

Durham DH99 1NS. The office should be asked for a probate valuation of the certificates and conformation that there are no other certificates registered in the deceased's name or in the name of the deceased jointly with another. The certificate of value will be required by the Capital Taxes Office if an Inland Revenue Account is submitted (see Chapter 10). An encashment form, or if the certificates are to be transferred, a form of transfer, should also be requested. It is possible to encash part only, rather than the total, of the holding, and this facility is useful where there are some certificates which have not yet been held for the full term and where early encashment would lose part of the interest payable.

If any certificates have been nominated (see page 69), this will be advised by the Controller.

Income bonds may be dealt with in the same manner as Savings Certificates, although it should be noted that correspondence should be directed to the Bonds and Stock Office in Blackpool (see page 57 for the address).

4. Post-war credits

These are certificates which were issued to employees in the early post-war years, and all of them should have been encashed some years ago. However, there are still many in circulation and if any in the deceased's name are found they should be sent for encashment to HMIT, PWC Centre, Ty Glas, Llanishen, Cardiff CF4 5TX, on completion of Form DC 351.

The certificates should be worth their face value plus an additional 38 per cent or thereabouts. The time to make claims *without* a certificate expired 31 December 1978 (SI 1978 No 662). Since that date, claims can only be made by producing one or more certificates. However, everyone who could produce certificates, and also everyone who could be traced by the post-war credits department (even if they could not produce certificates) has received payment. Therefore, even if certificates are found in the deceased's estate, it is not certain that they have any value, because repayment may have been made already. In this event the PWC department will return the certificates, stamped 'cancelled'.

5. Stocks and shares

These include registered and bearer shares and those not quoted on the Stock Exchange. Stocks and shares should be listed alphabetically, showing any unquoted shares separately for easy reference. It will be necessary to ascertain the number of shares held in private companies in relation to the total number of shares issued by that company, as the proportion is relevant to the value of the deceased's holding.

If the deceased left details of the brokers who normally managed his portfolio, they can be asked to prepare a probate valuation either from their own records, or from a schedule supplied to them. Stockbrokers usually prepare a valuation according to classification, e.g. government stocks, food, leisure, mining. As from 11 February 1986 all values of gilt-edged stocks are quoted 'clean', that is, after allowing for accrued interest, whereas previously valuations could be quoted 'ex dividend' etc. All 'gilts' are exempt from capital gains tax even on sales within twelve months of purchasing the holding.

The broker's valuation should be checked against a list of shares held, and any discrepancy dealt with. Share and dividend vouchers can be compared with the list of holdings and this might reveal a difference between the broker's list and the list from the bank or the personal representative. The brokers can be asked to verify the numbers of shares or the amount of stock held if there is any uncertainty. As dividend and interest cheques on stocks and shares are received a list should be prepared showing the gross amounts, tax credits, and net sums received. This may be used for preparing the income accounts (see Appendix 4), and as a checklist when re-issuing cheques in favour of the personal representatives after the grant has issued. Separate lists should be prepared for cheques received and payable up to the date of death, and for those payable after the death. Amounts payable up to the death will form part of the estate, and must be included in the deceased's tax returns for the period up to the death.

If there is any likelihood of delay in obtaining a grant of representation the death may be registered with the various registrars of the companies as soon as the death certificate is available, and the interest and dividend payments will then be withheld until the grant has been produced, at which time the cheques will be issued in favour of the personal representative.

Beneficiaries might wish to accept stocks or shares as part of their entitlement and it should be noted that the value passing for purposes of the administration will be the value as at the date of the transfer, and *not* the value as at the date of death. It will be necessary to obtain a separate date-of-transfer valuation for those holdings transferred to beneficiaries. Any increase or decrease in values should be included in the estate accounts. For the beneficiaries, the value passing for the purposes of capital gains tax will be the date-of-death value (s 49(4) CGTA 1979).

If there are unit trusts which have been taken over by another company, and are classified under new names, up-to-date details of the names and addresses may be found in the Unit Trust Year Book published by the Unit Trust Association, 65 Kingsway, London, or in Extel Publications.

Below are definitions of some stock exchange terms:

Capitalisation Issue: (normally called a 'scrip' or 'bonus' issue) which is a free issue of shares in proportion to the existing holding.

Common Stock: the term for ordinary shares in the USA and Canada.

Cum: means with the current dividend or other rights.

Ex: without the current dividend or other rights.

Final Dividend: the last distribution by a company for a trading period. The majority of companies pay two dividends per year, but some pay only one per year.

Fully Paid: where the nominal value of shares is fully paid up.

Gilt Edged (British Funds): the usual name for UK Government stocks.

Interim Dividend: this is a dividend on account of the total dividend for the current trading period paid by a company.

Par: a security's nominal value.

Portfolio: a list of the securities owned by an individual or an institution.

Rights Issue: issue of new shares in proportion to those held by existing share holders. The price of the issue is normally lower than the market price of existing shares.

A personal representative does not become a member of the company or companies in which the deceased held shares merely by registering the grant of representation. The shareholding remains in the deceased's name. The shares do not have to be registered in the personal representative to enable him to sell or transfer them. If the personal representative does not intend to sell or transfer a holding for some time, then it may be beneficial to transfer the holding into his name so that he is entitled, on behalf of the estate, to any member's privileges and rights in the company. A letter of request is used by a personal representative to transfer shares into his own name.

When an executor dies intestate, or when an administrator dies before selling or transferring the shares, the company registrars will require a grant of letters of administration *de bonis non*.

6. Life assurance

Letters should be sent to the insurance companies with whom the deceased held any policy, to ascertain whether the policy(ies) is valid, and if so, the value. The letter should quote the policy number and should be accompanied by the policy document and the premium receipt book if these are available. It is advisable to keep a photocopy of the policy in the file. However, the letter should not be delayed if these documents are not immediately to hand, although the insurers must be informed if any policy has been lost. The letter should also request a claim form for completion by the personal representative (subject to the claim being admitted), as this will save having to obtain a claim form after the grant has issued. Some insurance companies, however, will not release a claim form until the grant is produced. The death certificate should also be produced. *Note:* Insurance companies refuse to accept a photocopy of the death certificate even if the copy has been certified by a solicitor.

To claim the amount due to the estate, insurance companies will require sight of the death certificate, and the grant of representation. They will also need the original policy document, and the company's claim form completed by the executor. A few insurance companies may also require sight of the deceased's birth and marriage certificates depending on the type of policy, which is usually when the deceased held an investment bond. In cases where policy documents have been lost, the company will provide their own form of indemnity (lost policy declaration) for completion by the executor.

When the deceased was the proposer of any life assurance on the life of another, the surrender value of the policy should be obtained. At a later date the policy can be surrendered by the life assured or transferred to the life assured or another person, subject to the terms of the will or the entitlement under an intestacy. However, any dealings with the policy must be under the written instructions of the personal representative if it is dealt with by the solicitors.

Any life assurance on the life of the deceased which was proposed by another person does not form part of the deceased's estate and the proposer can make a claim on the policy by completing a claim form and producing a death certificate to the insurance company.

In case of difficulty in tracing an insurance company, the Registrar of Friendly Societies, the British Insurance Association or the Insurance Brokers Registration Council may be contacted; addresses and telephone numbers are given in Appendix 2. With regard to any dispute, the Insurance Ombudsman or the Personal Arbitration Service may be consulted (Appendix 2).

7. Schedule of securities

A schedule of securities should be prepared, covering all the matters discussed in paragraphs 2 to 6 above. Whether this is prepared by a bank, stockbroker, the personal representatives or their agents, it should show full and complete details of the assets, including values and reference numbers of bonds, certificates, policy documents and the like. All these details will be required to ascertain the total value of the estate to apply for a grant of representation (see Chapter 12).

8. Wages, salaries and private pensions

If the deceased was employed at the date of his death his employers should be advised of the death and asked if there are any arrears of salary, and any holiday pay due to the estate. The letter to the employer should also ask for details of the deceased's tax reference number and the address of his tax district (see page 77), and of any pension scheme to which he belonged.

A death certificate should be produced to the trustees of the pension scheme and details of the deceased's family should be provided, i.e. the full names of a spouse and the names and ages of any children who were financially dependent on the deceased. If the trustees require sight of any marriage certificate or birth certificate they will request them. Any lump sum benefit due to the estate will be advised but it is usual for the pension fund trustees to deal direct with the surviving spouse in relation to any pension due.

Most pensions are payable at the discretion of the trustees of the pension fund, and the personal representative(s) will have no say as to who receives the pension, although they will usually be given the opportunity to make a statement of the beneficiaries' claims.

If the deceased was a member of a trade union there may be an *ex gratia* payment made to the spouse or next of kin, which is usually paid direct and does not normally form part of the estate. There is often a collection of money made by the deceased's colleagues at his place of employment, but this is normally for the spouse or other next of kin and cannot be classed as an estate asset since it is not a benefit which the deceased would have received.

See page 78 for State pensions.

9. Self-employed pension plans

'Self-employed pension plans' are chargeable with inheritance tax *and* income tax.

Example:

A widow purchases a 'self-employed pension plan', and opts to have payments guaranteed for the first five years. The policy matures and she receives the pension, (which is taxable as her part of her earnings), for one year. She then dies, leaving four years to run under the terms of the guaranteed pension.

It is not possible to commute or assign this type of pension/annuity. The pension payments continue for four years to her beneficiaries and become part of their taxable investment income.

The widow's estate is liable for inheritance tax, and the remaining guaranteed payments form part of her assets.

It may be possible to negotiate a lower figure for the estate value because the pension/annuity (in this example) is payable over four years and cannot be assigned or commuted, and income tax will have to be paid. The Inland Revenue may accept a reduction equal to the amount of the basic rate income tax payable.

In cases where the policy holder dies before the policy has matured, the death benefits are tax free.

10. Annuities

(a) Securities and Investment Board Rules

Whenever a person applies for an annuity investment he enjoys a 14-day waiting period (a cooling-off period) during which time he can change his mind and cancel his application.

However, if that person dies within the 14-day period, the application is considered as having been completed. The result is that the capital investment made is not repayable to the deceased's estate (depending on the type of investment applied for).

11. Chattels

Assets which fall under the heading of personal chattels are as follows (s 55(1)(x) Administration of Estates Act 1925):

'carriages, horses, stable furniture and effects (not used for business purposes), motor cars and accessories (not used for business purposes), garden effects, domestic animals, plate, plated articles, linen, china, glass, books, pictures, prints, furniture, jewellery, articles of household or personal use or ornament, musical and scientific instruments and apparatus, wines, liquors and consumable stores'.

Chattels do not include any chattels used at the death for business purposes, or money or securities for money.

If the deceased's home is to be left unoccupied it is important that all valuable items are made secure, the easily portable items being removed from the property and kept in a safe place. The insurers may need to be advised of the removal for safekeeping of chattels if this affects the cover.

Personal representatives should be advised that family and friends should not help themselves to any items from the estate, whether it is for 'a keepsake' or because 'the deceased promised it to me'. Any claims of this nature can be dealt with at a later date, but in the meantime it should be strongly emphasised that everything forms part of the estate and nothing should be removed without the knowledge and permission of the personal representative, who is responsible to the beneficiaries. If there is a surviving spouse who inherits the chattels either under the will or intestacy, he or she may retain the chattels and the personal representative need not be involved a part from ascertaining the values, and obtaining a receipt from the beneficiary, if appropriate.

See page 148 as to the sale of chattels.

(a) Valuation

If the chattels are being retained after the grant, because they have been specifically bequeathed by the will or because a beneficiary wishes to take a chattel or chattels as part of his entitlement, they should be valued, and individual values should be obtained for items which are specifically mentioned in the will. Items or sets of items which have a value exceeding £500 should also be valued individually under descriptions which clearly identify them.

A professional valuation protects the personal representative. Where an agent is instructed to deal with the sale of a dwelling house, he will sometimes be prepared to provide an overall valuation of the household contents free of charge, but this should be checked before proceeding.

Where there are specific chattels left to individuals in the will, the valuer should be asked to prepare written valuations specifying the individual values. These values will be included in the distribution accounts (see Appendix 4).

Any single asset, or a set worth £500 or more should be described fully, and individual values given in the Inland Revenue Account (see Chapter 10). Where assets are sold within a reasonable period after the death, the gross amounts realised in the sale are the values to be submitted for inheritance tax purposes, even though the actual amounts received will be less the agent's charge. Agents charge around 17.5 per cent of the amount received on sale, plus removal charges, plus VAT.

Under the Consumer Protection Act 1994 it is difficult to dispose of certain chattels. All *soft furnishings* manufactured prior to 1988 and which do not carry the Fire Retardant warning triangle do not comply with the new regulations. This means that they could be a fire hazard. Auctioneers will therefore no longer sell foam filled and hazardous items through their auction rooms.

Electrical appliances: All electrical appliances will have to have a certificate showing that they have been tested, and passed as safe. Many auctioneers have dealt with this problem by employing a qualified electrician to test any items which have been sent for sale. All items which fail these tests cannot be exhibited for sale. Auctioneers are liable to a fine of up to £2,000 per article if they offer goods which do not pass the safety test.

Gas cookers and gas bottle heaters: These items also have to be tested and any items failing the test will not be accepted for sale.

These rules apply not only to auction houses but to all retail outlets. It has been suggested that these rules will eventually apply also to car boot sales.

Since the introduction of the Furniture and Furnishings (Fire Safety) Regulations 1988 (SI 1988 No 1324 as amended by SI 1990 No 2358 and SI 1993 No 207), upholstered furniture which does not comply cannot be sold at auctions. Electrical and gas appliances are also affected. This creates problems in valuing these types of chattels.

If there are chattels which are valuable or would be were it not for the Safety Regulations, personal representatives should consider if it would be worthwhile having the upholstering replaced so that the chattel complies with the regulations, so that the chattel could then be sold at auction.

If the chattels are not to be sold, they should be valued, and the estimated cost of reupholstery deducted from the valuation, the reduced value is then submitted as the date of death value. If the estimated cost of reupholstery exceeds the value of the article, then that chattel has a nil value. Electrical and gas appliances can be dealt with in a similar way.

(b) Jewellery, plate etc.

If for any reason it is not possible to obtain a professional valuation, a reasonable estimate of the open market value may have to be submitted when applying for the grant. A list may be prepared in which the items of gold, silver, plated articles, jewellery, stamp collections etc. should be described as fully as possible. There might be a previous valuation for insurance purposes among the personal effects which will assist in estimating the values for the grant. However, insurance values are usually higher than probate values and the items should therefore be valued when they are released from safe custody. A corrective account (see page 90) should, when appropriate, be submitted to the capital taxes office as soon as the true value of the estimated items is known.

Items of value in the deceased's possession at the date of death should be valued as soon as possible and thereafter can be handed over to the beneficiaries named in the will, if they are specifically mentioned. The beneficiary should, of course, give a receipt. The personal representative must satisfy himself that the estate is solvent before releasing any assets.

(c) Cars

The grant of representation is not normally needed to dispose of the deceased's motor car, and the notification of sale on the vehicle registration document may be marked '........ died on (date) and I am the personal representative'. The DVLC at Swansea usually accepts this without raising any query. If it is considered necessary, a photocopy of the death certificate can be included with the notification of sale or transfer. As soon as the vehicle has been disposed of, the deceased's motor insurers should be advised, and a request for a refund of premium made. The proceeds of sale are transferred to the estate. If a member of the deceased's family or another person entitled decides to accept the motor vehicle as part of his entitlement, he should be advised to insure the vehicle immediately before it is driven.

(d) Equipment on hire

Any equipment on hire to the deceased should be returned (or the hire transferred to the spouse by the hire company). If a television set is returned to a hire company or otherwise disposed of, the licence should be returned to TV Licensing, Bristol BS98 1TL, with a certified copy of the death certificate. Refunds are given (*a*) where a licence is purchased in error e.g. where a licence is already held or a licence is not required, or (*b*) part refunds are given for fully unused quarters of the licence.

12. Real property

(a) Valuation

When dealing with an estate where no inheritance tax liability arises, the personal representative might prefer to give his own estimated value of the dwelling house where it was owned by the deceased. However, if the home is to be sold, a valuation can usually be obtained free of charge if the valuers are instructed to deal with the sale.

Where inheritance tax is likely to be payable, a full valuation should be obtained, and, unless the dwelling is to be sold fairly promptly, the Capital Taxes Office will contact the local District Valuation Officer. The DVO may wish to inspect the property and will advise the personal representative of the value of the dwelling. It is advisable to instruct an estate agent to deal with the DVO if the value is disputed, as local estate agents are aware of current market trends and are in a position to discuss values with the District Valuation Officer, and the personal representative can accept the advice of the local agent which will safeguard him against any claim by the residuary beneficiaries.

If the house is sold at arm's length reasonably soon after the death, the amount realised on the sale will be taken as the value for inheritance tax purposes. If the sale takes place within four years of the death the sale value can be substituted for the probate value.

(b) Fire and contents insurance

The personal representative should ascertain at once if the house and contents are insured to the full market value of the contents and the full rebuilding costs of the building. If so, the insurers must be informed in writing of the death, and they should be advised of the names of the personal representative(s). If the insurance cover is not sufficient it should be increased to the correct amount immediately to safeguard the personal representative against any claim by the beneficiaries for loss.

When details of insurance cover cannot be found, insurance must be arranged immediately even at the risk of duplicating cover as this is preferable to risking the assets being left uninsured. If an insurance policy is subsequently traced, the emergency cover can be cancelled and the unused premium reclaimed.

It is difficult to find an insurance company who will accept the risk on an unoccupied property where the owner is deceased. Insurance cover may now be arranged through a scheme arranged with a leading insurance company by the Law Society.

When a property is sold any apportioned premium repayable must be included in the net estate and distributed to the beneficiaries.

Insurers must be advised if the property is left unoccupied as this may affect the cover.

(c) Caring for property left empty

During the warmer months, empty property should be checked regularly to make certain that water in the lavatory, sink and bath traps has not evaporated; taps should be opened from time to time and lavatories flushed to keep the waste pipes full of water so as to avoid the possibility of an inflow of air direct from the main sewer. If the personal representative, family of the deceased, or beneficiaries do not live in the area, a neighbour might agree to make regular visits to the dwelling.

In cold weather the personal representative should be advised to check that the mains water stop cock has been closed and the system drained. Taps should be left open to prevent the system filling again if the stop cock is faulty. Where central heating is fitted, the personal representative might decide to leave it switched on; but otherwise it is preferable to drain this too. Personal representatives should endeavour to arrange for a neighbour to watch the property in case of vandalism, and the neighbour should be given a telephone number and name of a person to contact if the need arises. The police should also be advised. Remember to advise the police when the property is sold.

These are obvious precautions, but it should be borne in mind that personal representatives are not used to dealing with such matters and are probably not experienced in the results of overlooking them. Insurance companies usually stipulate that the property should be visited regularly, and that the above precautions should be taken.

(d) Clearing the contents

When the dwelling has been cleared of furniture the local water company can be contacted and asked to confirm that the property is void for charges. The insurance company holding cover for the contents can be advised that the furniture has been disposed of, and the insurance cancelled. A claim may then be made for a refund of the apportioned premium, but if carpets and curtains have been left in the dwelling the insurance cover for these should remain in force in case of any loss or damage.

(e) Council tax

Any council tax not paid by the deceased is, of course, an estate liability. After the death there is no liability until six months after the date that the grant is issued. Thereafter the personal representatives are liable to pay council tax until the property is sold.

(f) Mail

Where the deceased's residence is left unoccupied, or a rented property is surrendered to the landlord, an application for redirection of mail should be completed (see Appendix 2). The application forms are obtained from the Post Office. Fees are currently:

   up to 1 month £6.00

   up to 3 months £13.00

   up to 12 months £30.00

To stop deliveries of unwanted junk mail to the deceased's residence, the personal representative should complete an application form which is obtained from Mailing Preference Services, Freepost 22, London W1E 7EZ.

The office of the local 'free newspaper' should be asked to stop deliveries to the empty property. These precautions may help to avoid giving notice to burglars and/or vandals that the dwelling is unoccupied.

13. Mortgages, rents and other debts due to the estate

The name of the personal representative or his agents, and an address, should be given to anyone who has a mortgage or a loan, or who rents property, from the deceased. All capital sums outstanding and interest thereon up to the death should be included in the list of assets (see page 87). Money received during the administration period should be noted and the money banked. Tenants should be advised to make payments either to the personal representative or his agents. If an agent is already acting for the deceased he should be advised of the death, and asked to make payments to the personal representative. A note of payments due and owing up to the date of death should be made and will be required for income tax returns. Payments received thereafter should be declared to the Inland Revenue when the administration has been completed, or at the end of each income tax period, and the standard rate tax will be payable.

Any debts due to the deceased for work carried out by the deceased and all other debts due under a contract, are enforceable by the personal representative. Such debts should be identified, quantified and included in the estate.

14. Foreign assets

It is the personal representative's duty to administer assets in accordance with the *lex loci* of the assets, and he must deal with the assets and debts and distribute the balance to the persons entitled. There can be problems in repatriating assets from abroad because many countries have exchange controls in varying degrees of severity, which prevent repatriation of assets. If the estate includes foreign property with a value in excess of £15,000, Form IHT 200 should be forwarded to the Capital Taxes Office irrespective of the total estate value. Full details of the information required by the CTO is given in Form IHT 10 which can be obtained from the Capital Taxes Office. Details of the information required by the Inland Revenue include shares and securities, bank accounts, land, timeshares, expenses and double taxation.

Assets held abroad will normally be dealt with only when the personal representative has produced a copy of the grant (and the will) which has been certified and sealed by the Probate Registry and bears the apostil in accordance with The Hague Convention 1961. This is obtained by forwarding the copy, sealed and certified by the registry to: The Legalisation Office, Foreign and Commonwealth Office, Petty France, London. The fee for this is currently £8.00. The foreign country's own succession laws will apply to the assets in that country.

In estates where inheritance tax is payable, and additional expenses have been incurred administering the assets abroad, the Inland Revenue may make an allowance from the value of the property.

If the personal representatives are unable to secure enough foreign assets to pay the liability to inheritance tax attributable to those foreign assets because of restrictions imposed by that foreign country, they may ask for payment of the tax to be deferred until sufficient assets have been recovered. If the eventual final sum obtained by the personal representative is not sufficient to settle the tax liability completely, the outstanding balance due may be waived by the Inland Revenue.

Note also that if tax arising on death is charged by the authorities in a foreign country on property situated in that country and there is a double taxation agreement in force with that country, a credit for the amount paid may be allowed against inheritance tax. However, the amount of the credit allowed cannot exceed the amount of inheritance tax due on that property.

15. Equitable interests

Details of any interests under a will, intestacy or settlement due to the deceased should be included in the estate assets. Where the interest has not been paid to the deceased, the solicitors or trustees dealing with the interest should be advised of the death, and when available, the grant should be produced to them to enable them to release the interest.

Where the deceased was a trustee of a settlement or a trust, his co-trustees must be informed of his death, and his death must be registered against the securities.

16. Nominated property

Nominated property is property covered by a form of nomination made by the deceased during his lifetime which names a certain person to receive the property on death, and the terms of the will cannot affect or cancel the nomination.

Nominated property, which is usually property held in the Trustee Savings Bank, the National Savings Bank or a friendly society, does not follow the rules of distribution on intestacy or the terms of a will. These sums can therefore be paid, subject to the amounts nominated, to the nominee without production of the grant of representation, although a certificate of clearance of inheritance tax may be required. Such a certificate is obtained from the Capital Taxes Office. A death certificate will of course be required. Production of the death certificate and completion of a form of receipt by the nominee is usually sufficient to obtain payment of the amounts nominated. The form of receipt is a standard form provided by the bank or friendly society which holds the account.

There are, however, some exceptions to the above. The National Savings Bank will not usually release nominated assets which have a value of £5,000 or more without production of the grant of representation; furthermore, before nominated assets of a value in excess of £25,000 are released, the National Savings Bank will require both the grant and a statement from the Commissioners of Inland Revenue stating either that no inheritance tax is payable or that any liability has been satisfied.

When writing to ascertain the value of assets held by these banks and friendly societies it should be specifically requested that details of nominations and the requirements for releasing the property to the nominee be given.

The facility for nomination has now been withdrawn by both the Trustee Savings Bank and the National Savings Bank, and any nomination made after 30 April 1979 with the Trustee Savings Bank, and after 30 April 1981 with the National Savings Bank, is of no effect.

There are many nominations still in existence, having been made prior to the above dates, and nominations may still be made with friendly societies. These usually relate to industrial pensions.

In claims for family provision (see page 167) the court may decide that the value of the nominated property should be added to the value of the estate when calculating any awards.

17. Personal representatives' bank accounts

If the executors or administrators are solicitors, accountants or other professional people an executor's account should be opened with a bank. A current account will usually be needed, but a deposit account may also be opened to earn interest for the estate during the period of administration. Where a personal representative who is not a professional does not require an executor's account, he should be asked to sign a letter of authority to open a building society account (see Appendix 5 for an example).

An executor does not incur any liability by leaving money in a bank if the will does not state that the money is to be invested. Where the will does give such a direction the executor is still entitled to leave money in a current account to deal with the estate administration. However, it is advantageous to place the money on deposit to earn interest for the beneficiaries.

If there is an executor's account, money received into the solicitor-executor's client account must be paid out immediately to the executor's account and must never be left in the client account.

All client money should be available on demand; therefore if personal representatives require sums of money to be invested for fixed periods on the money market, a written authority must be obtained from them before the money is so invested so as to indemnify the practitioner who arranges such an investment. Many banks now offer interest-earning current accounts.

Summary

- Collect all cash, which includes coins of the realm and any foreign currency. A coin collection will usually be classed as an asset 'other than' cash in hand.

- Collect all building society passbooks and bonds, and details, including statements if possible, of all bank accounts. Where any of these are held in joint names it may prove difficult to obtain the passbooks. In those circumstances you must obtain full details of the accounts and of the other joint holder or holders.

- There are several types of National Savings Bank investments including NSC's, premium bonds, income bonds, savings accounts etc. If you are uncertain the National Savings Bank will check their records on receiving your written request.

- If a post-war credit certificate is found among the deceased's papers, it does not prove that a repayment is due. All post-war credits were repaid a number of years ago, even if the certificates were not found.

- Full and complete details of all stocks and shares should be noted, including joint holdings, and a probate valuation obtained. Any dividends received during the administration should be returned to the registrars when a grant is available with a request for them to be reissued to the executors.

- Keep a photocopy of all life insurance policies on file in case any queries arise after the policies have been encashed. The death certificate issued by the registrar of deaths will have to be sent to the insurance company, as they will not accept certified copies.

- The deceased's employers will provide full details of any balance wages and holiday pay due, and details of pay and tax deducted for tax purposes. The firm's pensions' section will give details of any pension due to the estate or to next of kin.

- An estimate of the value of the personal chattels is usually all that is required but in those cases where IHT will be payable or where there are chattels of high or antique value, a professional written valuation should be obtained. Personal representatives should not allow any chattels to be removed until the matter of their valuation has been dealt with.

- A probate value of all realty must be obtained. It should be noted that in cases of a sale of realty within four years of the death which results in a lower value than the probate value, the sale value can be substituted for the probate value for the purposes of IHT.

- It is now possible to obtain a refund of part of a TV licence whereas previously no refunds were given.

- The local authority must be advised of the date of death so that any surviving spouse can obtain a reduction of council tax, where appropriate, or the estate can be classed as not liable to council tax until 6 months after the grant is received. Make a note on the file to advise the local authority of the date of the grant when it has been issued.

- If the surviving spouse remains in the property there should be no reason for mail to be re-directed. Otherwise, the Post Office mail re-direction request should be completed and sent to the Post Office as quickly as possible. Note that the cost of the re-direction must be prepaid.

Chapter 8

Identifying the estate liabilities

1. Debts owed by the estate

Details of all debts will be required. The following list covers most of the usual liabilities:

- gas, electricity and telephone;
- credit cards;
- local authority charges;
- water rates;
- property rental, ground rent, mortgage;
- clothing clubs;
- newspapers and milk;
- tax;
- National Insurance;
- television and other rental agreements;
- hire purchase and personal loan;
- mortgages etc.

If the estate is solvent, and there is a sum of cash in hand available, small debts such as newspaper bills or garage bills may be settled from the cash. Other creditors should be advised of the death but it is not necessary to produce a death certificate unless this is specifically requested.

Any items on hire should be returned immediately and a final statement requested.

Credit cards should be mutilated by cutting them in half; they should be returned to the credit card company(ies) with a request for a final statement. It should be noted that interest normally continues on amounts outstanding on credit card accounts, and these should be paid off as soon as possible.

If there are any library books among the deceased's possessions these should be returned to the library and the librarian should be advised of the death. If there is a library ticket but no books, it should be returned and the librarian should be asked to confirm that there are no books outstanding in the deceased's name. If there are any books missing, the estate may be charged with the replacement cost.

Final readings of gas, water and electricity meters should be obtained, and the authorities advised of the death. They will then make their own arrangements for the supply to be taken over by another person, if the property is sold or transferred. If the telephone is to remain in the property a final reading can be requested. If the property is to be sold and will remain empty until the sale, the personal representative can decide if the instrument is to be removed, or disconnected temporarily, to be reconnected when the sale is completed. If the apparatus is stolen from the property the estate will receive the bill for the replacement.

Foreign debts are dealt with in the same way as other liabilities, and if there are also foreign assets, the liabilities can be settled from those assets depending on the nature of both.

Any liabilities due after the date of death, e.g. gas, water and electricity accounts, will be a liability on the estate but are not deductible for the purposes of calculating inheritance tax liability or Probate Registry fees, which are both calculated on the amount of the net estate as at the date of death.

Most of the debts and liabilities of the deceased are enforceable against his personal representative, but specific acts which could only be carried out by the deceased, such as a contract to sing in an opera, or a high wire juggling act, obviously cannot be enforced.

2. The funeral and the funeral account

Where executors are appointed they are *prima facie* entitled to possession of the body and are responsible for its disposal. Under the Human Tissue Act 1961 the person who is lawfully in possession of the body may authorise removal of parts of the body for medical purposes.

The personal representatives often arrange for the funeral account to be sent to the solicitors who are dealing with the estate administration. It should be pointed out to them that the account cannot be settled until there is money available from the estate. Some undertakers offer discounts for early settlement of accounts, and if the personal representative wishes to take advantage of such a reduction he should make his own arrangements to settle the bill and reimburse himself from the estate at a later date. It is not good practice to make numerous payments from the firm's office account to enable clients to take advantage of discounts, and any disbursements should, whenever possible, be paid from money in client account, or the client should be asked to provide it. If money is not available for early settlement of the funeral account, payment will have to be made after the grant has been issued and the assets have been encashed.

If the deceased was a patient under the Court of Protection and there are funds in the Court Funds Office, the court will generally settle the funeral account from those funds, on request. Similarly, where the deceased held an account with the National Savings Bank, or certain other banks or building societies, the personal representative can apply to have the funeral account paid from that account.

When the funeral account is received it should be checked and if it includes charges for floral tributes, the undertakers should be asked to give the names and addresses of those who ordered the flowers, and they should be asked to pay the amount to the estate. It should be explained to the personal representatives that the estate bears the cost of the funeral but does not bear the cost of floral tributes from others.

The client should be advised also that the funeral account is the first charge against the estate assets. The term 'funeral expenses' in s 172 Inheritance Tax Act 1984 was initially construed as excluding the cost of a tombstone. The Board of the Inland Revenue has now taken the view that the term allows a deduction from the value of the deceased's estate for the cost of a tombstone or gravestone (Inland Revenue Statement of Practice SP7/87: *Inheritance Tax – deduction for reasonable funeral expenses*).

If there are any complaints about the service given or the cost of the funeral, these should be addressed to: National Secretary, National Association of Funeral Directors, 57 Doughty Street, London WC1N 2NE, or The Funeral Standards Council, 30 North Road, Cardiff CF1 3DY, or The National Association of Prepaid Funeral Plans, 618 Warwick Road, Solihull, West Midlands B91 1AA.

(a) Gravestone

There is no absolute right to erect a gravestone; permission must be given by the vicar of the diocese. Usually there are specifications of the size and type of gravestones which may be erected, and the inscriptions. If permission is refused an appeal can be entered for the request to be reconsidered. The Funeral Directors can give guidance on this. Normally, a gravestone is not erected or replaced (in cases involving family graves where an additional burial has taken place) for six to nine months. This is to allow the ground to settle after the burial.

The second charge against an estate is the administration costs, and thereafter all other claims – but see insolvent estates (page 140).

There are clients who are in financial difficulties but who run into further debt by arranging expensive funerals they cannot easily afford. There are also cases where the next of kin sell the deceased's home to pay for the funeral, which is a sad and often unnecessary state of affairs. Where there are obvious financial difficulties, the client should be advised to apply to the Social Security Benefits Agency for assistance before instructing the undertaker. If the funeral arrangements have already been made, the DSS should be advised, and they can contact the undertaker. Details of assistance in meeting funeral expenses are given on page 7.

Where the death has given rise to a claim being made to the Criminal Injuries Compensation Board, the claim should include a claim for the cost of the funeral, and a contribution toward the cost of the gravestone.

Where a body has been accepted for medical research, that department arranges the funeral. Where the deceased has left his body for medical research, or has left instructions that organs may be removed, e.g. for kidney transplants or corneal grafting, the local hospital must be informed of the death immediately, as delay can render the gift unusable. The heart, liver and kidneys must be removed within half an hour of the death; the eyes must be removed within six hours.

If the death has been reported to the Coroner, his consent is needed before the organs or body can be donated. If the whole body is to be donated, telephone the Anatomy Office of the nearest medical school (the London Anatomy Office for the London area). In case of difficulty, call HM Inspector of Anatomy in London. Bodies are refused if there has been a post mortem or if any organs (except the cornea) have been removed.

The fact that the deceased left his remains for research does not necessarily mean that they will be accepted. If the body is accepted, the research centre will make arrangements to collect it. If the next of kin wish to attend the funeral the research centre must be informed and they will advise of the funeral arrangements. The personal representative and the next of kin have no say in the method of disposal of the body, which will be decided upon by the research centre, and is usually by cremation.

A body may be kept for up to two years for medical teaching purposes.

(b) Moving a body out of England and Wales

If the body is to be removed out of England or Wales, only the Coroner can give permission. This has to be obtained at least four days before the body is removed, to enable the Coroner to carry out the necessary enquiries. Then a removal notice is issued on Form 194. Permission must be obtained in every case where a funeral is to take place outside England or Wales. The undertaker can be requested to deal with this procedure. Clients should be advised that these arrangements may take several weeks to complete, because not only is the Coroner involved, the Embassy or other official body of the country to which the body is to be removed must also agree, and very strict regulations have to be adhered to. Because of these possible delays, the funeral director may advise that the body should be embalmed.

3. Claims by the DSS

When, during his lifetime, the deceased was in receipt of payments from the Social Fund, the personal representatives might be contacted by the DSS enquiring about the value of the deceased's assets. This happens where the capital declared by the deceased when applying for benefit does not appear to tally with the value of the estate declared in the oath applying for the grant, suggesting that the recipient was not entitled to the payments. The DSS will ask for an explanation. If the personal representative does not disclose the assets making up the estate, the DSS may make a claim against the estate for the total amount of benefit paid to the deceased, and the only way to refute such a claim is to disclose the assets. It is often found that the assets are the dwelling house, insurance policies, chattels etc. and a minimal amount of money. In these cases, the DSS will confirm that they have no claim against the estate.

However, where the deceased received benefit to which he was not entitled, the DSS will ask for full details of all cash and securities from the date benefit was first paid up to the date of death. This can create problems when, for example, there were bank and building society accounts, because details of the balances in the accounts at specific dates will have to be obtained. If the deceased held a large amount of cash in hand the personal representative will be asked to establish the source of the cash. When full details have been disclosed to the DSS, any over-payment will be calculated by the DSS which will claim repayment from the estate.

It is usual for the DSS to write to the solicitor who is dealing with the application for the grant of representation, requesting full details of the deceased's estate. The information held by the solicitor is *confidential* and therefore it must not be disclosed to the DSS without the consent of the personal representative. This consent, if given, should be obtained in writing. If such consent is not given, and the personal representative intends to distribute the net estate, the provisions of s 27 Trustee Act 1925 should be drawn to the personal representative's attention in writing. The solicitor acting has no responsibility to the DSS but should advise the personal representative that they are likely to be persistent in their claim.

4. Income tax and capital gains tax

If the deceased employed an accountant during his lifetime, the accountant should be advised of the death. He can be asked to finalise the tax affairs up to the date of death, and he should be asked if he has any outstanding fees due, which will be a liability of the estate. The accountant will advise the details he requires to complete the deceased's tax affairs, and he will require the original grant to produce to the Inland Revenue. Any correspondence from the Inland Revenue should be passed on to the accountant so that he is fully aware, at all times, of the Inland Revenue's position.

To trace a chartered accountant who has moved or a firm of chartered accountants which has moved or changed name, contact The Institute of Chartered Accountants who may have up-to-date details (see Appendix 6).

Where no one was employed to deal with the tax affairs, the personal representative must ascertain the address and reference number of the deceased's tax district, and, where necessary, an income tax return should be requested to cover the tax period to the date of death. If there is any tax owed by the deceased this will be an estate liability, and any repayment of overpaid tax will form part of the estate assets. All cheques from the Inland Revenue for tax refunds are now crossed 'account payee only'. If the personal representatives require the cheque to be made payable to a third party, for example to the solicitors or accountants dealing with the administration of the estate, they must send their written authority to the Inland Revenue. If this is not done the Inland Revenue cheque will be made payable to the first named executor or to all of the executors. The Revenue may charge interest on overdue tax, but if the taxpayer died before the date the tax was due to be paid, personal representatives will be liable to interest from the date of the grant.

If the personal representative is unable to trace the deceased's tax district, he must deal with the tax affairs under his own tax district, and his own tax office should be informed. The estate will be liable for any tax due, but there will be no liability for tax against the personal representative personally unless he distributes the estate having failed to disclose any liability.

The personal representative is also responsible for tax liability during the period of administration, and it should be remembered that there are no 'personal allowances' for the personal representative as far as income received by the estate is concerned, but the basic rate of tax currently 25 per cent only is levied against all gross income received by the estate. However, where only small sums are involved, it is usually found that the Inland Revenue will not bother to collect the tax because, it appears, the cost of collecting small amounts outweighs the value of the tax collected. There does not appear to be any official ruling on this, and therefore all taxable income received into the estate must be reported.

Rates of income tax and allowances usually change with each budget; scales are readily available from the Inland Revenue. It may be discovered that the deceased failed to complete income tax returns, and should the personal representative need to complete returns for several years prior to death, the following income tax, capital gains tax and retirement pension tables will be of assistance.

Income tax

Tax year	Personal reliefs Single person	Married man or woman	Basic rate tax	Bands of taxable income assessed at basic rate
1989/90	2,785	4,375	25%	1–20,700
1990/91	3,005	4,725	25%	1–20,700
1991/92	3,295	5,015	25%	1–23,700
1992/93	3,445	5,165	25%	2,001–23,700
1993/94	3,445	5,165	25%	2,501–23,700
1994/95	3,445	5,165	25%	3,001–23,700
1995/96	3,525	5,245	25%	3,201–24,300

Capital gains tax

Tax year	Individuals	Trustees
1983/84	5,300	2,650
1984/85	5,600	2,800
1985/86	5,900	2,950
1986/87	6,300	3,150
1987/88	6,600	3,300
1988/89	5,000	2,500
1989/90	5,000	2,500
1990/91	5,000	2,500
1991/92	5,500	2,750
1992/93	5,800	2,900
1993/94	5,800	2,900
1994/95	5,800	2,900
1995/96	6,000	3,000

DSS basic retirement pensions

From	Single person weekly	Married couple (wife non-contributor) weekly
21 November 1983	£34.05	£54.50
26 November 1984	£35.80	£57.30
25 November 1985	£38.30	£61.30
28 July 1986	£38.70	£61.95
6 April 1987	£39.50	£63.25
11 April 1988	£41.15	£65.90
10 April 1989	£43.60	£69.80
9 April 1990	£46.90	£75.10
8 April 1991	£52.00	£83.25
6 April 1993	£56.10	£89.80
11 April 1994	£57.60	£92.10
10 April 1995	£58.85	£94.10

Capital gains tax

Any capital gains tax liability on sales of assets during the administration period is the liability of the personal representatives. During the remainder of the tax year in which the death occurred and the two years following, the personal representatives have the same annual allowance (currently £6,000) as an individual. After this period there is no annual allowance.

To ascertain the net chargeable gain the following calculations should be made.

(i) Total acquisition cost:

Purchase price, plus costs incurred e.g. estate agent's fees, surveyors, valuer, advertising, legal costs, stamp duty etc. plus indexation (see retail price index (RPI));

(ii) Sale price, less sale costs (as above) less annual exemption.

Retail price index

	1980	1981	1982	1983	1984	1985	1986
January	62.18	70.29	78.73	82.61	86.84	91.20	96.25
February	63.07	70.93	78.76	82.97	87.20	91.94	96.60
March	63.93	71.99	79.44	83.12	87.48	92.80	96.73
April	66.11	74.07	81.04	84.28	88.64	94.78	97.67
May	66.72	74.55	81.62	84.64	88.97	95.21	97.85
June	67.35	74.98	81.85	84.84	89.20	95.41	97.79
July	67.91	75.31	81.88	85.30	89.10	95.23	97.52
August	68.06	75.87	81.90	85.68	89.94	95.49	97.82
September	68.49	76.30	81.85	86.06	90.11	95.44	98.30
October	68.92	76.98	82.26	86.36	90.67	95.59	98.45
November	69.48	77.78	82.66	86.67	90.95	95.92	99.29
December	69.86	78.28	82.51	86.89	90.87	96.05	99.62

	1987	1988	1989	1990	1991	1992	1993
January	100.00	103.30	111.00	119.50	130.20	135.60	139.90
February	100.40	103.70	111.80	120.20	130.90	136.30	138.80
March	100.60	104.10	112.30	121.40	131.40	136.70	139.30
April	101.80	105.80	114.30	125.10	133.10	138.80	140.60
May	101.90	106.20	115.00	126.20	133.50	139.30	141.10
June	101.90	106.60	115.40	126.70	134.10	139.30	141.10
July	101.80	106.70	115.50	126.80	133.80	138.70	140.70
August	102.10	107.90	115.80	128.10	134.10	138.90	141.30
September	102.40	108.40	116.60	129.30	134.60	139.40	141.90
October	102.90	109.50	117.50	130.30	135.10	139.90	141.80
November	103.40	110.00	118.50	130.00	135.60	139.70	141.60
December	103.30	110.30	118.80	129.90	135.70	139.20	141.90

	1994	1995
January	141.30	146.00
February	142.10	146.90
March	141.50	
April	144.20	
May	144.70	
June	144.70	
July	144.00	
August	144.70	
September	145.00	
October	145.20	
November	145.30	
December	146.00	

The *indexation factor* is calculated as follows:

$$\frac{(RD - RI)}{RI}$$

where: RD is the RPI figure for the month of disposal; and
RI is the RPI figure for the month of acquisition.

The *indexation allowance* is then calculated as follows:
indexation factor × cost

Example:

Shares bought in April 1982 for £8,000
        sold in May 1986 for £15,000

Indexation factor: $\dfrac{\text{RD } (97.85) - \text{RI } (81.04)}{\text{RI } (81.04)} = 0.207$

Indexation allowance: $0.207 \times \text{cost } (£8,000) = £1,656$

Gain:

sale price	£15,000.00
less purchase price plus indexation allowance	
(£8,000 + £1,656)	£9,656.00
Gain =	£5,344.00

Capital Gains on purchase and sale of shares is 'pooled': see Chapter 11.

(a) Fees

Personal representatives may also make a deduction for CGT representing legal and accountancy fees in preparing the inheritance tax account and the cost of obtaining the grant of representation (*Richards Executors* (1971) 46 TC 626 (HL)). The following scales set out the fees allowed on the sale of chargeable assets (Revenue Statement of Practice SP7/81, updated for deaths after 5 April 1993),

Probate value of assets sold *(for deaths after 5 April 1981)*	*Fees allowed*
up to £40,000	1.75% of probate value of assets sold
£40,001 to £70,000	£700 divided among all of the assets in proportion to their probate value
£70,001 to £300,000	1% probate value of assets sold
£300,000 to £400,000	£3,000 divided as above
£400,001 to £750,000	0.75%
Over £750,000	By negotiation with the Inland Revenue

There are certain items which are exempt or partially exempt from capital gains tax liability and the most obvious as far as estates are concerned relate to chattels. From financial year 1989/90 onwards, a chattel sold for £6,000 or less in the financial year is exempt. For a chattel sold before tax year 1989/90, the exemption figure was £3,000 or less for each financial year.

For these calculations a chattel is a single item or several items making up a set e.g. a set of twelve chairs, or a three-piece suite.

There is no capital gains tax liability where an asset is transferred to a legatee, and for CGT purposes the beneficiary is deemed to have received it at date of death value.

The value, for the purposes of capital gains tax, of assets transferred should not be confused with the value of those same assets passing for the purposes of the estate accounts. For example, a shareholding transferred to one of several beneficiaries, say nine months after the date of death, is transferred at date of death value for capital gains tax purposes. But the date of death value is not used in calculating that beneficiary's entitlement (or part entitlement) from the estate, as this would almost certainly result in an unequal division of the assets. The shares transferred are re-valued at the date of transfer and it is this later value which is taken into account for the division of the estate.

Once it has been established that there is no further liability to tax, the personal representative, or the solicitors acting for him, should request a tax clearance from the Inland Revenue. If, thereafter, it is discovered that due to some administrative error by the Revenue authorities there is a further liability to tax, the personal representative will not be personally responsible if he has distributed the estate, but the tax authorities may still pursue the outstanding amount from the beneficiaries.

Where the deceased leaves a lawful widow she will be entitled to additional income tax relief during the remainder of the tax year in which her spouse died and for the whole of the year following; thereafter she will be entitled to the standard tax relief for single persons. The additional relief referred to above is called 'widow's allowance' and is an amount which increases the allowance to that given to a married man. (In 1995/96 £172.00 per year.)

As from 11 February 1986 all gilt stock valuations are quoted 'clean', i.e. accrued interest is included. This means that a vendor and purchaser will be allowed apportioned interest up to and as from the dealing. Care should also be taken to include this correctly in income tax returns.

From 11 February 1986 also, all 'gilts' are exempt from capital gains tax even if a sale takes place within twelve months of purchase.

Tax arrears may be waived wholly or partially in certain circumstances if they arise because the Inland Revenue fails to deal properly and in time with a person's tax details. Normally, the concessions shown below only apply if the taxpayer has not been notified by the end of the tax year which follows the year in which the arrears of tax arose. The current remissions are as follows when the arrears were first notified on or after 23 July 1985:

Gross income	*Proportion remitted*
Less than £8,500	All
£8,501–£10,500	75%
£10,501–£13,500	50%
£13,501–£16,000	25%
£16,001–£23,000	10%

For pensioners, £2,500 is added to the gross income bands shown above. The gross income limits are varied from time to time, and fuller details are to be found in the Inland Revenue booklet IR1.

When tax has been paid on income received during the administration period the residuary beneficiaries should be given tax deduction certificates (Form R185E – supplies of this form may be obtained from the Inland Revenue) showing the amount of tax deducted from their share of the income. Beneficiaries should be advised to send the R185E to their own tax district, and if they are not liable for tax, they can reclaim all or part of the tax suffered. Any beneficiary who is liable to tax in the higher brackets will be charged for the amount of the difference between his higher rate tax and the standard rate already deducted.

By virtue of s 696 Income and Corporation Taxes Act 1988, the Inland Revenue will not 'look through' residuary income paid to persons having an absolute interest in residue. This means that the Inland Revenue will not seek to differentiate between bank and building society interest, dividends etc. The whole of the income should be included in the tax deduction certificate for repayment or for assessment for higher rate tax. This applies only to persons ordinarily resident in the United Kingdom; it does not apply to persons who are not resident.

However, share dividends are now taxed at 20 per cent, and should be shown separately from other interest which is taxed at 25 per cent.

5. Inheritance tax

All property owned by the deceased at the date of his death is liable to assessment for inheritance tax. In addition, all gifts made by the deceased during the seven years before his death are brought into account in calculating the inheritance tax liability.

Certain lifetime transfers are exempt:

(i) transfers of value in any one year not exceeding £3,000 (from 6 April 1981).

   Any unused exemptions from a previous year may be brought forward, but unused exemptions may be carried forward one year only;

(ii) transfers of value to any one person in any one tax year not exceeding £250 (from 6 April 1980).

   Any gift of £250 which is given to a person who also receives a gift of £3,000 will not count as an exempt transfer. The total is £3,250, and the smaller sum will be reported as a non-exempt gift;

(iii) regular gifts out of income which do not affect the transferor's standard of living;

(iv) gifts to a bride or groom in contemplation of marriage with the following limits:

   • £5,000 from a parent;

   • £2,500 from a bride, groom, or grandparent;

   • £1,000 from any other person.

Other points to note:

(a) There is no lifetime charge on gifts between individuals, gifts into accumulation and maintenance trusts, and trusts for the disabled – provided that the transferor lives for at least seven years from the date of the gift. The same rules apply for interest in possession trusts.

(b) There is a lifetime charge (i.e. half the death rate) on lifetime transfers involving companies and gifts into and out of discretionary trusts.

(c) Any chargeable transfers made within seven years of death are brought into account as a cumulative total. Gifts made more than three years before the death may benefit from tapering relief. It should be noted that tapering relief only reduces the tax on the gift, not the value of the gift itself, and so makes no reduction in the tax on the estate. Tapering relief operates as follows:

Years between transfer and death	*% of full rates*
0–3	100
3–4	80
4–5	60
5–6	40
6–7	20

(d) The personal representative will be responsible for enquiries into gifts made during the seven-year period prior to the death and the responsibility for the tax payable will be that of the recipient primarily but with recourse to the estate as necessary.

(e) The rate scale is as follows:

Scale £	*Tax rate – %*
Deaths on or after 17 March 1987	
0–90,000	Nil
90,000–140,000	30
140,000–220,000	40
220,000–330,000	50
Over 330,000	60
Deaths on or after 15 March 1988	
0–110,000	Nil
Over 110,000	40
Deaths on or after 6 April 1989	
0–118,000	Nil
Over 118,000	40
Deaths on or after 6 April 1990	
0–128,000	Nil
Over 128,000	40
Deaths on or after 6 April 1991	
0–140,000	Nil
Over 140,000	40

Deaths on or after 10 March 1992

0–150,000	Nil
Over 150,000	40

Deaths on or after 6 April 1995

0–154,000	Nil
Over 154,000	40

(f) Gifts with reservations, for example where the donor gifts the house but reserves the right to live in it or where the donor gifts an insurance policy but keeps the right to the benefits from it, will be treated in the same way as other gifts and those between individuals will not be taxed at the time of the gift. However for gifts involving insurance policies, the charge will be made at the time of the gift, depending on the recipient.

Where the transferor dies within seven years of making a transfer and where the inheritance tax remains unpaid by a transferee twelve months after the end of the month in which the transferor dies, the personal representative is liable for the inheritance tax. He must consider pursuing the transferee to reimburse the estate (see 2.(*a*) on page 164).

Obviously inheritance tax is a highly complex subject and the appropriate books should be consulted for full details of exclusions, exemptions and reliefs.

The rates are as follows:

Inheritance tax interest

Interest period	*Interest rate*	
06.12.86 to 05.06.87	172 days	8%
06.06.87 to 05.08.88	427 days	6%
06.08.88 to 05.10.88	61 days	8%
06.10.88 to 05.07.89	273 days	9%
06.07.89 to 05.03.91	608 days	11%
06.03.91 to 05.05.91	61 days	10%
06.05.91 to 05.07.91	61 days	9%
06.07.91 to 05.11.92	489 days	8%
06.11.92 to 05.12.92	30 days	6%
06.12.92 to 05.01.94	396 days	5%
06.01.94 to 05.10.94	273 days	4%
06.10.94 to		5%

Summary

- The personal representatives are *prima facie* entitled to possession of the body and are responsible for its disposal.

- Personal representatives should ascertain, as soon as possible if the deceased has completed a kidney donor or other donor card and if he has donated his body for medical research. If so, the personal representatives should get in touch with the appropriate authorities immediately.

- They should also check that there are sufficient assets in the estate to pay the funeral account, and they should be advised that this is the first charge against the estate assets.

- If not, they should be advised to contact the DSS before making the funeral arrangements.

- If the deceased was in receipt of DSS payments to which he was not entitled, the DSS will make a claim against the estate.

- Personal representatives should make certain that there are no income tax or CGT liabilities outstanding before distributing the estate.

- If the deceased was liable to pay income tax the personal representatives must complete a final tax return up to the date of death.

- The personal representatives must also use their best endeavours to find out if the deceased made any lifetime gifts which might be Potentially Exempt Transfers (PETs).

- The probate value of the deceased's estate can be below the IHT threshold, but any PETs could raise the value to make the estate liable to IHT.

Chapter 9

Preparing for the Inland Revenue Account and the application for the grant

1. All of the estate held jointly

Where all of the assets are held in the joint names of the deceased and his lawful spouse the assets pass by survivorship and there is no liability to inheritance tax. There should therefore be no reason to obtain a grant of representation to administer the estate. If there are one or two assets in the deceased's sole name it may be possible to transfer these to the spouse without a grant (see below; and see also page 167 as to the Inheritance (Provision for Family and Dependants) Act).

2. Small payments

Under section 6 Administration of Estates (Small Payments) Act 1965 it may be possible to deal with the deceased's assets, or part of the estate, without the need for a grant of representation. This relates to small sums of £5,000 (for deaths after 11 May 1984).

The figure of £5,000 refers to the value of individual assets and not the value of the entire estate. The amounts are increased from time to time by the Treasury.

It should be noted that this provision is permissive not obligatory. Account holders can be requested to consider dispensing with production of a grant when small amounts are being dealt with, but they may ask the person dealing with the estate to swear or affirm a statutory declaration before the asset is released. Clearly, if one account holder insists on a grant of representation, there will be little point incurring the expense of swearing or affirming individual declarations. If there are numerous small accounts, the cost of swearing individual declarations for each will almost always exceed the cost of obtaining a grant.

When dealing with stocks and shares and realty a grant must be obtained even if the total value of the estate is below the limits set out above.

There are six sets of Regulations governing National Savings Investments. In the past, all six were aggregated and a grant was required where the aggregated total exceeded the small payments limit (currently £5,000). The National Savings Bank will now normally release assets without a grant if each one does not exceed £5,000. If a grant is required for any one, the grant will usually be required to release all of the others.

3. Realty only

In estates where the deceased is survived by a spouse leaving only the matrimonial home in the deceased's sole name, thus necessitating a grant, and leaving only enough personal estate (or insufficient personal estate) to settle the funeral account, district judges and registrars have a discretion to remit or reduce probate fees. Full details should be supplied to the Probate Registry before an application for a grant is submitted.

In such cases of hardship, the spouse should be advised to make an application on legal aid to deal with the administration of the estate, which would cover the cost of making the application for a grant. Legal aid should cover the cost of the commissioner's fees, but does not meet the probate court fees.

In addition, the spouse may apply to the DSS for assistance in meeting the cost of the funeral, as explained on page 73–74.

4. Schedule of assets and liabilities

The schedule of assets and liabilities used to ascertain the extent of the deceased's estate can now be expanded and used as a day-to-day record of the administration (see Appendix 3). The schedule can be filled in to show when banks etc. have been contacted, or when a death certificate has been requested, exhibited and returned to the file. Notes can show if assets are to be encashed or transferred, and estimated values can be entered, to be replaced thereafter with the correct values when these are known. When the information has been received, and the details have been noted on the schedule, this can be used to prepare the personal representative's application for a grant.

Summary

- If all of the deceased's assets are held in joint names beneficially with another person then the assets will pass by survivorship and there should be no need to obtain a grant of probate.

- Under s6 Administration of Estates (Small Payments) Act 1965 it is usually possible to deal with assets valued at £5,000 or less without production of probate.

- In cases of hardship, for example where the only asset is the realty, the beneficiary should be advised to make an application for legal aid to deal with the administration. Additionally, the beneficiary should be advised to apply to the DSS for assistance to meet the cost of the funeral.

- Prepare a schedule of the assets and liabilities of the estate as quickly as possible with estimated values, where necessary. These estimated values can be amended when the true probate values are known.

Chapter 10

The Inland Revenue Account and inheritance tax

1. Introduction

Depending on whether the deceased died before or after 18 March 1986, the liability will be to capital transfer tax or to inheritance tax (see page 90). The procedure for accounting for either tax is the same, and the remainder of this chapter applies equally to inheritance tax as to CTT.

Having ascertained the total value of the estate, the next stage is to decide whether or not an Inland Revenue Account will be required, and if so, to prepare the Account which will be filed with the application for the grant (see Chapter 12).

2. Excepted estates

For deaths after 3 August 1981 certain estates can be classed as 'excepted estates' and an Inland Revenue Account is not required. Certain conditions have to be satisfied, and the cash limits are increased from time to time:

(i)   the total value of the estate (including joint and nominated property) must not exceed:

£125,000 for deaths on or after 1 April 1991
£125,000 for deaths on or after 1 April 1991
£115,000 for deaths on or after 1 April 1990
£100,000 for deaths on or after 1 April 1989
£ 70,000 for deaths on or after 1 April 1987
£ 40,000 for deaths on or after 1 April 1983
£ 25,000 for deaths before 1 April 1983

(Before 1 April 1990 joint property included the full value of any joint property passing by survivorship, but now includes only the value of the deceased's beneficial interest in joint property);

(ii) of the property passing, not more than £15,000 (for deaths after 1 April 1989) represents the value of the property situate out of England and Wales.

Valuation limits applicable to deaths before this date are:

£10,000 for deaths after 1 April 1987
£2,000* for deaths after 1 April 1983

*(or 10% of the gross estate, whichever is higher)
£1,000 for deaths before 1 April 1983;

(iii) the deceased must have died domiciled in England and Wales, and have made no lifetime gifts chargeable to inheritance tax (or CTT);

(iv) the grant must not be limited, e.g. to settled land or personalty only;

(v) the estate comprises only property passing by intestacy or the deceased's will, by nomination or beneficially by survivorship.

If all the above conditions are fulfilled, the oath will include the words 'to the best of my/our knowledge, information and belief, the gross estate passing under the grant does not exceed [£145,000, £125,000, £115,000, £100,000, £70,000 as appropriate]'.

If there is any doubt whether an estate is excepted or not, the matter should be referred to the Capital Taxes Office, Ferrers House, PO Box 38, Castle Meadow Road, Nottingham NG2 1BB, not to the Probate Registry. The Document Exchange number of the Capital Taxes Office is 'DX 701201 Nottingham 4 (pre-grant DX 701202 Nottingham 4)'. The telephone number is (0115) 974 2400.

3. Forms of Inland Revenue Account

If the estate is not 'excepted', an Account must be prepared. There are several different forms currently in use, but the following are most frequently encountered:

(i) IHT 200 where the deceased died domiciled in the UK on or after 18 March 1986;

(ii) IHT 201 in cases of domicile outside England and Wales (after 18 March 1986);

(iii) IHT 202 for estates not exceeding the threshold above which inheritance tax is payable, where the deceased died domiciled in the UK on or after 18 March 1986, and where the estate is comprised only of property passing under the will, under intestacy, by survivorship, or by nomination.

Form 37 (in which realty must be described) and Form 40 (in which stocks and shares are listed) are sometimes not included when Form 202 is received; stock may be obtained on request. Alternatively, the loose-leaf Forms 37 and 40 enclosed with Form 200 can be photocopied if required. The Capital Taxes Office does not appear to object to a photocopy of these forms.

The Inland Revenue has produced forms for inheritance tax as listed below with their CTT equivalents. CAP forms may be used for inheritance tax; and CAP forms will continue to be used for events which occurred before the introduction of inheritance tax. Many of the IHT forms can be obtained from major Post Offices, but CAP forms can be obtained only from the Capital Taxes Office.

The following is a list of the forms currently in use:

Account/Form	Description
IHT 1	Complete guide to inheritance tax.
IHT 2	Inheritance tax on lifetime gifts.
IHT 3	Inheritance tax – an introduction.
IHT 8	Alterations to an inheritance following a death.
IHT 9	Information to provide with an Inland Revenue Account.
IHT 10	Inheritance tax and foreign property.
IHT 11	Payment of inheritance tax from National Savings.
IHT 26	Statement of Domicile.
IHT 37	Schedule of land and interests in land.
IHT 40	Schedule of stocks and shares.
IHT 100 (*CAP C-5)	Account of transfer of value (IHT).
IHT 101 (*CAP C-7)	Account of a chargeable event (IHT).
IHT 110 (*CAP 210)	Guidance notes on completion of IHT 100.
IHT 111 (*CAP 212)	Guidance notes on completion of IHT 101.
IHT 200 (*CAP 200)	Inland Revenue account where the deceased died domiciled outside the UK on or after 18 March 1986.
IHT 201 (*CAP 201)	Inland Revenue Account where the deceased died domiciled outside the UK on or after 18 March 1986, or where s 267 IHTA 1984 applies.
IHT 202 (*CAP 202)	Inland Revenue Account (net estate below threshold).
IHT 210 (*CAP 213)	Guidance notes on the completion of Inland Revenue Accounts.
FORM CAP D3	Corrective Accounts.
FORM CAP 30	Application for clearance certificate.
FORM CAP 38	Claim for loss on sale of land.
FORM SECT 5	Claim for loss on sale of investments.
FORM A5c	Account for unadministered property.

[*Previously]

Where it has not been possible to arrive at exact values, reasoned estimates of the open market value should be included in the Inland Revenue Account for correction later. Before applying for a clearance certificate (see page 95), the personal representative must report any changes in the value of the estate to the Capital Taxes Office and a corrective account is submitted in Form CAP D3. If the corrections are very few, it may be possible to report the changes by letter and dispense with Form CAP D3, subject to the agreement of the Capital Taxes Office.

For deaths after 13 March 1975 the accounts need not be sworn, but must be signed by the personal representative. All values can be rounded down to the nearest £1.

4. Inheritance tax

Schedule 4 Finance Act 1975 Part III requires the personal representative to submit an account of the property which formed the estate immediately before the death. The personal representative(s) is liable for the tax on unsettled property, and on settled land devolving in or vesting in him, and the beneficiaries are equally liable for the whole of the tax, but not until the property has been vested in them.

The personal representative must deliver an account of the estate to the Capital Taxes Office within twelve months of the death, or within three months from first acting if this is later. Tax is due six months after the death and personal representatives must pay all tax for which they are liable on delivering the account, unless they elect to pay tax by instalments on the instalment option property (i.e. realty, agricultural property, business assets). Interest is payable on all tax outstanding as from the end of the sixth month after the death (see Interest rates below).

For deaths after 15 March 1983, payments may be made in ten annual instalments on option property but the whole of the tax outstanding in respect of individual property becomes immediately payable when a property is sold.

A personal representative who fails to deliver an account of the estate assets to the Capital Taxes Office will be liable to a penalty not exceeding £50, and if the failure continues he will be liable to further sums not exceeding £10 per day for each day he fails to deliver. The Probate Registry will not issue a grant in an estate where an account is required but is not delivered with the application, until the account is delivered or until the district judge or the registrar is satisfied that any tax due has been paid.

The rates are as follows:

Inheritance tax interest

Interest period		*[Interest rate]*
16.12.86 to 05.06.87	172 days	8%
06.06.87 to 05.08.88	427 days	6%
06.08.88 to 05.10.88	61 days	8%
06.10.88 to 05.07.89	273 days	9%
06.07.89 to 05.03.91	608 days	11%
06.03.91 to 05.05.91	61 days	10%
06.05.91 to 05.07.91	61 days	9%
06.07.91 to 05.11.92	489 days	8%
06.11.92 to 05.12.92	30 days	6%
06.12.92 to 05.01.94	396 days	5%
06.01.94 to 05.10.94	273 days	4%
06.10.94 to		5%

5. Completing the Inland Revenue Account

The complexities of inheritance tax and capital transfer tax are clearly beyond the scope of this book, and the appropriate works should be consulted on matters such as exemptions and reliefs. The following points, however, are worth noting here.

Form IHT 9 suggests information to be provided with the Inland Revenue Account which should help to finalise the case more quickly. It will be very helpful to consider IHT 9 before completing the IHT account.

When using Form 200 the amount of tax payable (if any) should be calculated, and it should be indicated if the tax on realty, business property, or agricultural property (where these are not entitled to 100 per cent relief) is to be paid by annual instalments. (Reminder! the assets must have been owned for at least two years before the death (s 117 Inheritance Tax Act 1984 (a farm must have been occupied by the deceased for the purposes of agriculture during the last two years before the death. If the farm is tenanted, the deceased must have owned it for the last seven years prior to the death).) Tax on personalty is payable before applying for the grant, and payment must be made to the Capital Taxes Office and a receipt obtained on the Inland Revenue Account which is then sent to the Probate Registry with the oath and probate fees (plus wills and codicils) when appropriate (see page 124). Failure to make these payments on applying for a grant will result in the refusal of the application and the grant will not issue until they have been made.

If there is no tax payable, e.g. where the whole estate passes to the surviving spouse, this should be clearly marked on the back page of Form 200 and the papers may be sent direct to the Probate Registry.

Assets which are exempt from tax (e.g. to the spouse or gifts to charity) should be clearly specified in the Account. Enquiries concerning inheritance tax and capital transfer tax should be directed to the Capital Taxes Office and not to the Probate Registry.

Property held by the deceased and another person or persons on a beneficial joint tenancy passes to the survivor or survivors, and does not devolve on the personal representative of the deceased. Care should be taken to enter this correctly in the Inland Revenue Account to avoid overpayment of probate fees and tax.

Numerous applicants are failing to reply to the questions about settled property in Form IHT 200 (section 5 – top of page 8 of that form). The Capital Taxes Office has issued a reminder to practitioners.

6. Payment of inheritance tax

If inheritance tax is not paid on the due date interest is charged by the Inland Revenue. Inheritance tax is due six months after the end of the month in which the death occurs. Interest on unpaid tax is charged from the following day after it is due. When the executors have elected to pay inheritance tax on realty by instalments, interest is charged from the day after the instalment falls due, and is charged on the whole of the outstanding tax.

Personal representatives may pay a sum of money in to the Inland Revenue (Financial Services Office) and this is placed on deposit to stop interest charges. The Inland Revenue will pay interest on all money deposited in excess of the inheritance tax due. The interest rate from 6 December 1992 is 5 per cent. The CTO will advise, in Form IHT 4 the interest rates between stated dates. The rates change from time to time.

Payment of inheritance tax should be made to: Inland Revenue (A), Financial Services Office (Cashier), Barrington Road, Worthing, West Sussex, BN12 4XH. Or by Britdoc to Inland Revenue (A), Financial Services Office (Cashier), DX 90950, Worthing 3.

Enquiries about inheritance tax should be made to: Capital Taxes Office, Ferrers House, PO Box 38, Castle Meadow Road, Nottingham NG2 1BB; tel. 0115 974 2400. Or Britdoc, Capital Taxes Office, DX 701202, Nottingham 4.

As a result of the Cheques Act 1992 all cheques from the Inland Revenue are crossed 'account payee only'. Where personal representatives require payment to be made to another person or persons (for example to the solicitors/accountants dealing with the administration of the estate) they must send their written authority for the Inland Revenue to make payment to that third party.

The Capital Taxes Office suggest that this written authority should be sent to them when details of amendments to the estate assets or liabilities are sent, or with the application for the clearance certificate.

If the estate includes foreign property with a value in excess of £15,000, Form IHT 200 should be forwarded to the Capital Taxes Office irrespective of the total estate value. Full details of the information required by the CTO is given in Form IHT 10 which can be obtained from the Capital Taxes Office. Details of the information required by the Inland Revenue include shares and securities, bank accounts, land, timeshares, expenses and double taxation.

7. Financing the payment of tax

Until the grant is received the assets in the estate are frozen and this usually means that a loan has to be taken out to pay the initial inheritance tax or capital transfer tax, enabling a grant to be issued. Loans from banks to pay this should be taken out on a 'loan account' and not on an overdraft account. Interest charged on loan accounts for the purpose of paying the tax may be offset by the Inspector of Taxes against an income tax liability of the estate. Tax relief for loans is limited to the interest charges on the loan during one year from the issue of the loan. This may be set against the income for that year, and any balance may be set against income of previous years. If the income is insufficient to enable all of the interest charges to be set off, the personal representative may apply to have it set off for the following year and later years. This application should be made to the Inspector of Taxes and not to the Capital Taxes Office or the

Probate Registry. Loan account interest for payment of inheritance tax may be set off against tax, but interest charged on loans to pay Probate Court fees is not allowed to be set off, and should be borrowed on an overdraft account or a separate loan account.

If the deceased held money in a building society account, it is often possible to get agreement from the building society to withdraw a cheque payable to the Inland Revenue to pay the initial inheritance tax, such a cheque being drawn from the frozen accounts in the deceased's name. The solicitor will normally be expected to give an undertaking to the society to produce the grant as soon as it is issued, and he should obtain written authority from the personal representative to deal with the payment of tax in this manner. The decision whether to arrange a bank loan or seek a cheque from the building society rests entirely with the personal representative. To avoid the expense of a bank loan, it may be worth checking whether any of the beneficiaries have funds of their own available.

If the deceased was a patient under the Court of Protection there may be sufficient funds held by the court to pay all or part of the inheritance tax. An application should be made to the Court Funds Office for part or all of the funds to be released for these purposes.

Executors should also approach the surviving joint owner of joint bank or building society accounts to consider providing the inheritance tax, interest free, to the executors to enable them to obtain the grant of probate. If the chattels are to be sold, these can be sold without production of the grant.

If the deceased held premium savings bonds, or other investments in the National Savings Bank, or bank accounts elsewhere valued at less than £5,000, it might be possible to realise these assets under the Administration of Estates (Small Payments) Act 1965.

8. Payment in kind

Any person liable to pay inheritance tax or capital transfer tax may make an application to settle the liability by payment in lieu of the tax, which can take the form of, *inter alia*, land and buildings, works of art, manuscripts and books (see Sch 4 para 17 Finance Act 1975 as amended by s 12(1) National Heritage Act 1980 and SI 1983 No 879). Offers to settle the tax liabilities in this manner should be made to the Capital Taxes Office who will advise on procedure. The Museums and Galleries Commission deals with the day-to-day administration of this system.

9. Clearance certificate

An application for a clearance certificate (s 239 IHTA 1984) to the effect that all tax liability has been discharged is made in duplicate on Form

CAP 30 by the personal representative after he has ensured there are no further assets or liabilities to be reported and that all tax and interest due has been paid. A sealed copy of Form CAP 30 will be issued by the Capital Taxes Office as conformation that on the information submitted it appears there is no further liability.

If a house is sold within four years after the death at a value lower than the probate value; the lower value can be substituted for the probate value.

Summary

- When full details of an estate have been ascertained, it will be possible to see whether or not an Inland Revenue Account is required.

- If an estate is an excepted estate, an Inland Revenue Account is not required.

- An excepted estate is:
  - An estate where the total value including joint and nominated property does not exceed £145,000 for deaths on or after the 6 April 1995.
  - Joint property includes only the value of the deceased's beneficial interest in that joint property.
  - Not more than £15,000 of the property passing should represent the value of property situate out of England and Wales.
  - The deceased must have died domiciled in England and Wales and have made no lifetime gifts chargeable to IHT.
  - The grant must not be limited.
  - The estate must comprise only of property passing by the deceased's will or by intestacy, by nomination or beneficially by survivorship.

- There are several forms of Inland Revenue Account and those most commonly in use are Forms IHT 200 and IHT 202.

- The personal representative must deliver an account of the estate to the Capital Taxes Office within twelve months of the death. If the personal representative did not commence to act until some time after the death, he must deliver the account within three months from first acting if this is later than twelve months after the death.

- IHT is due six months after the death on personalty and realty unless the personal representative chooses to pay inheritance tax in instalments on the realty. If this is the case then the first instalment is due from the end of the sixth month after the death.

- Personal representatives failing to deliver an account may be liable to a penalty for each day they fail to deliver the account.

- The Inland Revenue will provide a Form IHT 9 which suggests the information to be provided with the Inland Revenue Account.

- It may be helpful to consider IHT 9 before completing the Form 200.

- Where personal representatives are unable to provide the initial inheritance tax to apply for a grant of representation they should be advised to consider requesting an advance from any building society account owned by the deceased.

- Another method of raising money is to apply to the deceased's bank or other bank to open a loan account and to issue a cheque payable to the Inland Revenue for the inheritance tax. The bank will require the executors to complete a first proceeds form, and an undertaking to exhibit the grant as soon as it is issued.

- If the deceased was a patient under the Court of Protection an application can be made to that court to release part or all of the funds for these purposes.

- Personal representatives may apply to settle inheritance tax liabilities by way of payment in lieu of tax. This can take the form of land and buildings, works of art, manuscripts and books etc. The Museums and Galleries Commission deals with the day-to-day administration of this system.

- When all of the inheritance tax due on an estate has been paid the executors should apply for a clearance certificate from the Capital Taxes Office on Form CAP 30.

Chapter 11

Income tax, capital gains tax and inheritance tax

1. Income tax

A tax year runs from 6 April in one year to 5 April in the following year. There are three different rates of income tax which are:

- the lower rate of 20%
- the standard rate of 25% and
- the higher rate of 40% (see the following tables).

Personal income tax

Taxable income	1990/91	Tax rate
1–20,700		25%
over 20,700		40%

Taxable income	1991/92	Tax rate
1–23,700		25%
over 23,700		40%

Taxable income	1992/93	Tax rate
1–2,000		20%
2,001–23,700		25%
over 23,700		40%

Taxable income	1993/94	Tax rate
1–2,500		20%
2,501–23,700		25%
over 23,700		40%

Taxable income	1994/95	Tax rate
1–3,000		20%
3,001–23,700		25%
over 23,700		40%

Taxable income	1995/96	Tax rate
1–3,200		20%
3,201–24,300		25%
over 24,300		40%

In most cases, each individual's income is taxed at source either:

(a) through pay as you earn (PAYE) deducted by the employer at source from their earnings;

(b) by tax being deducted and shown as tax credits on dividends and income payments from investments, or deducted at source by banks; or

(c) through building societies (unless a person has applied to have the income paid gross).

There are many sources of income which are exempt for income tax purposes, the more usual sources are:

(i)   National Savings Certificates;

(ii)   redundancy payments up to stated limits;

(iii)   the first £70 of interest from National Savings Bank ordinary accounts;

(iv)   disability living allowance;

(v)   disability working allowance;

(vi)   attendance allowance;

(vii)   child benefit.

Income tax is calculated on the income received by an individual during a tax year.

2. Allowances

For income tax everyone has a tax free allowance.

(a) Tax allowance

Single persons have a personal tax allowance (currently £3,525 per year) which means that they may receive income up to that amount in a tax year which is not liable to income tax.

For married couples, this means that they each have their own personal relief of £3,525 in the tax year, and there is also additional tax relief available which is called married couple's relief. This additional relief is usually given against the husband's earnings, but the couple may elect to have the married couple's relief transferred to the wife's earnings, or shared between them. This can be beneficial where the wife's income is greater than her spouse's, or where the husband's income is not sufficient to render him liable to income tax. For the tax year 1994/95 the married couple's allowance is given by way of a reduction in income tax. This is calculated by taking 20 per cent of the married couple's allowance. For the tax year 1995/96 this will be 15 per cent of the married couple's allowance.

Table of allowances

	Personal	Married couple
1990/91	3,005	1,720
1991/92	3,295	1,720
1992/93	3,445	1,720
1993/94	3,445	1,720
1994/95	3,445	1,720 × 20% (see para above)
1995/96	3,525	1,720 × 15%

Examples

Example 1. A single man (under 65 years) earning £20,000 per year in 1995/96 would be liable to tax of:

(Salary £20,000)	Personal allowance £3,525	Taxed at 20% £3,200	Taxed at 25% £13,275	Taxed at 40% NIL
		Tax £640	Tax £3,318.75	Total tax £3,958.75

Example 2. A married man (under 65 years) earning the same salary in the same year would pay:

(Salary £20,000)	Personal allowance £3,525	Taxed at 20% £3,200	Taxed at 25% £13,275	Taxed at 40% NIL
		Tax £640	Tax £3,318.75	Total tax £3,958.75

LESS married couple's allowance, £1,720 × 15% £258.00

= £3,700.75 tax

Example 3. A single man (under 65 years) earning £50,000 per year in 1995/96 would pay:

(Salary £50,000)	Personal allowance £3,525	Taxed at 20% £3,200	Taxed at 25% £21,100	Taxed at 40% (everything over £24,300) = £22,175	
		Tax £640	Tax £5,275	Tax £8,870	Total tax £14,785

(b) Age allowance

Where persons are aged between 65 and 74 years, or are over 75 years old, an additional allowance known as age allowance is available.

Age 65 years or over to under 75 years

	Personal	Married couple (husband or wife over age limit)	Income limits
1990/91	3,670	2,145	12,300
1991/92	4,020	2,355	13,500
1992/93	4,200	2,465	14,200

1993/94	4,200	2,465	14,200
1994/95	4,200	2,665 × 20% (see Tax allowance, page 98)	14,200
1995/96	4,630	2,995 × 15%	14,600

Age over 75 years

	Personal	*Married couple (husband or wife over age limit)*	*Income limits*
1990/91	3,820	2,185	12,300
1991/92	4,180	2,395	13,500
1992/93	4,370	2,505	14,200
1993/94	4,370	2,505	14,200
1994/95	4,370	2,705 × 20% (see Tax allowance, page 98)	14,200
1995/96	4,800	3,035 × 15%	14,600

Age allowance is reduced by £1 for every £2 of income which is in excess of the above income limits until the standard allowances are reached.

Example

A man aged over 75 years receives taxable income of £12,600 in 1990/91. This exceeds his income limit of £12,300 by £300. The age allowance of £3,820 (for 1990/91) is therefore reduced by £150 (one-half of the £300 excess) leaving his age allowance for that year at £3,670 (£3,820 minus £150).

If the same man in the same year receives taxable income of £13,950, this income exceeds that year's income limit by £1,650. His tax relief of £3,820 for that year should be reduced by £825 (one-half of £1,650). This reduces his tax allowance to £2,995 (£3,820 minus £825). However, the standard allowance for that year is £3,005. Therefore his allowance is reduced only to the standard allowance of £3,005.

There are other allowances available including widow's bereavement allowance and blind person's allowance (as discussed below).

(c) Widow's bereavement allowance

A lawful widow is entitled to her own annual allowance, and in addition, a widow's allowance, for the remainder of the tax year in which her spouse died, and for the whole of the following tax year. The amount allowed for widow's allowance is the same as the amount allowed for married couple's allowance which is currently £1,720 per year. For tax years 1994/95 and 1995/96 the allowance is given by way of a reduction in income tax which is calculated by taking 20 per cent of the allowance in 1994/95 and 15 per cent in 1995/96.

(d) Blind person's allowance

Blind person's relief is available to a person who is registered blind. A married couple who are both blind may each claim the allowance. A married blind person may transfer unused blind person's relief to the spouse whether or not the spouse is blind.

1990/91	1991/92	1992/93	1993/94	1994/95	1995/96
1,080	1,080	1,080	1,080	1,200	1,200

(e) Dividends

Since tax year 1993/94, dividends from shares are all taxed at 20 per cent, which means that the shareholder receives a dividend of 80 per cent, and a tax credit of 20 per cent. Annual income tax returns now allow for these tax credits at 20 per cent to be shown separately from all other income which has been taxed at 25 per cent, and all untaxed income.

(f) Income tax returns

Income tax returns must show if income was received net of tax or gross so that the income tax liability can be assessed correctly.

Income tax liability is calculated as follows:

(i) The total income received during the tax year.

(ii) Less, the individual's annual allowances, for example, personal allowance, married couple's allowance (see 'allowances' for married couple's allowance for 1994/95 onwards), age allowance etc., and this leaves the income which is taxable.

(iii) Tax at the lowest rate (currently 20%) is calculated on the first band (currently £3,200).

(iv) Tax at the next rate (currently 25%) is calculated on all income within the next band (currently up to £21,000).

(v) All income over £24,300 is taxed at the next rate (currently 40%) which is the highest rate of tax charged.

(g) Administration of estates

Personal representatives are liable for income tax on all untaxed income received into an estate during the administration period. No tax free allowances are available to them. All of this income is taxed at 25 per cent. Personal representatives are not entitled to pay the lower rate tax of 20 per cent and they are not liable to tax at the higher rate of 40 per cent, because, as personal representatives, they are not assessed as individuals.

If there is an income tax repayment due to the estate the Inland Revenue will send a Form R 27 to the personal representative for completion.

When dealing with the administration of an estate the personal representative must finalise the deceased's tax affairs up to the date of death. This means the personal representative must complete a tax return for the period from the 6 April prior to the death up to the actual date of death. The deceased's personal allowances will be given for the whole of the tax year in which he dies even if he dies half way through the tax year. Where the deceased leaves a widow, the married couple's allowance is given only up to the date of death. However, his widow is entitled to widow's bereavement allowance from the date of death for the remainder of that tax year and for the whole of the following tax year. The personal representative should also check that tax returns have been completed and submitted to the Inland Revenue for previous tax years. Where there is no evidence of this, the personal representative should ask the Inland Revenue to confirm that tax returns have been submitted for the last tax year before the death, and for previous tax years. It is often helpful to obtain a copy of the previous year's tax return (from the Inland Revenue if necessary) as this is a method of checking the deceased's income producing assets.

If the deceased received very little income, it is probable that he was not required to complete annual tax returns. Confirmation must be obtained from the Inland Revenue.

The personal representative must declare the deceased's income and any capital gains.

Any tax due from the deceased up to the date of death is an estate liability, and any repayment of tax due to the deceased prior to the date of death is an estate asset. Either of these must be included in Form IHT 200 or other form used.

3. Tax during administration

Untaxed income received into the estate during the administration period must be declared to the Inland Revenue by the personal representative, and any income tax must be paid from the estate. Similarly, any capital gain incurred during the period must be declared, and any capital gains tax paid from the estate. If the administration of the estate continues over more than one tax year, the personal representative must declare all untaxed income, and all capital gains at the end of each tax year. When the tax has been paid, he can issue tax deduction certificates (Form R 185E) to the beneficiaries. The beneficiaries can then send the tax deduction certificate to their own tax inspector to reclaim any overpaid tax, or be taxed for any additional rate tax liability if they are higher rate taxpayers. Remember to submit Inland Revenue Form R 59 to the deceased's tax district.

The Inland Revenue may raise assessments for up to three years after the end of the year of death. They may make assessments for the period of six years prior to the date of death.

(a) Limited interests

Up to 5 April 1995 income paid to a beneficiary with a limited interest (e.g. a life interest) is treated as his income for the tax year in which the income is paid to him.

(b) Absolute interests

Up to 5 April 1995 income paid to a beneficiary with an absolute interest is treated as his income for the tax year in which the income was earned.

Within three years from the end of the year in which the administration was completed the income figures are revised by the Inland Revenue. For limited interests, the income received is calculated on a day-to-day basis over the administration period. For absolute interests the income received is calculated for each tax year during the administration period.

(c) New rules

From 6 April 1995 new rules apply, and income from estates will only be treated as the income of the beneficiaries for the tax year in which it is paid to the beneficiary. This might not create tax problems for beneficiaries of small estates, but in estates receiving large amounts of income, the beneficiaries could find that the income received increases their tax liability to the higher rates of tax.

(d) Charities

Charities are entitled to reclaim any income tax suffered on the share of the estate due to that charity. The personal representative should, therefore, provide the charity with an Inland Revenue Form R 185E, and also complete Inland Revenue Form 59 and send this to the deceased's tax district.

(e) Beneficiaries

From 6 April 1995 the Inland Revenue treat income payments to residuary beneficiaries as the recipient's income for the tax year in whch the income was received by that beneficiary (see Tax during administration).

(f) Income arising during the administration period

For tax year 1992/93 income from banks, building societies etc. was liable to tax at 25 per cent. Share dividends were also taxed at 25 per cent. Bank and building society interest was received net of tax, and in the following examples it has been grossed up.

Examples

Example 1. Tax year *1992/93*

	£
Bank/building society interest (grossed up)	133.33
less tax at 25%	33.33

income net of tax	100.00
Dividends (gross)	1,600.00
less tax credit at 25%	400.00
net dividend	1,200.00

If there is only one beneficiary, the personal representatives should provide that beneficiary with a tax deduction certificate on Form R 185E. The separate sources of income would not have to be shown and the R 185E would contain the following information:

Gross income	Tax	Net income paid
1,733.33	433.33	1,300.00

Example 2. Tax year *1993/94 and thereafter*

	£
Bank/building society interest (grossed up)	133.33
less tax at 25%	33.33
income net of tax	100.00
Dividends (gross)	1,600.00
less tax credit at 20%	320.00
net dividend	1,280.00

The personal representatives should show separately the sources of income to show tax deducted at 25 per cent and at 20 per cent. The R 185E should contain the following information:

	Gross income	Tax	Net income paid
dividends	1,600.00	320.00	1,280.00
building society	133.33	33.33	100.00
Totals	1,733.33	353.33	1,380.00

Where there is more than one beneficiary sharing the net estate, the Form R 185E for each beneficiary would show the portion of income to which each of them is entitled (see Tax during administration).

4. Capital gains tax

There are three different rates of CGT depending on an individual's income tax rate, the rates are:

- the lower rate of 20%
- the standard rate of 25%
- the higher rate of 40%.

CGT is charged at the same percentage as an individual's top slice of income tax. Therefore, for a standard rate tax payer the CGT rate is 25 per cent.

For a higher rate tax payer the CGT rate is 40 per cent.

A husband and a wife are assessed separately.

For capital gains tax, individuals have an annual allowance of £6,000

(1995/96) of gains which are tax free. Husband and wife both have this allowance making £12,000 between them.

CGT annual allowances

Tax year	Individuals	Trusts
1990/91	£5,000	£2,500
1991/92	£5,500	£2,750
1992/93	£5,800	£2,900
1993/94	£5,800	£2,900
1994/95	£5,800	£2,900
1995/96	£6,000	£3,000

(a) Indexation

In order to calculate the correct capital gain, reference should be made to the retail price index table on page 108, to calculate the indexation allowance.

For disposals before 30 November 1993 use of indexation could create a loss, or increase a loss, for CGT purposes. From 6 April 1995 indexation relief will not be allowed to create or increase a CGT loss, but it will be allowed to reduce a gain to zero.

A special transitional relief applied in the interim for disposals made by individuals and trustees of existing settlements but this did not apply to personal representatives.

(b) CGT calculation

To ascertain the net chargeable gain the following calculations should be made

    (i)   Total acquisition cost:
        Purchase price, plus costs incurred; e.g. estate agent's fees, surveyors, valuer, advertising, legal costs, stamp duty etc., plus indexation.

    (ii) Sale price:
        less sale costs (as above), less annual exemption.

(c) Shares

There is no CGT liability on gains from the sale of gilt edged stocks.

(d) Pooling

Securities purchased in the same company, at various dates, by the same person, in the same capacity, are pooled and considered to be a single asset. This asset can, of course, increase or decrease if more of the same security are purchased, or if any are sold.

Example

'A' purchases shares in the same company at various periods:

		Retail price index		
January	1986	(96.25)	500 shares	cost £700.00
July	1986	(97.52)	500 shares	cost £875.00
March	1988	(104.1)	1,000 shares	cost £900.00
April	1990	(125.1)	250 shares	cost £450.00

Each time additional shares are purchased, the existing pool is indexed, and the cost of the newly purchased shares is added giving the new overall value of all of the shares now held viz:

Purchase date	Nominal	Cost	Indexed pool
January 1986	500	£700	£700

July 1986 (500 shares purchased)

indexed rise;
January 1986–July 1986

$$\frac{97.52 - 96.25}{96.25} \times £700 = £9.24$$

Additional shares	500	£875	£875.00
New totals	shares 1,000	cost £1,575	pool £1,584.24

March 1988 (1,000 shares purchased)

indexed rise;
July 1986–March 1988

$$\frac{104.1 - 97.52}{97.52} \times £1,584.24 = £106.89$$

Additional shares	1,000	£900	£900.00
New totals	shares 2,000	cost £2,475	pool £2,591.13

April 1990 (250 shares purchased)

indexed rise;
March 1988–April 1990

$$\frac{125.1 - 104.1}{104.1} \times £2,591.13 = £522.70$$

Additional shares	250	£450	£450.00
New totals	shares 2,250	cost £2,925	pool £3,563.83

In April 1993, 1,250 shares are sold for £1,900

indexation;
April 1990–April 1993

$$\frac{140.6 - 125.1}{125.1} \times £3,563.83 = £441.56$$

$$= £4,005.39$$

| Shares sold | (1,250) | (£1,625) | (£2,225.22) |
| New totals | shares 1000 | cost £1,300 | pool £1,780.17 |

The indexed value of the 1,250 shares sold =

$$\frac{1,250}{2,250} \times £4,005.39 = 2,225.22$$

Proceeds of the sale of 1,250 shares, £1,900 less indexed cost £2,225.22

LOSS = £325.22

(e) Shares held at 31 March 1982

The values of shares held on 31 March 1982 which are sold *after* 5 April 1988 are 're-based', that is, their value is the market value as at 31 March 1982.

The general rule for re-basing is that on a disposal after 5 April 1988 it is assumed that the holding was sold on 31 March 1982 and repurchased immediately at its market value at that date. The person selling the shares must have held them on 31 March 1982.

(f) Chattels

Each chattel sold for £6,000 or less is exempt for CGT. For these purposes a chattel may be a single item, or several items making up a set; for example a set of twelve chairs or a three-piece suite.

Disposal of chattels, either by sale or as a gift may be liable to a CGT charge if the value exceeds £6,000. Even if such an asset should be destroyed (for example by fire) it may be charged. The gift of a chattel between spouses, however, is exempt so long as the spouses are living together at the time of the gift. The spouse is considered to have received it at the price and at the date the donor purchased it.

When a chattel is sold for a price in excess of £6,000 the method of calculating the capital gain is shown below (being five-thirds of the difference between the amount realised on the sale and the figure £6,000).

Examples

Example 1. Chattel sold for £9,000
Less £6,000
= £3,000 × 5/3
Capital gain (A) £5,000

Compare this with the actual gain:
Chattel purchased for £3,000
Chattel sold for £9,000 (as above)
Capital gain (B) £6,000

The chargeable gain is £5,000 (A) being the lesser of the two calculations above (A) or (B). If this is the only chargeable gain in a year there is no CGT liability (it is less than the annual exemption of £6,000).

Example 2 Chattel sold for   £14,500
                Less   £6,000
                              = £8,500 × 5/3
                Capital gain (A)   £14,166
Compare this with the actual gain:
                Chattel purchased for £4,500
                Chattel sold for   £14,500 (as above)
                Capital gain (B)   £10,000
The chargeable gain is £10,000 (B) being the lesser of the two calculations above (A) or (B).

If this is the only chargeable gain in a year CGT is charged on £10,000 less the annual exemption of £6,000, therefore the net gain is £4,000 charged at the relevant percentage for capital gains tax.

5. Administration of estates – CGT

Any CGT liability on the sale of estate assets during the administration of the estate is the liability of the personal representatives.

Personal representatives get the same relief as an individual (£6,000 per year as above) during the remainder of the tax year in which the death occurred, plus the two following years. After this period, they get no annual allowance, until they become trustees after finalising the administration of the estate.

(a) Charities

CGT exemption is available to charities who are residuary legatees. To take advantage of this the personal representative should show in the estate accounts (even the draft estate accounts) that the shares or other assets have been appropriated to the charity, and he should write to the charity advising them that the appropriation has taken place.

The charity may then write to the personal representative with instructions to sell the assets on behalf of the charity, and the personal representative then sells as bare trustee, and the charity is not liable to CGT on any gains made on the sale.

Retail Price Index

	1980	1981	1982	1983	1984	1985	1986
January	62.18	70.29	78.73	82.61	86.84	91.20	96.25
February	63.07	70.93	78.76	82.97	87.20	91.94	96.60
March	63.93	71.99	79.44	83.12	87.48	92.80	96.73
April	66.11	74.07	81.04	84.28	88.64	94.78	97.67
May	66.72	74.55	81.62	84.64	88.97	95.21	97.85
June	67.35	74.98	81.85	84.84	89.20	95.41	97.79
July	67.91	75.31	81.88	85.30	89.10	95.23	97.52
August	68.06	75.87	81.90	85.68	89.94	95.49	97.82
September	68.49	76.30	81.85	86.06	90.11	95.44	98.30
October	68.92	76.98	82.26	86.36	90.67	95.59	98.45
November	69.48	77.78	82.66	86.67	90.95	95.92	99.29
December	69.86	78.28	82.51	86.89	90.87	96.05	99.62

	1987	1988	1989	1990	1991	1992	1993
January	100.00	103.30	111.00	119.50	130.20	135.60	137.90
February	100.40	103.70	111.80	120.20	130.90	136.30	138.80
March	100.60	104.10	112.30	121.40	131.40	136.70	139.30
April	101.80	105.80	114.30	125.10	133.10	138.80	140.60
May	101.90	106.20	115.00	126.20	133.50	139.30	141.10
June	101.90	106.60	115.40	126.70	134.10	139.30	141.10
July	101.80	106.70	115.50	126.80	133.80	138.70	140.70
August	102.10	107.90	115.80	128.10	134.10	138.90	141.30
September	102.40	108.40	116.60	129.30	134.60	139.40	141.90
October	102.90	109.50	117.50	130.30	135.10	139.90	141.80
November	103.40	110.00	118.50	130.00	135.60	139.70	141.60
December	103.30	110.30	118.80	129.90	135.70	139.20	141.90

	1994	1995
January	141.30	146.00
February	142.10	146.90
March	142.50	147.50
April	144.20	149.00
May	144.70	149.60
June	144.70	
July	144.00	
August	144.70	
September	145.00	
October	145.20	
November	145.30	
December	146.00	

A proportion of the costs incurred by the personal representatives to obtain a grant of representation can be set off against a capital gains tax liability. It is accepted that those costs are incidental to the acquisition of the assets of the estate by the personal representatives.

The Inland Revenue have (provisionally) agreed to the following amounts:

Allowable expenditure	Estate value (gross)
1.75% of probate value of assets sold	Up to £40,000
£700 which has to be divided between all of the assets in proportion to their probate value	£40,001 to £70,000
1% probate value of assets sold	£70,001 to £300,000
£3,000 which has to be divided between all of the assets in proportion to their probate value	£300,001 to £400,000
0.75% of probate value of assets sold	£400,001 to £750,000

The Inland Revenue will negotiate the amount of allowable expenditure on values over £750,000.

There is no CGT liability when an asset is transferred to a beneficiary *in specie*. The beneficiary is deemed to have received it at its date of death value.

6. Inheritance tax

Inheritance tax (IHT) is chargeable on a person's net estate at death, which includes certain lifetime transfers (but there are exemptions, as noted below). The first £154,000 (1995/96) of net estate is exempt and the balance is taxed at 40 per cent (currently). Chargeable lifetime gifts are taxed at 20 per cent.

The rate scale is as follows:

Scale £	Tax rate – %
Deaths on or after 17 March 1987	
0 – 90,000	Nil
90,000 – 140,000	30
140,000 – 220,000	40
220,000 – 330,000	50
Over 330,000	60
Deaths on or after 15 March 1988	
0 – 110,000	Nil
Over 110,000	40
Deaths on or after 6 April 1989	
0 – 118,000	Nil
Over 118,000	40
Deaths on or after 6 April 1990	
0 – 128,000	Nil
Over 128,000	40
Deaths on or after 6 April 1991	
0 – 140,000	Nil
Over 140,000	40
Deaths on or after 10 March 1992	
0 – 150,000	Nil
over 150,000	40
Deaths on or after 6 April 1995	
0 – 154,000	Nil
over 154,000	40

The personal representatives cannot obtain a grant of representation until an IHT account, detailing all of the deceased's estate, has been receipted by the CTO, unless the estate is an excepted estate (see below) or the account shows that there is no liability or no immediate liability to tax. (IHTA 1984, Pt VIII.)

(a) IHT account

Where an IHT account is required it must be sent to the CTO within one year of the death (this is calculated from the end of the month in which the death occurred).

If no one starts to deal with the estate for a long time the one year time limit is not relevant, but as soon as a person commences the administration of the estate, the IHT account must be sent to the CTO within three months of the commencement of the administration. Generally, when IHT is payable, the tax due on the value of the personalty is payable immediately the account is sent to the CTO, and IHT on the value of the realty may be paid in ten annual instalments (if the personal representatives have elected to pay by instalments), the first instalment being payable six months after the end of the month in which the death occurred.

(b) Receipted account

After the initial IHT has been paid, the CTO will return the account (receipted) to the personal representatives. The receipted account is then forwarded to the Probate Registry with the application for the grant.

In cases where the oath shows that the estate is not liable for IHT, the IHT account does not have to be sent to the CTO before applying for the grant, it can be sent immediately to the Probate Registry with the grant application.

When an estate is an 'excepted estate' an account is not required unless the CTO gives written notice requiring an account to be submitted.

(c) Penalties

A personal representative who fails to deliver an account of the estate assets to the Capital Taxes Office will be liable to a penalty not exceeding £50, and if the account is not then delivered he will be liable to further sums not exceeding £10 per day for each day. A Probate Registry cannot issue a grant in estates where an account is required until either the account is produced showing that no IHT is payable, or showing a receipt from the Inland Revenue.

(d) Liability for IHT

The beneficiaries are equally liable for the whole of the IHT, but not until the property has been vested in them.

(e) Excepted estates

For deaths after 3 August 1981 certain estates can be classed as 'excepted estates' and an Inland Revenue Account is not required. Certain conditions have to be satisfied, and the cash limits are increased from time to time.

(i) The total value of the estate (including joint and nominated property) must not exceed:

- £145,000 for deaths on or after 6 April 1995,
- £125,000 for deaths on or after 1 April 1991,
- £115,000 for deaths on or after 1 April 1990,
- £100,000 for deaths on or after 1 April 1989,
- £70,000 for deaths on or after 1 April 1987,
- £40,000 for deaths on or after 1 April 1983,
- £25,000 for deaths before 1 April 1983.

(f) Joint property

Before 1 April 1990 joint property included the full value of any joint property passing by survivorship, but it now includes only the value of the deceased's beneficial interest in joint property e.g. jointly owned matrimonial home, the deceased's share is considered to be 50 per cent.

(ii) Of the property passing, not more than £15,000 (for deaths after 1 April 1989) represents the value of property situated outside of England and Wales.

Limits applicable to deaths before this date are:

- £10,000 for deaths after 1 April 1987
- £2,000* for deaths after 1 April 1983
- £1,000 for deaths before 1 April 1983

*(or 10% of the gross estate, whichever is higher).

(iii) The deceased must have died domiciled in England and Wales, and have made no lifetime gifts chargeable to inheritance tax, CTT or PETs which have become chargeable.

(iv) The grant must not be limited, e.g. to settled land or personalty only.

(v) The estate must comprise only property passing by intestacy or the deceased's will, by nomination or beneficially by survivorship.

(g) Oath

If all of the above conditions are fulfilled, the oath will include the words 'to the best of my knowledge, information, and belief, the gross estate passing under the grant does not exceed (£145,000, £125,000, £115,000, £100,000, £70,000 as appropriate)'.

If, during the administration, further assets are discovered and the estate is no longer 'excepted', this fact must be reported to the CTO within six months of discovery of the additional assets.

If there is any doubt whether an estate is excepted or not, the matter should be referred to the CTO, not to the Probate Registry.

(h) IHT in instalments

The assets for which the instalment option is available are: dwellings, buildings, land, timber, business interests. When an asset which is the subject of the instalment option is sold, the IHT, or the balance IHT and interest, becomes immediately payable in full.

When personal representatives have elected to pay by instalments, the CTO will send an assessment to them before each instalment becomes due. The assessment will show the annual instalment due, which is one-tenth of the total IHT, and it will show the amount of interest payable which is calculated on the whole of the outstanding IHT, and not just on the amount of the annual instalment.

(j) Interest rates

Interest rate	Interest charge per £1 per day
6%	0.000164383
7%	0.000191780
8%	0.000219178
9%	0.000246575
10%	0.000273972
11%	0.000301369
12%	0.000328767

Interest period	Transfers on death
01-10-75 to 31-12-79 (1553 days)	6%
01-01-80 to 30-11-82 (1065 days)	9%
01-12-82 to 30-04-85 (1882 days)	6%
01-05-85 to 15-12-86 (594 days)	9%
16-12-86 to 05-06-87 (172 days)	8%
06-06-87 to 05-08-88 (427 days)	6%
06-08-88 to 05-10-88 (61 days)	8%
06-10-88 to 05-07-89 (273 days)	9%
06-07-89 to 05-03-91 (608 days)	11%
06-03-91 to 05-05-91 (61 days)	10%
06-05-91 to 05-07-91 (61 days)	9%
06-07-91 to 05-11-92 (489 days)	8%
06-11-92 to 05-12-92 (30 days)	6%
06-12-92 to 05-01-94 (396 days)	5%
06-01-94 to 05-10-94 (273 days)	4%
06-10-94 to date	5%

If the deceased is domiciled in the UK, all of his assets, (including assets out of the UK) are liable to be assessed for IHT.

When the deceased dies domiciled out of the UK, only the UK assets are liable to IHT.

Lifetime transfers are PETs (Potentially Exempt Transfers) which become exempt transfers if the donor survives the transfer by seven years, and has not reserved any benefit for himself. Certain small gifts are exempt (see *(m)* below). If the donor fails to survive the transfer by seven years it is added back into the estate for IHT purposes. IHT on the transfer is calculated on the value of the transfer at the date it was made, but tax is charged at the IHT rates applicable at the date of death. If the donor survives the transfer for more than three years but less than seven years taper relief is available. It must be understood that it is the tax chargeable which is tapered, and not the value of the transfer.

(k) Taper relief

Years 1–3	the whole of the transfer is chargeable
Year 4	80% of IHT
Year 5	60% of IHT
Year 6	40% of IHT
Year 7	20% of IHT
Over 7 years	the whole of the transfer is exempt.

(l) Nil rate band

If the value of a lifetime transfer (or transfers) is less than the nil rate band (currently £154,000) the tapering relief is not operative because there is no IHT chargeable below this amount, and therefore there can be no tax saving.

(m) Exempt transfers

Certain other lifetime transfers are exempt:

(i)   A gift in any one year not exceeding £3,000. Any part of that annual gift of £3,000 may be carried forward (one year only), to the following tax year, and may be added to the £3,000 gift allowance for that second year.

   Example: "A" makes a gift of £2,000 to his nephew in 1992, and makes no other gifts. The unused £1,000 may be carried forward to 1993 and he can then make a gift of £3,000 plus the unused £1,000 making £4,000 in total. If, however, he only gives £3,000 in 1993, the brought forward £1,000 can no longer be carried forward and the gift exemption for that amount from 1992 is lost. As will be seen from this example, a person must first of all utilise the annual £3,000 before using any 'brought forward unused amount' from the previous year.

(ii) Transfers of value to any one person in any one tax year not exceeding £250. As there is no limit to the number of £250 transfers in any one year, there can be no unused gifts of this amount to be carried forward to the following year.

   However, if a transfer of £250 is made to a person who also receives £3,000 from the same donor in the same tax year, the £250 is not counted as an exempt transfer. In this case, the £3,000 is an exempt transfer, but the £250 is a Potentially Exempt Transfer (PET) which will not fall out of account until the donor has survived the transfer by seven years.

(iii) Regular gifts out of income which do not affect the transferor's standard of living.

(iv) Gifts to either a bride or a groom in contemplation of marriage, but with the following limits:

   – £5,000 from a parent;

   – £2,500 from a bride, groom, or a grandparent;

   – £1,000 from any other person.

(n) Gifts with reservation

A gift with reservation is not an exempt gift or a PET. For example, a person makes a gift of his house to his sister, but he reserves the right to live in that house as part of the gift.

(o) Transfer to spouse

The entire value of a transfer to a lawful spouse is exempt if the spouse is domiciled in the UK. If the spouse is not UK domiciled, only £55,000 is exempt.

(p) Gifts to charities

All gifts to charities are exempt.

(q) Gifts to political parties

All gifts to political parties are exempt.

(r) Gifts for national purposes

These include gifts to national museums, The National Heritage, The National Trust etc. These are exempt.

(s) Gifts for public benefit

These include writings, paintings, land and buildings, etc. The Treasury decide if a gift falls into any of these categories, and if they are of merit.

(t) Realty

When the estate includes realty, and where that realty is sold within four years after the death, the executors may apply to the CTO to substitute the sale value for the probate value only if the amount realised on sale is 5 per cent lower than the probate value, or £1,000 less than the probate value, whichever is the lower value.

(u) Losses on shares sold

An overall net loss incurred on the sale of stocks and shares which have been sold within one year of the date of death, in estates where inheritance tax has been paid, should be reported to the Capital Taxes Office, and a claim for relief submitted under Inheritance Tax Act 1984, s 179. Such claims must be made on Form SECT 5. The gross proceeds, that is the actual amount received from the buyer before any deductions, are used in calculating the amount of the loss. The claim for relief is applicable only if the total amount realised is less than the date of death value of all of the shares. A claim is not applicable where some of the shares have been sold at a loss, others have been sold at a gain, and the overall result is a gain.

(v) IHT refunds

A refund of IHT may be claimed on the amount of the loss. If, instead of a loss, the overall result is an increase over the probate values, the gain does not have to be reported to the CTO as there is no increased liability to IHT. However, there could be a CGT liability, depending on the amount of the gain.

(w) Quoted securities

If quoted securities are suspended after the date of death, it will not be possible to sell those shares. But the estate will still be liable to IHT on the probate value (if the estate is liable to IHT).

For deaths after 15 March 1992, if a quoted investment is suspended within the first year after the death, the personal representative can apply for the value of the security (on the first anniversary of the death) to be substituted for the probate value. Where this results in an over-assessment of IHT, he should claim a refund from the CTO.

(x) Unpaid IHT on gifts

Where IHT on a lifetime gift remains unpaid twelve months after the death of the donor, his personal representative is liable to settle the IHT, and pursue the recipient of the gift to reimburse the estate.

(y) Relief for business or agricultural property: Transfers of value and chargeable transfers made on or after 10 March 1992

Agricultural property: conditions

IHT relief is available on the transfer of agricultural property, subject to various conditions.

The relief is 100 per cent and 50 per cent for transfers after 9 March 1992 (relief previously was 50 per cent and 30 per cent).

(i) The property must have been *occupied* by the transferor, for agricultural purposes, for two years prior to the transfer.

OR

(ii) The property must have been *owned* by the transferor for seven years prior to the transfer, and have been occupied by the transferor or by another person for agricultural purposes.

If the transferor has control of a company, and that company occupies the property, the transferor is considered to *occupy* the property.

If the transferor has inherited the property from an estate he is deemed to have owned it from the date of death; and

If the deceased former owner was the spouse, the time it was owned/occupied by the deceased spouse is added to the transferor's period of ownership/occupation.

The 100% relief is available if:

(1) The transferor enjoyed the right to vacant possession, or the right to obtain vacant possession within one year.

(2) The transferor had a beneficial entitlement to his interest since prior to 10 March 1981, and,

(2a) he would have been able to claim the 50% relief which was available between 6 April 1976 and 10 March 1981 if he had sold the property.

(2b) His relief would not have been restricted to the 1000 acres or £250,000 limit which was applicable between the dates at (2a).

(2c) Between the dates 10 March 1981 and the date of transfer the interest he held did not give him the right of vacant possession (see (1) above).

(3) The property is let on a tenancy on or after 1 September 1995.

Business property: conditions

The conditions for relief from IHT on transfers of relevant business property are as follows:

(1) The business must be a qualifying business (and this includes a profession or a vocation) but not a business which is carried on otherwise than for gain.

(2) The asset must be relevant business property (see (A) below) and must have been owned by the transferor for a minimum period (see (B) below).

  (A) Relevant business property –

  Sole traders or a partner's interest in a partnership.

  Partnership shares in a trading partnership.

  Shareholdings with over 25% of the voting power in an unquoted trading company (the shares must have been held for two years).

  (B) Minimum period of ownership –

  The asset must have been owned by the transferor for a minimum of two years immediately prior to the transfer,

  or

  the asset replaced other property which qualified and both properties were owned by the transferor for a minimum of two years out of the five years immediately prior to the transfer (IHTA 1984 ss 106 and 107(1)).

(3) Inherited property –

  This is treated as having been owned from the date of death. If the property was inherited from a spouse, the property is treated as having been owned from the date the deceased spouse owned it.

Summary

Income tax

- The tax year runs from 6 April in any one year to 5 April the following year.

- There are three rates of income tax: the lower rate of 20 per cent; the standard rate of 25 per cent and the higher rate of 40 per cent.

- In most cases, an individual's income is taxed at source.

- Many sources of income are exempt for income tax purposes including National Savings Certificates, redundancy payments up to stated limits, the first £70 of interest from National Savings ordinary accounts, disability pensions, attendance allowance, child benefit and widow's pensions.

- A single person is entitled to a personal tax allowance. Married couples are each entitled to married couple's relief in addition to their own personal relief. Other allowances available include widow's bereavement allowance and a blind person's allowance.

- Personal representatives are liable for income tax on all untaxed income received into an estate during the administration.

Capital gains tax

- There are three rates of capital gains tax equivalent to the rates of income tax (see above).

- Individuals have an annual allowance of £6,000.

- In order to calculate the correct capital gain, reference should be made to the retail price index.

- Any CGT liability on the sale of the assets during the administration of the estate is the liability of the personal representatives.

- A proportion of the costs incurred by the personal representatives to obtain a grant of representation can be set off against a CGT liability.

Inheritance tax

- IHT is chargeable on a person's net estate at death. Various exemptions and reliefs are available to lessen the impact of tax.

- The personal representatives cannot obtain a grant of representation until an IHT account detailing all of the deceased's estate has been receipted by the Capital Taxes Office.

- A personal representative who fails to deliver an account of the estate assets to the CTO will be liable to a penalty.

Chapter 12

The grant of representation

The term 'grant of representation' includes a grant of probate and all other types of grant. This general description may be used in standard letters and saves having to prepare different standard letters for use with different types of grant (see Appendix 2).

In cases where the value of individual assets does not exceed £5,000, it may be possible to administer the estate without applying for a grant (see page 86).

1. Types of grant

Several types of grant may be applied for:

Probate: The grant issued to the executor(s) named in the will (see Chapter 4).

Double probate: Issued after the original grant of probate in various circumstances; e.g. where power was reserved to an executor, and he now wishes to take up the appointment (see page 28). If power was originally reserved to more than one, the oath for double probate should reserve power again to any continuing non-acting executors. This grant confers the same powers on the executor as the original grantor. This process may be repeated by any other non-acting executor to whom power has again been reserved.

'Save and except': A grant issued to an executor to deal with part of the estate, for example, the deceased's business affairs only where the testator has appointed different executors to deal with the other estate.

'Caeterorum': The grant issued after the grant 'save and except', to enable the rest of the estate to be administered.

'Cessate': Where the first grant ceases to operate, for example where a minor attains his majority, or where an attorney took letters of administration (with the will) for use and benefit, and the donor of the power of attorney now wishes to obtain a grant (see page 31).

Special executors: Appointed for settled land and, for example, after a 'save and except' grant.

Settled land: A grant to administer land which was vested in the deceased at the date of his death which was settled previously (and not by his will) and which remained settled land notwithstanding his death.

Letters of administration (with the will): When no executors have been named, or named executors do not, or cannot, prove the will (see Chapter 5).

Letters of administration: Issued to the person or persons entitled where the deceased died intestate (see Chapter 6).

Pendente lite: Issued to protect the estate where there is an action pending in Chancery concerning the validity of the will, or the entitlement to the grant. The grant is made to the person agreed by both parties in dispute, or to a person appointed by the court. Application may be made only at the Principal Registry.

Ad colligenda bona: A limited grant ordered by a district judge or a registrar to enable the estate to be protected until a full grant is issued. Subject to the registrar's discretion under s 114 Supreme Court Act 1981, two persons or a trust corporation must be appointed where there is a minority or a life interest (see page 49).

De bonis non: When the personal representative appointed cannot continue with the administration of the estate, and the estate is left partly unadministered. The most common example is where a sole personal representative dies, and there is no chain of representation. The grant is in respect of the unadministered estate and can be of letters of administration with or without the will *de bonis non*.

Durante absentia: Any person can apply for this grant after one year has elapsed since the deceased died and the personal representative was residing out of England and Wales. An application may be made to the Chancery Division for similar powers, i.e. the appointment of a judicial trustee.

2. Waiting period

No grant of probate or letters of administration (with the will) is normally issued until seven clear days after the death have elapsed, and no grant of letters of administration is normally issued until fourteen clear days have elapsed since the death. However, in very exceptional circumstances a request for earlier issue will be considered. A statement of the relevant facts must accompany the application, which may be made by letter, although it is advisable to telephone either the Principal Probate Registry (0171 936 6974) or one of the District Probate Registries (see Appendix 6), to ascertain the precise requirements. The leave of only one district judge or registrar is required to issue a grant within the seven and fourteen-day periods (r 6 Non-Contentious Probate Rules 1987).

Since the waiting periods are very short, the need to obtain a grant earlier is very unusual but it may arise, perhaps where there is a real danger of loss of value of the assets. An example is the completion of an urgent conveyancing transaction.

3. Reason for grants

A grant is required for all the estate of a deceased which devolves on his personal representatives, and which cannot be released from its source without legal proof of title. The grant enables the personal representative to collect in and administer the deceased's property for the benefit of the legatees and devisees, creditors and residuary beneficiaries.

With certain exceptions (see page 86), the grant has to be produced to those concerned to establish the personal representative's authority to deal with the deceased's estate.

4. Nil estates

The court has jurisdiction to issue a grant of representation even if the deceased left no estate (see page 42), but an application for a grant in these circumstances must be accompanied by a sworn statement by the applicant showing why such a grant is required. The statement can take the form of an additional clause in the oath.

5. Application for the grant

The personal representative should use his best endeavours to ascertain the exact values of the assets and liabilities, as explained in Chapters 7 and 8. At times exact figures cannot be ascertained and estimated values have to be used in the application for the grant. In these cases, it must be shown that the values are estimates, and when the true values are known, they should be reported to the Capital Taxes Office for inheritance tax purposes (see below).

Having ascertained the values, or estimated values, the personal representative can now apply for a grant of representation. This is done by completing a form of oath (see Appendix 5 for forms) and filing it, together with the other documents required, at the Probate Registry. There are many standard pre-printed forms of oath available. Unless the personal representative is applying for a grant in person, only a solicitor holding a current practising certificate or other persons as specified in the Courts and Legal Services Act 1990 (see Preface), may prepare the oath.

(a) Settling oaths

If there is any doubt about the way an oath should be prepared, a draft may be sent or taken to the Probate Registry to be checked, and thereafter it may be engrossed and sworn (or 'affirmed') by the personal representative. This procedure is known as 'settling oaths' and a fee (currently £5) is charged for this service. The fee may be paid either when the draft is submitted to be settled, or when the application for the grant is made. It is advisable to take advantage of this facility where unusual oaths are needed or where any doubt exists, as this avoids having to ask the personal representative to re-swear (or 'affirm') an oath which has been rejected due to error.

Settled drafts should be returned to the Registry when the oath is submitted.

(b) Probate

The oath for executors must show the full names and the address at the date of death of the deceased, including any alias(es) with an explanation for any alias. If the address on the will differs from the address at the date of death, the testator's address at the date of the will should be inserted preceded by the words 'formerly of'. The age of the deceased must be included, but if the exact date of birth is not known, it should be shown that the deceased was born 'in or about (year)'.

The name and address of the person extracting the grant must be included at the head of the oath (r 4(2) Non-Contentious Probate Rules 1987), and members of the Document Exchange should include their Britdoc numbers at the head of the oath in addition to their full address.

The full names, addresses and occupations (see page 29) of the executors should be shown, with an explanation of any differences between the names in the will and the executors' true names (see page 33). If not all of the named executors are applying for the grant, the oath should clear off the rest, showing the reason why the other executors are not taking up the appointment (e.g. death, power reserved, renunciation). The description of the acting executors (e.g. 'two of', 'the surviving', see page 32) should also be included. If power is reserved to an executor (see page 28) his name should be inserted following the words 'power reserved to ....' and the oath should therefore contain the statement 'and I/we further make oath and say that notice of this application has been given to the executors to whom power is to be reserved'. If there is a codicil(s), references in the oath to the will should be followed by the words 'with [one, two, or as appropriate] codicil[s]'. Any limitation or condition (see page 23) must be dealt with specifically, and the oath should show that the condition or limitation has been fulfilled.

The oath must contain a statement that notice of the application has been given to all non-acting executors. Where a firm of solicitors is appointed as executors, but the partners are not actually named, and where all of the partners do not or cannot apply for probate (a maximum of four executors may prove at any one time: s 114(1) Supreme Court Act 1981) the oath must also state that those partners applying are (or were) partners in the named firm at the date of the will. The statement that notice of the application has been given to all non-acting partners need not be included, and notice need not be given to them if another partner in the firm applies for a grant.

If the estate is an 'excepted estate' (see page 88) the oath should show the 'gross' estate as not exceeding £145,000, £125,000, £115,000, £100,000, £70,000, £40,000, or £25,000 as appropriate for the date of death, and the net estate as not exceeding £200,000, £100,000, £70,000, £40,000, £25,000, £10,000 as appropriate to indicate the net estate on which probate fees are payable (see page 124).

Where the estate is not 'excepted' an Inland Revenue Account will be required in Form 200 or 202 (see page 89). This should be completed, and the gross and net figures from the Form 200 should be inserted into the oath. If inheritance tax is payable, the Form 200 should show if the personal representatives elect to pay the tax on instalment option property in annual payments. Tax on personalty is payable at the time of the application, but if the application for the grant is not submitted until after the first instalment becomes due, this will also be payable on application, plus interest at the rate current at the date of application.

Cheques for payment of inheritance tax should be sent to the Inland Revenue, with the Inland Revenue Account. The Account will be receipted and returned and can then be sent to the Probate Registry with the oath. Cheques should be sent by British Document Exchange to the Capital Taxes Office, DX 90950 Worthing 3, or by post to:

Financial Services Office (IHT cashiers),
Inland Revenue,
Barrington Road,
Worthing,
West Sussex BN12 4XH.

See page 137 for Capital Taxes Offices.

Cheques for Probate Registry fees are made payable to HM Paymaster General. The full names of the deceased should be written on the back of the cheque, in block capitals. This will assist the Probate Registry in identifying the application if the cheque bounces. The application should stipulate, in a covering letter, how many sealed copies of the grant are required and the cost should be added to the probate fee (currently 25p per copy).

The personal representative should be asked to read the oath (and the Inland Revenue Account if there is one) and if the documents are agreed, the Inland Revenue Account may be signed; the date of signing should be inserted. The oath with the will and codicil(s) if any, may be sworn or 'affirmed' and the oath should show the date and place of swearing or 'affirmation' and the name of the commissioner for oaths.

If an executor lives out of the area, the documents may be sent to him first, and thereafter signed/sworn or 'affirmed' by any other executor living locally. A cheque for the commissioner's fees can be sent to the executor out of the area, and it should be made payable to him personally as the name of the commissioner will not normally be known.

(c) Letters of administration (with the will)

The oath is prepared in the same way as an oath to lead a grant of probate (above), but there must in addition be an explanation of why no executor is proving the will (see page 39). The right of the applicant to apply is shown, clearing off anyone with a prior right to the grant. The will (and codicil(s)) must be exhibited when affirming or swearing the oath.

(d) Letters of administration

The application for letters of administration should show the names, address(es) and age of the deceased, together with his description (bachelor, spinster, etc.; see page 49). The name and address of the extracting solicitors must also appear. The full names, address and description of the applicant should be inserted and the oath should clear off anyone with a prior right to the grant. See also page 50 as to the administrators' oath.

(e) Fees

Commissioner's fees are currently £5.00 plus £2.00 for each exhibit. Therefore, an executor's oath plus the will costs £7.00 to swear or affirm; the oath, will and one codicil costs £9.00.

The Inland Revenue Account is no longer exhibited as it is not required to be sworn for deaths after 13 March 1975. The correct probate fees should be calculated on the net value of the estate and for applications from 1 August 1989, the scale is as follows:

Net estate not exceeding	Fee payable
£10,000	nil
£25,000	£40
£40,000	£80
£70,000	£150
£100,000	£215
£200,000	£300
£300,000	£350
£400,000	£400
For each additional £100,000 or part thereof	£50

Cheques are payable to HM Paymaster General. Note that Probate Registry fees can be waived in cases of hardship (see page 87) (remember to print the full names of the deceased on the back of the cheque ((b) above)).

The following do not attract fees:

(i)   nominated property;

(ii)   assets not in England or Wales;

(iii)   Civil Service gratuities;

(iv)   joint property which passes by survivorship.

(f) Sealed copies

Since the original grant should not be sent out when releasing assets, in case it is lost, the appropriate number of sealed copies should be requested from the Probate Registry with the application. By checking the number and type of assets, the number of sealed copies required can be ascertained. For example, if there are various bank and building society accounts in the same town, it ought not be necessary to purchase a copy for each and every separate account. Where there are stocks and shares to be sold or transferred, one copy will suffice for the gilts with the Bank of England, and if the dealings are through a stockbroker, he will not need a copy for every separate holding. Photostat copies are not normally acceptable by company registrars. The Probate Registry fee is currently 25p per sealed copy.

(g) Extra copies of the grant

If extra copies of a grant are needed after the grant has been issued, the charge is £2.00 for the first copy and 25p for each additional copy.

(h) Filing the oath

The oath, will, codicil(s), Form 200/202 and the cheque to the Probate Registry can now be presented to the Registry. If sent by post they should be sent first class.

There are no territorial limitations on the jurisdiction of District Probate Registries; generally an application for a grant may be made to any District Probate Registry or to the Principal Registry, but there are some exceptions.

Some clients may suggest that the application for the grant be made to a Probate Registry which is as far away as possible from the deceased's residence, in the hope that details of the estate will not be published in the local newspaper. Clients should be advised that it matters not in which registry the application is made, as all details are forwarded to the Principal Registry, from which newspapers may obtain details of every grant issued. As clients tend to believe it is solicitors who provide information to the press, it is good for public relations if they are made absolutely clear on this point, and it can also be explained that after the grant has issued, anyone may obtain a copy of it, and of the will, on paying the appropriate fee.

If the application is in order, the grant should be received in about one week. The original grant can be produced to the Inspector of Taxes if required by him (see page 76), and if it needs to be returned quickly, the return will be speeded by sending a photocopy also.

If the sale of any real property is imminent it is preferable to retain the original grant until the sale has been completed, and send it to the Inspector of Taxes thereafter.

6. Error in the oath

If there is an error in the oath submitted to obtain the grant, the oath may be returned by the Probate Registry. If the error is only minor, the matter may be resolved by a certificate from the solicitor, but the district judge or the registrar will indicate his requirements. In more serious cases, the oath will need to be corrected and re-sworn. After the correction has been made, the oath should be re-sworn, preferably before the commissioner before whom the original oath was sworn. The commissioner must initial in the margin of the oath each amendment that has been made. He must then add a new jurat commencing with the words 're-sworn by' etc. If a different commissioner is used for the re-swearing, then where the will is exhibited, the will must be re-marked by the deponent and signed by the commissioner. If the required correction or addition is lengthy, the oath may need to be re-typed in its entirety, and re-sworn as above. If the oath has already been submitted to the Probate Registry and has been returned, and it has to be re-drafted, the re-drafted oath should be sworn in the usual way but the original returned oath should be re-submitted together with the re-drafted oath after the re-drafted document has been sworn.

If an oath has to be re-sworn, it must be re-sworn by *all* of the deponents; not just by one of them. Clearly care should be taken to avoid any error.

Any errors in, or additions to, an Inland Revenue Account after it has been submitted to the Capital Taxes Office are dealt with by way of a letter showing the corrections (if minor only); otherwise a corrective account signed by the personal representative must be submitted. This must be done before applying for a clearance certificate (see page 95).

7. Error in the grant

When received, the grant should be checked, and if it contains any official error, it can be corrected by the Probate Registry, and re-issued without any formality. The original grant and all the office copies must be returned to the issuing registry within 14 days of issue if corrections are needed.

8. Effect of the grant

A grant of probate is accepted in all courts in England and Wales, Scotland and Northern Ireland as evidence of the formal validity of the will, of due execution (see page 138) and as evidence of the executor's title. A grant of administration is accepted in all courts as conclusive evidence of the intestacy of the deceased.

Grants of probate and letters of administration are accepted as evidence of the personal representative's title, and as authority to release the deceased's estate to the personal representative.

On the other hand, no grant is conclusive proof of the death, or of the identity of the personal representative.

9. Property covered by a grant of representation

The original grant is made in respect of all the estate of a deceased which devolves on his personal representative. Thus it does not cover nominated property or property held on a beneficial joint tenancy (e.g. bank or building society accounts or a dwelling-house held in joint names), which do not form part of the estate passing under the grant.

10. Change of solicitor (in contentious business)

If a client needs to change to another solicitor after the application for a grant has been submitted, a letter of consent from the first solicitor should be lodged with the district judge or the registrar, together with the applicant's authority to the new solicitor, and the case can then be transferred to the new solicitor appointed. Where a client decides to change solicitor after the grant has issued, the details of the solicitors as shown on the grant may not be altered.

11. Grants limited to settled land

(a) Intestacy

If a tenant for life dies intestate, then priority to obtain a grant of administration limited to settled land belongs to:

    (i) the special executors in regard to settled land constituted by s 22 Administration of Estates Act 1925;

    (ii) the trustees of the settlement at the time of the application;

    (iii) the personal representative(s) of the settlor (if the settlement is created by a will or an intestacy).

(r 29 Non-Contentious Probate Rules 1987 as amended by the Non-Contentious Probate (Amendment) Rules 1991)

(b) Testacy

If the general executors of the tenant for life are also the trustees of the settlement at the date of death, they may apply for a grant of probate including settled land, and deal with both matters under the same grant. Special executors may have power reserved or they may renounce as may ordinary executors, but if a special executor renounces the grant limited to settled land, he may not, if he is also one of the executors of the tenant for life, join in a grant of probate 'including settled land'.

There can be no chain of executorship through a special executor of settled land.

Where the settlement is created by the will of the estate owner, the will is a trust instrument, and the personal representative(s) of the testator holds the land on trust. Capital money from the sale of settled land is not in itself settled land, although land purchased with the capital money becomes settled land under the settlement.

A settled land grant is not required in respect of a tenant for life if the land ceases to be settled and there is no continuing life interest on such death. A normal grant of representation may be obtained; no reference to the settled land is made in the oath, and the value of the land is not included in the amount of the deceased's estate on the oath. If the tenant for life leaves no free estate, an application for a nil estate grant (see page 121) is made to enable the legal estate in the land to pass to the remainderman. The value of the settled land must be declared for inheritance tax, and the trustees of the settlement are liable for any tax payable on the value of the land.

Any trustee in office at the date of death of the life tenant who thereafter retires from the trust, is not cleared off by his retirement, and he must renounce before a grant can be made to a person with a lower title.

The Probate Registry fee for a grant limited to settled land is currently £2.00 (see Non-Contentious Probate Fees Order 1981, Fee 3(b)).

Where the settlement is created by the will or arises under an intestacy, and there are no trustees of the settlement at the death of the life tenant, the personal representatives of the settlor are deemed to be trustees until other trustees are appointed. A sole personal representative (unless a trust corporation) is required to appoint an additional trustee to act with him.

12. Probate in solemn form

An action may be commenced to have the will proved in solemn form by a person whose interest would be adversely affected by a grant of probate in common form. A personal representative might apply to prove in solemn form if, for example, he believes that an application to prove in common form might be opposed, or if the validity of the will is in doubt. A grant in solemn form follows an order of the Chancery Division. The difference between a grant in common form and a grant in solemn form is that the former is revocable, whereas a grant in solemn form is not (but see below), provided that proper notice has been given. The procedure for proof in solemn form is by revocation action to put the person who has obtained a grant in common form to proof of the will in solemn form.

There are two exceptions to the rule that a grant in solemn form is not revocable and these are:

(i)   if, subsequent to the decree, a later will is found;

(ii) the judgment may be set aside if it has been obtained by fraud.

The following persons may put an executor or other person(s) interested to prove the will in solemn form:

(i)   the surviving spouse or others entitled on an intestacy or their personal representative;

(ii) a legatee, a devisee, or the personal representative of either, if the person proving the will intends to suggest that the legacy is not valid, and to have it omitted from probate;

(iii) an executor, a legatee, a devisee (or the personal representative of these) who is named in any other testamentary instrument, and whose interest is adversely affected by the will.

The following may put an executor to proof of the will in solemn form only before probate in common form is issued:

(i)   a creditor to whom administration has been granted;

(ii)   any other person holding a grant of representation as appointee of the court but not having a beneficial interest in the estate.

Summary

- There are many different types of grant which may be applied for in addition to grants of probate and letters of administration (with a will).

- Unless there are very exceptional circumstances, no grant of probate or letters of administration (with the will) will be issued until seven clear days after the death and no grant of letters of administration will be issued until fourteen clear days have elapsed.

- Grants are required to provide legal proof of title to the personal representatives to enable them to administer an estate.

- It is possible for a grant to be issued even if the deceased left no estate. In these circumstances the application for a grant must also be accompanied by a sworn statement showing why such a grant is required.

- The application for the grant should be made as soon as possible after ascertaining the values of the assets and liabilities. However, if there is an unavoidable lengthy delay, the grant can be applied for on estimated values in the first instance. When full values are known, they can then be reported to the Capital Taxes Office for inheritance tax purposes.

- In cases where there is any doubt about the way an oath should be prepared, a draft may be sent to a Probate Registry to be 'settled' by the registrar. When the application is made the settled draft should be returned to the Registry with the oath.

- For an application for a grant of probate the full names and address and date of death of the deceased must be shown and any alias included with an explanation for the aliases. Where the testator's address at the date of death differs from the address in the will the last address should be inserted followed by the words 'formerly of' and the address in the will included thereafter.

- The full names, addresses and occupations of the executors should be shown and any non-acting executors should be cleared off. An application for a grant of letters of administration (with the will) should be prepared in the same way and, in addition, should include an explanation of why no executor is proving the will.

- For grants of letters of administration the same details of the deceased should be included together with the full names, addresses and descriptions of the applicants. Anyone with a prior right to the grant of letters of administration should be cleared off.

- Probate court fees must be paid at the time the application for a grant is made and cheques should be made payable to HM Paymaster General.

- The full names of the deceased should be printed on the back of cheques payable to HM Paymaster General.

- Sealed copies of the grant should be requested at the time the application is made and these cost 25p each (currently).

- There are no territorial limitations on the jurisdiction of District Probate Registries and an application can be made to any District Probate Registry or to the Principal Registry.

- If the Probate Registry discover an error in the oath this will usually be returned to the applicant by the Registry. If the error is only minor the matter may be resolved by a certificate from the solicitor. In more serious cases the oath may need to be corrected and re-sworn.

- The grant should be checked as soon as it is received and if it contains any official error the grant and all of the copies should be returned to the issuing Registry immediately or, at any event within fourteen days of issue. A correct grant and office copies will then be issued.

- A grant of probate is accepted in all courts as the form of validity of the will, and as evidence of the executor's title. Grants of probate and letters of administration evidence the personal representative's title.

- No grant is conclusive proof of the death, or of the identity of a personal representative.

- A grant of representation covers only the estate of the deceased devolving on his personal representatives. It does not cover nominated property or beneficially held joint property.

- It is possible to obtain a grant limited to settled land.

- Any person whose interest would be adversely affected by a grant of probate in common form may commence an action to have the will proved in solemn form. A grant in solemn form follows an order of the Chancery Division. A grant in common form is revocable whereas a grant in solemn form is not.

Chapter 13

Collecting in the estate

Once the grant has been issued, the next task is to realise the assets and then to distribute them in accordance with the will or the intestacy rules.

1. The personal representative's liabilities

The personal representative is liable for the deceased's obligations, and any claim against the deceased which was enforceable by suing the deceased during his lifetime is enforceable against the personal representative.

If the deceased had entered into a contract, for example, to sell his home, the personal representative is bound to complete the sale. Any liability for tax by the deceased passes to his personal representative in his representative capacity, and he is bound to utilise the estate assets to satisfy the liability plus any penalties incurred.

The liability of the personal representative is limited to the value of the estate assets. Any tort committed by the personal representative is his own personal responsibility, but if it was committed by him or his agent during the reasonable management of the estate he may be indemnified out of the estate assets.

2. Notices for claims

It is most important that the personal representative is fully aware of all the assets and liabilities, and he should not distribute the assets until he is certain. When full details are known, the liabilities should be settled in full before any distribution is made. Where there is a valid will the executor derives his authority from the will, and he can advertise for claims before the grant issues. In an intestacy, the administrator derives title from the grant, and cannot advertise until the grant has issued.

If the financial affairs of the deceased are well known to the personal representative there may be no need to place advertisements for claims against the estate. This decision must of course rest with the personal representative, who must be advised of the circumstances in which advertisements are necessary, and of his duties to the beneficiaries and to any creditors of the deceased. Whether or not advertisements are placed, the form of receipt to be signed by the residuary beneficiaries where the deceased died testate should include an indemnity for the personal representative against all and any claims against the estate that might arise after the estate has been distributed. Examples of advertisements for claims are given in Appendix 5.

Personal representatives should safeguard themselves from any claim by inserting notices for claims in the London Gazette, and in a newspaper local to the deceased's residence, and in any other area where he owned land. The notice should give not less than two months (see s 27 Trustee Act 1925) in which to claim, and consideration should be given to possible claims under the Inheritance (Provision for Family and Dependants) Act 1975 (see page 167), as circumstances warrant. A note of the date of the expiration of the claims period should be made on the front of the estate file, and a diary note should also be made. When a personal representative distributes the estate after the end of the period for claims against the estate, he is not liable for any claims of which he has not had notice. But, if he is aware of a claim, even though no written claim has been received in response to the advertisement he is liable for that claim.

Even if no claim has been received, the personal representative should realise, and should be reminded that there are the most obvious debts in most estates, e.g. rent, local authority charges, services, credit cards, mortgages. Debts on which interest continues to run should be paid as soon as possible.

3. Calling in the assets

The next stage is the physical collection in of the assets. All the matters considered in Chapter 7 should be referred to again.

If the personal chattels are to be sold following the issue of the grant, it is preferable that they be sold by auction as the best price will be deemed to have been obtained at auction rather than by private sale (but see page 63 chattels). Any antique items should be dealt with separately from the general items, and should be included in an 'antiques sale' if at all possible. Personal representatives should be advised against employing house clearance 'specialists' who usually advertise in the local newspapers, because chattels sold by this method will not have been sold for an open market value, and the personal representative may be open to a claim by the beneficiaries. The personal representative must be able to show items were sold at arm's length and beneficiaries cannot dispute values realised in a properly conducted auction sale.

Office copies of the grant together with claim forms, passbooks etc., should be sent out, and those assets not accruing interest may be called in first. When there is money available the funeral account should be paid and receipts for all payments obtained. When the estate is solvent the debts accruing interest charges may be settled next to limit the estate's liability.

When a property has been completely cleared of furniture a claim may be made to have it declared void for general rate and water charges. A final account, or an apportioned refund of these charges may be dealt with at the same time, as appropriate. Personal representatives are not expected to speculate whether stock and share values will increase or decrease, and it will be found that stockbrokers will normally recommend that these be disposed of as and when the grant is issued.

As each asset is encashed, transferred or otherwise dealt with the schedule of assets and liabilities (see Appendix 3) should be expanded further, and the cash amounts received in, or assets retained or transferred can be shown. This will show at a glance which assets have been dealt with, and which are outstanding. A system of this nature provides an immediate guide when answering clients' queries about progress in winding up the estate.

Similarly, notes can be made to show when debts have been settled, and this is a check to make sure that nothing is overlooked.

An additional schedule should be made for stock and share holdings, showing which are to be transferred and those being sold, and also when dividend/interest cheques have been returned to the company secretary for reissue and when they are received. These schedules make the work of drawing up the estate accounts very much easier.

Since the introduction of the Furniture and Furnishings (Fire Safety) Regulations 1988 (SI 1988 No 1324 as amended by SI 1990 No 2358 and SI 1993 No 207), upholstered furniture which does not comply cannot be sold at auctions. Electrical and gas appliances are also affected. This creates problems in valuing these types of chattels.

If there are chattels which are valuable or would be were it not for the Safety Regulations, personal representatives should consider if it would be worthwhile having the upholstery replaced so that the chattel complies with the regulations. The chattel could then be sold at auction.

If the chattels are not to be sold, they should be valued, and the estimated cost of reupholstery deducted from the valuation, the reduced value is then submitted as the date of death value. If the estimated cost of reupholstery exceeds the value of the article, then that chattel has a nil value. Electrical and gas appliances can be dealt with in a similar way.

4. Rent and other receipts

Payments of rent on property owned by the deceased will continue, and the persons liable for rent payments should be advised as soon as possible of the deceased's death, and asked to make all future rent payments to the personal representative or his agent until further notice. If the deceased appointed collecting agents they can be allowed to continue, as necessary, always remembering that they make a charge for so doing which is based on the amount of money they collect in, and money they receive should be paid over to the personal representative. This can then be placed in an income account until either the property is sold or transferred to a beneficiary. Rent received during the period of administration is gross income which is liable to income tax, and must be reported to the Inland Revenue, and tax paid thereon. If the will (if any) makes provision for the distribution of income these provisions are dealt with by the personal representatives.

5. Annuities

(a) Securities and Investment Board Rules

Whenever a person applies for an annuity investment he enjoys a 14-day waiting period (a cooling off period) during which time he can change his mind and cancel his application.

However, if that person dies within the 14-day period the application is considered as having been completed. The result is that the capital investment made is not repayable to the deceased's estate (depending on the type of investment applied for).

Annuities which are payable, or continue payable after the death, will form part of the estate assets and an actuarial valuation of the annuity policy should be obtained.

Dividends and interest on investments received should be recorded as explained on page 59.

When the application for the grant was made all income, from whatever source, which had accrued up to the date of death, but which had not been received, should have been included in the value of the estate.

6. Settling the debts and liabilities

All claims must be settled before legacies either specific or pecuniary are paid, or, in the case of intestacy, before the assets are distributed under the intestacy provisions. Only after satisfying all liabilities can the residue be distributed by the personal representative. Should he fail to do this then any outstanding debt may be claimed against him personally.

(a) Income tax and capital gains tax

When the grant is received the original may be sent to the Inspector of Taxes. If there is a tax return to be completed, and if an accountant is instructed, it may be sent to him for production to the Inland Revenue, and thereafter it should be returned to him as soon as possible. Where an original is forwarded direct to the Inland Revenue it is helpful to send also a photocopy as this enables the tax authorities to return the original very quickly.

All gross income received during the administration period is taxable and must be declared to the tax authorities, and tax paid.

But interest arising on National Savings Certificates is exempt. Interest received from the Capital Taxes Office from overpaid inheritance tax is not liable to income tax (Sch 4 para 19(4) Finance Act 1975). Personal representatives cannot be liable for higher rate tax because, as personal representatives, they are not 'individuals'.

Payment of tax is the personal representative's responsibility, and in this capacity, no tax free allowances are available, and the whole of the income is assessed. The personal representative may make application to the Inland

Revenue to have interest charges accrued on a loan account from which inheritance tax was paid, taken into account, but interest accrued on an overdraft account is not allowable.

(b) The funeral account

If the estate is insolvent, only the funeral account should be paid, and all the assets should be collected in before attempting to calculate the amount available to pay other creditors. The testamentary expenses and debts are payable in full before the other creditors are considered.

The cost of a memorial headstone is now classed as 'reasonable funeral expenses' (see page 74).

(c) Verification of claims

All claims made against an estate must be verified, and creditors are put to proof and must substantiate their claims to the personal representative if proof is not otherwise readily available as, for example, in the cases of gas and electricity.

(d) Order of application of assets

The statutory order of application of assets to pay liabilities and debts for deaths after 1925 applies to unsecured debts; a secured debt is payable primarily out of the property on which it is charged.

Subject to the terms of the will (if any) the order of priority of the real and personal estate used to pay funeral, testamentary and administration expenses, debts and liabilities is as follows:

(i) property not disposed of by the will (for example, where a partial intestacy arises);

(ii) property included in a gift of the residue;

(iii) property included in specific gifts;

(iv) property charged with paying the debts;

(v) pecuniary legacies;

(vi) property devised or bequeathed specifically;

(vii) property under a general power of appointment.

If a testator creates a general fund out of all his estate both real and personal to pay his debts and thereafter the legacies, the statutory order does not apply. Neither does it if the testator directs payment of debts out of personalty, or the residue is gifted; subject to payment thereout of funeral and testamentary expenses and debts.

7. The estate accounts

The estate accounts can now be taken a stage further. See Appendix 4 for an example of estate accounts.

The cover of the accounts should ideally give details of the deceased and the personal representative(s), and a synopsis of the will or distribution. The name and address of the acting solicitors can be appended.

On the first page all the assets and their values at the date of death should be listed (see Chapter 7). It may be helpful to beneficiaries to list first the assets jointly held and the remaining assets thereafter, showing the higher value assets first. Where there are stocks and shares these can be scheduled separately, and the total alone entered into the list of assets.

After the assets, the debts are listed (see Chapter 8), the funeral account first, and the remaining liabilities in reducing value order. The total of the liabilities is subtracted from the total assets, and the net balance carried forward. The 'brought forward' figure is followed by additional credits received during the administration period (e.g. premium bond prizes). The estate liabilities during the administration then follow (e.g. valuation fees, final rates, telephone, gas and electricity charges, probate court fees and inheritance tax paid), followed by the solicitor's fees.

A separate income account can itemise dividends and income receipts.

Finally, the accounts show the beneficiaries and the amounts due to them, taking into account any assets transferred to each person, and any interim payments on account, and the account ends with the balancing totals.

If the distribution is particularly involved, a separate distribution account may be added as an additional page to the accounts.

Before commencing the final distribution, the accounts should be agreed by the personal representatives and then a full copy of the accounts should be sent to each residuary beneficiary for approval and acceptance, and an indemnity for the personal representative can be added. Thereafter the estate can be distributed as explained in Chapter 14.

If inheritance tax has been paid, it is very helpful to keep a note showing the dates of all letters and other correspondence to and from the Capital Taxes Office. These dates will be used when applying for a clearance certificate Form CAP 30 (see page 95). The other alternative is to file all such correspondence separately, and it is then easily accessible for reference if any inheritance tax query is raised.

The next schedule is essential – a record of any changes in values of the estate assets and liabilities, which will be needed for the corrective affidavit (D3) required before the clearance certificate is issued. A note of the dates and amounts of inheritance tax payments can be made on this same schedule.

All correspondence to the Capital Taxes Office should be addressed to the Controller at one of the addresses listed below, and letters should quote either the CTO reference or, if no reference has yet been given, quote the name of the deceased and the date of death.

If you are dealing with the CTO in England and Wales cheques should be posted to:

Financial Services Office (IHT cashiers)
Inland Revenue
Barrington Road
Worthing
West Sussex
BN12 4XH
or
DX 90950
Worthing 3
or
Inland Revenue
Capital Taxes Office
Ferrers House
PO Box 38
Castle Meadow Road
Nottingham
NG2 1BB
or
DX 701201 Nottingham 4
(Pre-grant DX 701202 Nottingham 4).

Useful numbers:

CTO	Fax: 0115 974 2432
Inheritance Tax General Enquiries:	Phone: 0115 974 2400
Customer Service	Phone: 0115 974 2424
Stationery	Fax: 0115 974 3030

Shares Valuation Division
Inland Revenue
Shares Valuation Division
Fitz Roy House
PO Box 46
Castle Meadow Road
Nottingham
NG2 1BD
DX 701203 Nottingham 4

Useful telephone numbers:

General Enquiries about Share Valuation	0115 974 2222
Foreign Enquiries	0115 974 2300
Share Option Enquiries	0115 974 2355
Customer Service	0115 974 2374
Fax:	0115 974 2197

Northern Ireland

BT = Level 3
Dorchester House
52–58 Great Victoria Street
Belfast BT2 7QL
0232 236633

Scotland

EH = Mulberry House
16 Picardy Place
Edinburgh EH1 3NB

or DX ED 305
031 556 8511

8. Resealing grants

Grants issued by a country to which the Colonial Probates Acts 1892 and 1927 apply may be resealed by application to the Principal or District Probate Registry. When resealed, the grant will be effective as if it had been made in England and Wales, and it may then be used to administer estate in England and Wales.

A grant of probate, letters of administration (with the will) or letters of administration of an estate of a person domiciled in England and Wales issued within that jurisdiction, is recognised in Northern Ireland and Scotland, and is not required to be resealed. This is a reciprocal arrangement. However, a grant may be issued within the jurisdiction in respect of an estate in England and Wales even though the deceased may have been domiciled in Scotland or Northern Ireland, but in this case the grant will be limited to estate in England and Wales and will not be suitable for use in other countries.

English grants can be resealed to deal with foreign assets in countries to which the Colonial Probates Act 1892 and 1927 apply, and similarly, grants issued by the courts in those countries can be resealed in the United Kingdom. The resealing of an English grant in another country is simplified by appointing a solicitor in that country to act as an agent, in much the same way as London solicitors are appointed as agents by country solicitors. If no firm of solicitors is listed for the country in question, the Embassy or other official body representing the country should be approached for assistance.

(a) Exhibiting an English grant

It is often necessary to exhibit the grant in a country to which the Colonial Probates Acts do not apply, and, if English is not the official language of that country, it is usually found that a certified translation of the grant into the language of that country is required, and the certification may be made by that country's embassy or by the Foreign and Commonwealth

Office in London. The foreign lawyer of that country will advise what he requires. An affidavit dealing with the law relating to inheritance in England and Wales may also be required and this will also need to be translated and certified as above. There are firms in most cities who specialise in these matters, and who will deal with the arrangements for both the translation and the certification.

(b) Certified copies and exemplifications

At times an exemplification may be required by a foreign court. This is a copy of the English grant plus an exact copy of any will. A testimonium clause is added and is signed by a judge. The Family Division seal is added and the document shows the name and address of the extracting solicitor. Where the grant is issued by a District Probate Registry, the exemplification is obtained from the same registry.

Application for a certified copy of a will or a grant may be made to the District Probate Registry in which the will was proved or from which the grant issued. Where the grant issued from the Principal Registry, a written application for a certified copy should be addressed to the York District Registry. The certified copy is an exact copy of the document and bears the court seal.

(c) Channel Islands

To deal with assets situated in Jersey will normally require a Jersey grant of representation. This can only be obtained by the personal representative appearing before the Judicial Greffier of the Royal Court of Jersey. However, a person authorised by a special power of attorney can apply on behalf of the personal representative. An example is given in Appendix 5. The following documents are required to prepare a power of attorney:

- (i) the deceased's full names;

- (ii) his last address;

- (iii) the maiden name of a deceased married female;

- (iv) her husband's full names;

- (v) the place and date of death;

- (vi) the names and addresses of executors or administrators (where any of these are female include her maiden name);

- (vii) the relationship of administrators to the deceased.

The following are required to obtain a grant:

- (i) (if probate) a copy of the will and a copy of the grant, both of which must be certified by the district judge or the registrar and bear the court seal (do not send the original grant as this will be retained by the Jersey Court) (see (b) above for certified copies);

(ii) a statement of the value of the assets in the Channel Islands;

(iii) the death certificate;

(iv) a professional indemnity from the solicitor in England and Wales to the advocate, if requested;

(v) confirmation of whether there are any Channel Island residents who are beneficiaries;

(vi) if no English grant has been obtained an affidavit of foreign law will be required giving notice that the will or administrator's power is 'good' and would be sufficient if an application for a grant was needed in England.

On 27 March 1990 the Probate (Amendment) (Jersey) Law 1990 came into force. This amended the Probate (Jersey) Law 1949, and exempts certain small estates from the requirement to obtain a Jersey grant. The exemption applies only to the estates of persons not domiciled in Jersey.

Where an individual asset in Jersey does not exceed £5,000, the person holding the asset may release it 'to such person or persons as appear to be entitled to receive it under a Will or intestate succession, without a Jersey Grant'. The limit of £5,000 applies to individual assets, not to the total value of the estate in Jersey.

This amendment enables the person holding an asset to require production of either or both of the following:

(i) documentary evidence of the claimant's entitlement to receive the asset;

(ii) security (not exceeding the value of the asset) in the form and amount stipulated by the holder of the asset.

Although the nature of the documentary evidence is not stipulated, the probable requirement is a sealed and certified copy of the English grant or a death certificate, and an affidavit from an English lawyer.

There is no estate duty payable in Jersey, however it is necessary to purchase Probate Stamps according to the value of the estate situate in Jersey. This amount is calculated as follows and is due to the Royal Court of Jersey:

Value of estate	*Probate stamp duty*
Not exceeding £5,000	Nil.
Not exceeding £10,000	£50.00.
Not exceeding £50,000	£50 for each £10,000 or part of £10,000.
to exceed £50,000	£250 in respect of the first £50,000, plus £75 for each additional £10,000 or part thereof.

A further charge of £1.00 is also payable to the court in respect of registering a power of attorney or affidavit.

9. Administration of insolvent estates

If the valuation of the estate (see Chapters 7 and 8) has revealed any possibility that the estate may be insolvent (s 421(4) Insolvency Act 1986, and Administration of Insolvent Estates of Deceased Persons Order 1986), no liability should be settled until full details of all claims are known, and until the expiration of the period for claims stipulated in the advertisements for claims has expired.

The administration of an insolvent estate can be dealt with in three ways:

(1) Administration by the Chancery Division.

After a creditor applies for an order under RSC Order 85. If a creditor will join as a defendant with the personal representative, the personal representative may make the application.

(2) Administration out of court by the personal representative.

(3) Administration in bankruptcy.

This can be dealt with after an insolvency administration order has been made. A petition for an insolvency administration order may be made by:

(i) A personal representative but only on the grounds that the estate is insolvent.

(ii) A creditor if the amount of his debt would have supported a petition for bankruptcy during the deceased's lifetime.

(iii) A person bound by the deceased's voluntary arrangement as approved by his creditors.

(iv) The official petitioner if a criminal bankruptcy order was made against the deceased.

The petition for an insolvency administration order must be served on the personal representative.

Administration in bankruptcy allows for more extensive remedies to be pursued than those available to a personal representative administering the estate outside bankruptcy.

Whether an estate is administered in or out of bankruptcy, the same rules apply.

(a) Secured creditors

If a creditor holds a mortgage, charge, lien or other security over the deceased's property he is a secured creditor.

A secured creditor may choose one of several ways to prove for his debt:

(i) He may rely on that security and not prove for the debt.

(ii) He may realise that security and prove for the balance of the debt.

(iii) He may surrender his security and prove for the entire debt.

(iv) He may set a value on his security and prove for the balance of the debt.

(b) Debts

Certain debts under the Financial Services Act 1986 and s 49 of the Banking Act 1987 cannot be proved until all other claims plus interest have been settled in full (Insolvency Rules: Rule 12.3(2A) (a) and (b)).

Fines imposed on the deceased for offences, obligations under orders made in family or domestic proceedings, and obligations under certain confiscation orders are not provable at all.

(c) Interest

Where a debt bears interest, the interest up to the 'commencement of bankruptcy' forms part of the overall debt. This is defined as the date of the insolvency administration order by the Administration of Insolvent Estates of Deceased Persons Order. However, this does not cover estates which are administered otherwise than in bankruptcy, and it is thought that interest in these estates should be calculated up to the date of death.

The Bankruptcy Act limited interest to 5 per cent until all other debts had been paid, but the Insolvency Act does not impose this limitation.

(d) Order of priority

(1) Secured creditors:

By realising his security a secured creditor takes precedence but if he proves for his debt he is an unsecured creditor.

(2) Preferred debts (preferred by statute):

The expenses incurred by a Trustee of a deed of arrangement (Deeds of Arrangement Act 1914) or by a supervisor of a voluntary arrangement (Insolvency Act 1986) are a first charge over an estate, and take precedence over bankruptcy expenses, funeral testamentary and administration expenses.

(3) Bankruptcy expenses (where an estate is being administered in bankruptcy):

These are subject to a specific order of payment laid down by the Insolvency Rules (r 6.224).

(4) Funeral, testamentary and administration expenses:

When the estate is administered outside bankruptcy these have priority over the Schedule 6 preferred debts (Schedule 6 Insolvency Act 1986).

(5) Preferential debts:

These are payable after the previously listed debts have been settled in full.

Preferential debts rank equally among themselves and, if necessary, they abate proportionately.

There are six categories of preferential debts listed in Schedule 6 Insolvency Act 1986.

(a) Certain debts due to the Inland Revenue:

  (i) Tax which the deceased should have deducted from his employees under PAYE in the twelve months before the death

  or

  (ii) by way of deductions from payments made to subcontractors in the construction industry.

(b) Certain debts to HM Customs and Excise:

  (i) VAT referable in the six-month period before the death;

  (ii) car tax due at death and which became due in the twelve months before the death;

  (iii) general betting duty or pool betting duty recoverable from an agent collecting stakes or gaming licence duty due at death which became due in the twelve months before death.

(c) Class 1 or 2 social security contributions which became due in the twelve months before death or Class 4 social security contributions assessed on and due from the deceased at his death and up to 5 April next before the death, but not exceeding in total one year's assessment.

(d) Amounts due on account of contributions to state and occupational pension schemes.

(e) (i) Up to four months' remuneration to employee or former employee, but not exceeding such amount specified by the Secretary of State (currently £800);

  (ii) holiday remuneration to an employee or a former employee;

  (iii) money loaned to pay (e)(i) or (e)(ii);

  (iv) money which the deceased was ordered to pay under Reserve Forces (Safeguard of Employment) Act 1985 not exceeding such amount as specified by the Secretary of State.

(f) Money due in respect of levies under Arts 49 and 50 or any surcharge for delay under Art 50(3) ECSC Treaty and Art 6 of the Decision of the High Authority of the Coal and Steel Community.

(e) Ordinary debts

These are debts which are not in the above classes but are not deferred debts (see below). Ordinary debts rank equally, and must abate equally between themselves. NOTE: A judgment debt is an ordinary debt.

(f) Interest on preferential and ordinary debts

After preferential and ordinary debts have been paid in full, any surplus is applied towards interest due since the date of death.

(g) Deferred debts

(a) debts in respect of credit provided by the person who was the deceased's spouse at the time of death and interest from the time of death;

(b) advances to a partnership by way of loan being interest varying with the profits or sums due for the price of the goodwill of a business where this takes the form of a share in the profits.

Debts whose proving is deferred are debts which cannot be paid until all the other debts and expenses have been paid in full.

Notices for claims against the estate must be advertised to ascertain the full extent of the insolvency, and these should be inserted in the local newspaper for the area where the deceased lived; if he ran a business in a different area, an advertisement should also be placed in a newspaper covering that area. In addition, a notice must be placed in the London Gazette; as this must be pre-paid it is advisable to telephone to establish the current charges before submitting the advertisement. The advertisement must be signed by a practising solicitor. The Office of the London Gazette is HMSO Publications Centre, Gazette Office, Room 410, Nine Elms Lane, London, SW8 5DR. The cost is £32.00 plus VAT, plus £1.45 for a copy of the Gazette. (Tel: (0171) 873 8300.) See Appendix 5 for forms of notice.

A creditor may still submit a claim after the expiry of the period for claims, so long as he has not delayed by wilful default, and as long as there are still assets remaining. He is not allowed to disturb any distribution made before his claim, nor delay payments to others.

If at the time of distribution any creditor has disappeared, the personal representative must retain sufficient money to meet the claim, and must not divide the money among the other creditors.

Where the partners in a firm of solicitors or accountants are named as executors, they must obtain written agreement from all of the creditors that they may charge and be paid their fees from the estate before they commence the administration. Where a person or persons other than partners in a firm are named as executors, they are entitled to obtain professional advice and charge those professional fees against the estate.

Summary

- A personal representative is liable for all of the deceased's obligations. Any claim which was enforceable against the deceased during his lifetime is enforceable against his personal representatives.

- A personal representative's liability is limited to the value of the estate assets.

- A personal representative should be advised to consider inserting notices for claims in the local newspaper if the deceased owned realty and also in the London Gazette.

- Personal representatives must obtain the best possible price in the sale of assets and, ideally, should place on deposit all money received by them during the estate administration.

- The personal representatives should settle all of the estate liabilities. The first claim against any estate is the funeral account.

- Personal representatives should make certain that all tax liabilities have been settled before commencing to distribute the estate.

- All claims made against an estate must be verified and personal representatives should put creditors to proof of their claim.

- When all of the assets have been collected in, and all liabilities settled, estate accounts should be prepared showing all of this information.

- The accounts should show all pecuniary and specific legacies, if any, and distribution of the residue.

- Grants issued by any country to which the Colonial Probates Acts apply may be resealed in this country. When resealed, a grant will be effective as if it had been made in England and Wales. Similarly, English grants can be resealed to deal with foreign assets in countries to which the Colonial Probates Act applies.

- An exemplification is sometimes required by a foreign court. This is a copy of the English grant, plus an exact copy of any will, to which a testimonium clause is added and the document is signed by a judge or a District Probate Registrar.

- Where there are assets in Jersey, a Jersey grant of representation is normally required unless the asset does not exceed £5,000 when it may be released to the person entitled without the need to obtain a Jersey grant.

- There is no estate duty payable in Jersey, but Probate Stamp duty is payable.

- An estate is either solvent or insolvent. It is insolvent if there are insufficient assets to settle all of the liabilities. If an estate is insolvent it can be dealt with in three ways:

(1) Administration by the Chancery Division.

(2) Administration out of court by the personal representative.

(3) Administration in bankruptcy. Whether an estate is administered in or out of bankruptcy, the same rules apply.

● Where the partners in a firm of solicitors or accountants are named as executors, they must obtain the written agreement from all of the creditors that they may charge and be paid their fees from the estate before they commence the administration. Where the personal representatives are persons other than partners in a firm, those personal representatives are entitled to obtain professional advice and charge those professional fees against the estate.

Chapter 14

Distribution of the estate

1. Tax clearance

Before distributing the estate finally among the persons entitled, the personal representative should obtain a certificate from the Inspector of Taxes stating that all liability to income tax and capital gains tax from the estate has been satisfied. Similarly, a clearance certificate should be requested from the Capital Taxes Office for inheritance tax. The procedure for this is explained on page 95.

2. Executor's or administrator's year

It is generally accepted that after a period of one year from the date of death the personal representative should have realised the estate assets and settled the liabilities; while this should not be taken as a fixed rule, the onus lies on him to substantiate reasons for delay. All of the assets in which the deceased had a beneficial interest may be used to settle the liabilities (but see page 135).

Personal representatives are not liable if there is any loss caused by their having postponed a sale beyond the period of one year after the death, if they acted in their reasonable discretion.

The personal representative is under no obligation to distribute the estate of the deceased before the expiration of a year from the date of death, but after that period has elapsed, a legatee or other person interested in the estate may call on the personal representative to give an account of his actions to date. Any legacies which remain unpaid twelve months after the date of death become eligible for interest from that date up to the date of payment.

3. Carrying on the deceased's business

It is the responsibility of a personal representative to preserve the estate assets and he may carry on the deceased's business, or appoint agents to do so, to enable him to sell it as a going concern. He will not be liable for a breach of trust if he has acted in good faith. He may not utilise the general estate assets to enable him to carry on the business; he may only use the business assets, unless the testator has authorised the general assets.

If it is found to be impossible to carry on the business with the funds available, an application should be made to the court for directions; this is made by originating summons.

4. Principles of distribution

Where the deceased died testate the assets are distributed according to the terms of the will. Specific legacies are transferred to the beneficiary, and a receipt must be obtained. If realty passes, the appropriate deed can be prepared and the property transferred to the person entitled. Where there is realty owned jointly, a death certificate is placed with the title deeds, leaving the property in the name of the survivor or survivors. If the property was held as tenants in common, the deceased's interest must be dealt with as part of the estate, by sale or an assent as with property owned solely by the deceased.

Where the deceased died intestate, the assets are distributed according to the intestacy rules; see the table on pages 44–47.

5. Chattels

At the time of valuing the personal chattels, separate values should have been obtained for items or sets of items which have an individual value in excess of £500 (see page 62), to ensure correct distribution. A separate value should also be obtained for items specifically referred to in the will, or specific items which are desired by a beneficiary as part of his or her entitlement under the will or intestacy, and this can be taken into account when distributing the estate. Where two or more people would like the same specific items, and agreement cannot be reached, and the executor has not been given the final decision in such matters under any will, that item should be included with other chattels in a sale by auction (but see page 63(a) chattels).

If the personal representative has already allowed a beneficiary to remove any items from the estate, that item having been specifically mentioned in the will, it may be possible to obtain agreement from the beneficiary to have the article valued. In certain instances it is impossible to obtain a valuation from the beneficiary, and that person may then be obliged to have a valuation made, by placing an over-estimated value on it, leaving the beneficiary with the option of either accepting the over-estimate, or proving the true value by valuation. Failing these the personal representative must use his best endeavours to estimate the value. To avoid such problems the personal representative should be advised not to distribute any of the assets until a valuation has been obtained.

Under intestacy, of course, the chattels pass to the surviving spouse, and the problems referred to above do not arise very frequently. Should there be no spouse surviving then the chattels are dealt with with the rest of the estate.

When dealing with the estate the personal representative must be advised to obtain professional advice, e.g. from a stockbroker, with regard to stocks and shares. Personalty which is to be sold is best dealt with through an auction (see page 132 para 4), and realty should be valued or sold by a competent valuer or estate agent.

It is usually quite difficult if not impossible to sell the deceased's clothing, linen etc., although auctioneers will set up a rail of clothing if asked to do so. Personal representatives may decide to give these items to charity. If so, they should be advised to obtain written agreement from the residuary beneficiaries.

Since the introduction of the Furniture and Furnishings (Fire Safety) Regulations 1988 (SI 1988 No 1324 as amended by SI 1990 No 2358 and SI 1993 No. 207), upholstered furniture which does not comply cannot be sold at auctions. Electrical and gas appliances are also affected. This creates problems in valuing these types of chattels.

If there are chattels which are valuable or would be were it not for the Safety Regulations, personal representatives should consider if it would be worthwhile having the upholstery replaced so that the chattel complies with the regulations, the chattel could then be sold at auction.

If the chattels are not to be sold, they should be valued, and the estimated cost of reupholstery deducted from the valuation, the reduced value is then submitted as the date of death value. If the estimated cost of reupholstery exceeds the value of the article, then that chattel has a nil value. Electrical and gas appliances can be dealt with in a similar way.

6. Stocks and shares

(a) Transfer

When stocks and shares are to be transferred to a beneficiary the holdings to be transferred should be re-valued, as the actual value passing for the purposes of the administration will be that at the date of the transfer, and not the date-of-death value. The new valuation should be compared with the probate valuation, and the beneficiary should be informed and asked to confirm if the transfer is still desired. In so far as capital gains tax is concerned the value passing to the legatee is the value at the date of death (i.e. the probate value); a legatee is assumed to have acquired an asset at market value at date of death (s 49(4) Capital Gains Tax Act 1979). Transfer forms should be completed showing the transfer from the personal representative to the beneficiary, and these should be sent to the company registrars, together with the share certificates, and a sealed copy of the grant. Any interest or dividend cheques in the deceased's name should be forwarded at the same time, to be reissued to the personal representative.

Where the personal representative is also the beneficiary he may, after the grant has issued, transfer the holdings to himself, and the transfer is effected by the use of a letter of request by a personal representative to himself. Other transfers of stocks and shares are made on a stock transfer form. If it is desired, the stockbroker will deal with the transfer of the holding.

Stocks and shares held jointly can be transferred to the surviving joint holder by sending the share certificate with a death certificate to the company registrars.

The transfer of stocks and shares to a beneficiary no longer attracts stamp duty, and the transfers no longer need to be seen in stamp offices (Stamp Duty (Exempt Instruments) Regulations 1987). The transfer usually falls within one of the following categories:

(i) the conveyance or transfer of property the subject of a specific devise or legacy to the beneficiary named in the will (or his nominee);

(ii) the conveyance or transfer of property which forms part of an intestate's estate to the person entitled on intestacy (or his nominee);

(iii) the appropriation of property within s 84(4) Finance Act 1985 (death: appropriate in satisfaction of a general legacy of money) or s 84(5) or (7) of that Act (death: appropriation in satisfaction of any interest of the surviving spouse, and, in Scotland, also of any interest of issue);

(iv) a conveyance or transfer of property which forms part of the residuary estate of a testator to a beneficiary (or his nominee) entitled solely by virtue of his entitlement under the will.

If an administrator, or an executor dies intestate, a grant of letters of administration *de bonis non* will be required to deal with the shares.

(b) Gains on shares sold

Capital gains tax liability should be calculated on any gains made by the estate on the sale of shares or realty during the administration period, and it should be noted that personal representatives are entitled to the same capital gains allowances as an individual for the period up to the date the administration is completed, or during the year in which the death occurred, no matter how late in the year the death occurred, plus two full years thereafter, whichever is the shorter period. If the administration continues thereafter, there is no allowance, and it may be preferable to appropriate or transfer assets to the beneficiaries so that they can make use of their personal allowances.

(c) Losses on shares sold

Any total net loss incurred on the sale of stocks and shares which have been sold within one year of the date of death in estates where inheritance tax has been paid may be reported to the Capital Taxes Office, and a claim for relief submitted under Sch 10 para 15 Finance Act 1975. Such claims must be made on Form SECT 5. The gross proceeds, that is the actual amount received from the buyer before any deductions, are used in calculating the amount of the loss. The claim for relief is applicable only if the total amount realised is less than the date of death value, not for a loss suffered on some shares, where other shares have realised a gain, and the overall total is a gain.

A refund of inheritance tax may be claimed on the amount of the loss, but if a gain has been made, instead of a loss, this is not a matter which has to be reported, and there is no increase in the liability for inheritance tax.

(d) Losses on shares due to quoted securities being suspended

If quoted securities are suspended after the date of death the shares cannot be sold. However, the estate still has to pay inheritance tax on the probate value.

For deaths after 15 March 1992, if a quoted investment is suspended within the year after the death, the personal representative can claim for the value of the security on the first anniversary of the death to be substituted for the probate value.

7. Purchasing prohibition on personal representatives

Because a trustee may not put himself in a position of conflict of interest, a personal representative may not, without the sanction of the court or without specific permission in the will, purchase any item from the estate of which he is a personal representative, neither may he sell to another personal representative of that estate either directly or indirectly. Additionally, he is prohibited from obtaining the property through a circuitous arrangement whereby someone else purchases the property on behalf of the personal representative, or by the personal representative purchasing the property for someone else who then makes a gift, or sells it back to the personal representative. Where there was a pre-existing contract between the personal representative and the deceased, the personal representative may conclude the transaction, although extreme caution must be exercised in so doing.

When an executor/trustee is also a beneficiary, he may accept items from the estate as part of his entitlement.

Where an executor is also a legatee in a will it is presumed that the legacy is given to him in consideration of his accepting the appointment. If he does not accept the appointment but claims entitlement to the legacy he must show circumstances in the will which show this presumption to be wrong. However, the presumption is rebutted where the will leaves the legacy to the executor as a relative or friend, as a remembrance, or where the legacy is of residue.

In wills where it is clear that the legacy is attached to the appointment of the legatee as executor, and where the executor does not act, whether by choice or not, he is not entitled to the legacy. An example of this is 'I appoint . . . . to be the executor of this my will and I give him the sum of £100 if he accepts the appointment'. A legacy to an executor is not entitled to any priority and it is liable to abatement the same as other legacies.

8. Abatement

Where the deceased died testate, all general legacies, including those left to executors, and the testator's spouse, and all annuities, are liable to abate in equal proportions if there is insufficient in the estate to pay them in full. For these purposes, no distinction is made between legacies contained in the will and those in codicils.

If the charging clause does not allow for legal fees to be paid in priority, the fees also abate.

If the personal representative voluntarily pays a legacy in full he will be compelled to treat all other legacies likewise as he will be deemed to have admitted that the value of the estate is sufficient to do so. If it is not possible to extract this remedy from the personal representative personally, the other legatees may be allowed recourse to claim against the legatee who has been paid in full, unless the shortfall in the assets occurred after the payment was made.

If the payment in full of a legacy was made by mistake, and without the approval of the other beneficiaries, the court may compel a legatee to repay the legacy.

In the estate of an intestate, where another beneficiary with a prior or equal claim appears after the estate has been distributed, the recipients of the estate can be compelled by the appearing beneficiary, to repay the excess proportion received by them.

9. Application of assets to pay legacies

Pecuniary legacies are primarily payable out of the cash realised from any assets which the will does not dispose of. Legacies payable out of the estate generally are paid from the personalty, and where this is insufficient, recourse is made to the realty, unless a contrary intention is expressed in the will.

10. Interest on legacies

If the will directs that a legacy be paid immediately after the death, that legacy carries interest from the date of death. As the personal representative is not bound to distribute the estate before one year from the date of death, other legacies paid within this period do not carry interest, but interest is payable on unpaid legacies after the period of one year. Costs incurred on paying pecuniary legacies fall on the residue, whereas, generally, the cost of transferring specific legacies (for example post and packing) fall on the legatee, unless the will states otherwise.

11. Pending actions and claims

A personal representative should be warned that if any distribution is made while proceedings for family provision (see page 167) or other claims are pending, any distribution is made at his own risk. Similarly, any distribution made before the end of six months from the date of death, may leave the personal representative liable, due to a possible claim under the Inheritance (Provision for Family and Dependants) Act 1975.

12. Distribution on intestacy to deceased's child

Any money or property advanced to a child of an intestate deceased prior to death or on the marriage of such a child (including any life, or less, interest, and including property covenanted to be paid or settled) must be brought into account by the personal representative to preserve equality among the children before dividing the residue among them. These advances are to be taken as being paid or settled as part of the share of such child. If any child of the intestate predeceases him but leaves issue, those issues are entitled to take equal shares of that part of the estate which his, her or their parent would have taken if living.

The Law Reform (Succession) Bill, which had its second reading in February 1995, includes a recommendation to abolish the 'Hotchpot' rule (subs 2).

13. Minor beneficiaries

Minor beneficiaries, both under a will and on an intestacy, who have not attained their majority are unable to give the personal representative a valid receipt for their entitlement. This should be invested in the name of the personal representative. A record should be kept with details of the full names of the minor, his present address, the date he attains his majority, the name of the trust, the names and addresses of the trustees, and short details of the investments. If the investments are deposited with the solicitors by the personal representative a copy of the will (if testate) and a copy of the estate account may also be kept with the securities.

Minor children who marry under the age of 18 inherit their share of the intestate's estate without having to wait until they attain their age of majority.

Where a minor is absolutely entitled, s 42 Administration of Estates Act 1925 allows the personal representatives to appoint trustees; it will often be convenient to appoint the child's parents. The personal representatives can then transfer the legacy or other entitlement to the trustees.

When dealing with estate where remote members of the family are entitled to share in the estate and matters appear to be complex, it is recommended that a family tree be prepared (see page 47).

14. Missing beneficiaries

A simple method of tracing missing beneficiaries, and one which is overlooked with surprising frequency, is a check in the local telephone directory. Advertisements naming the missing person and his last known address, and requesting information, are also extremely revealing although they can produce a vast amount of unhelpful information and 'mistaken' claimants, and they can be very time consuming.

A letter addressed to a missing beneficiary may be sent under an explanatory covering letter to Special Section A, Room 101B, DSS Records Branch, Newcastle-upon-Tyne. If the DSS can trace the addressee, it will forward the letter to him. The letter to the DSS should state the date of birth of the missing person.

If the person still cannot be traced, a search can be made among the registers held in London at St Catherine's House which has taken over the function traditionally associated with Somerset House. It is often simplest to employ a specialist firm of agents to carry out the search.

If all attempts to trace a missing beneficiary fail, the personal representative can either pay the sum into court (see page 156), or take out a missing beneficiary indemnity with one of the insurance companies. This latter course appears to be the better solution as it enables the personal representative to complete his duties fully, and avoids the possibility of a legacy being left unclaimed, possibly forever.

15. Illegitimate children

Illegitimate children of a woman dying intestate on or after 1 January 1927 take the same interest as legitimate children, and for deaths on or after 1 January 1970 illegitimate children of either parent have the same rights of succession as legitimate children, and also issue of legitimate children who have predeceased.

For deaths intestate after 4 April 1988, the administrator's oath need not contain the description 'lawful' or 'natural' when referring to relatives other than the spouse (s 1 Family Law Reform Act 1987). See also Chapter 6, at page 49.

16. Lapse of gifts

It should be noted that gifts in a will lapse on the predecease of a beneficiary, unless there is specific provision to the contrary. If the gift is in the nature of residue the subject thereof will fall into residue. A residuary bequest that lapses will not pass to the other residuary beneficiaries unless the legacy is in the nature of a class gift, but will be distributed as on intestacy. A table of the distribution of intestacy is given on page 43. However, where the beneficiary was a child or remoter issue who died leaving issue, the gift does not lapse but devolves in one of two different ways depending on whether the deceased died before or after 1 January 1983. In the case of deaths before 1 January 1983 a beneficiary being a child of the deceased who died in the lifetime of the deceased is deemed to have survived and died immediately after the deceased. The effect of this assumption, which is provided for under s 33 Wills Act 1837, as amended from the above date by the Administration of Estates Act 1982, is that the legacy will fall in and form part of the estate of the legatee, and passes under his or her will or intestacy.

Section 19 Administration of Justice Act 1982 provides that a gift to a child or remoter descendant of a testator who predeceased the testator and left issue living at the testator's death will take as a gift to such issue living at the testator's death unless a contrary intention is expressed in the will. This section applies only in cases where the testator died on or after 1 January 1983. The legacy under the will to any beneficiary who survives the testator but thereafter dies before the legacy is paid over, is payable to the estate of the beneficiary.

17. Payment of legacies, receipts and certificates of tax deducted

Where the personal representative knows beneficiaries personally, the legacies can be paid to the persons entitled and a receipt obtained. However, in all cases where the beneficiaries are strangers to the personal representative it is imperative that the personal representative should establish the identities and addresses of legatees before making payments to them. Identity may be established by asking the beneficiaries to provide proof of identity or by asking the beneficiaries to reply to relevant questions about the deceased person, for example by providing the surname of the deceased and then asking the beneficiaries to provide the deceased's first name and address, and by establishing their relationship with the deceased (if appropriate).

A copy of the clause in a will which refers to a legacy can be given to the legatee, and a copy of the estate accounts can be given to the personal representative and the residuary beneficiaries for approval, and thereafter payment can be made.

Any legatees receiving interest should be given a statement of that interest. Residuary beneficiaries receiving net interest from temporarily invested money, or a share in interest and dividends from stocks, shares and investments should be given a full breakdown, and a tax deduction certificate (if appropriate) on Form R 185E after the tax has been paid by the personal representative. By virtue of s 696 Income and Corporation Taxes Act 1988, the Inland Revenue will not 'look through' residuary income paid to persons having an absolute interest in residue. This means the Inland Revenue did not seek to differentiate between bank and building society interest, dividends, etc. However, as dividends are now paid net of tax of 20 per cent, this should be shown separately on the R 185E. The whole of the income should be included in the tax deduction certificate for repayment (if appropriate) or for assessment for higher rate tax. This applies only to persons ordinarily resident in the United Kingdom, and does not apply to persons who are not resident.

The personal representative should be careful to obtain receipts for payments made. Letters sending the legacy payments should include a specific request for a receipt for such payment. He should also have the estate accounts approved by the residuary beneficiaries before paying out the amounts due. If any fragile specific gifts are to be posted to beneficiaries the beneficiary should be asked to fund the cost of insuring the article, failing which the beneficiary should be asked to collect the article. It is wise to send specific legacies of a high value by way of one of the security firms, and the beneficiary should meet the cost of so doing, unless the will directs otherwise.

If the personal representative cannot obtain a receipt and discharge because of the mental incapacity or minority of a beneficiary; or if it is not practicable to find out whether the beneficiary is still alive, he may pay the fund into court (see page 156).

Executors are entitled to a receipt only from pecuniary legatees, and this constitutes a sufficient discharge, but they are entitled to a receipt and approval of the accounts from the residuary legatee. The pecuniary legatees receive their legacy and not a copy of the accounts, whereas those receiving the residue are given a copy of the estate accounts, and the personal representative is entitled to have the accounts approved before paying out.

When distributing the estate the personal representative should provide the beneficiaries with a statement of gross interest, less tax deducted therefrom, and this is done on a certificate of deduction of tax, Income Tax Form R 185E. The beneficiaries should present this form to their own tax districts. The personal representative should request a clearance certificate from the Inspector of Taxes showing that all liability to tax from the estate has been cleared. He should also complete a Form CAP 30 (see page 95) in duplicate to obtain a clearance certificate in respect of inheritance tax from the Capital Taxes Office, if there was an inheritance tax liability.

In cases of intestacy, and where the surviving spouse has a life interest, that spouse should include in his personal income tax return the payments of income made to him; these are treated as income for the year of payment. Within three years of the end of the year in which the administration is completed, the figures are revised. The income applicable to the life tenant is deemed to accrue on a day-to-day basis during each tax year covered by the administration period. Thereafter the income is included in the tax returns on an 'arising basis'. The person dealing with the tax returns will need to know the payments of income and the dates of those payments. Once the administration is completed he will also require details of the net income arising during that period, the length of that period, and subsequently the income due to him for each tax year.

Personal representatives have a statutory right to pay money into court (s 63 Trustee Act 1925, s 36 Administration of Justice Act 1965). There is justification for so doing if there is the problem of their obtaining a valid discharge from a beneficiary (e.g. where the beneficiary is mentally incapable, a minor or cannot be traced). After payment into court the personal representative(s) continue as trustees but lose their discretionary powers in relation to the fund paid in. Personal representatives can be forced to pay into court, and an application for this is by way of originating summons by the interested party (RSC O 85 r 4).

18. Remuneration of personal representatives

(a) Costs and expenses

Personal representatives are entitled to an indemnity from an estate in respect of any costs and expenses incurred in the proper execution of their duties. They are empowered to instruct a solicitor to transact any business, and to pay him from the estate (s 23 Trustee Act 1925). However, the Act does not allow payment where separate personal representatives instruct separate solicitors. Personal representatives must not make or cause to be made any unnecessary payments from the estate, and they should therefore agree to instruct a solicitor jointly. Any personal representative instructing a separate solicitor, knowing that another firm is already acting for the estate, will be personally responsible for his costs. If a beneficiary takes legal advice in respect of the administration of the estate, he will not be entitled to claim his costs from the estate.

A personal representative is not allowed to make any profit out of his office, and therefore, he is not entitled to remuneration for acting (unless this is specifically provided for in the will), but solicitors, accountants, trust companies etc. may charge their fees if the will authorises them to do so. If the 'charging clause' has been omitted from a will, and the beneficiaries wish the professional person to accept the appointment, written agreement should be obtained from all of the persons concerned, in the first instance, to meet the fees. If agreement from all persons concerned is not forthcoming, and of course any minority would prevent this, the other persons must agree to meet the fees between them, and ideally written agreement from each of them to be liable for the whole of the debt, should be obtained.

Notwithstanding the above, an administrator *pendente lite* may be granted remuneration by the court, and where a trust corporation is appointed co-grantee without an authority for making its charges, the court can empower that corporation to charge for its services.

(b) Solicitors' remuneration for non-contentious business

This is governed by The Solicitors' Remuneration Order 1972 (SI 1972 No 1139) which provides in Article 2 that the remuneration for non-contentious business shall be such sum as may be fair and reasonable having regard to all the circumstances of the case and in particular to:

(i) the complexity of the matter or the difficulty or novelty of the questions raised;

(ii) the skill, labour, specialised knowledge and responsibility involved;

(iii) the time spent on business;

(iv) the number and importance of the documents prepared or perused without regard to length;

(v)   the place where and the circumstances in which the business or any part thereof is transacted;

(vi)   the amount or value of any money or property involved;

(vii)   whether any land involved is registered land within the meaning of the Land Registration Act 1925;

(viii) the importance of the matter to the client.

A yardstick may be applied in assessing the proposed charges, and for non-contentious probate and administration of estates. The Law Society suggests 1 per cent of the gross value of the free estate less the residence, with 0.5 per cent being allowed for the residence itself; the percentages may be adjusted as appropriate along the guidelines set out by The Law Society (see *The Law Society's Gazette* 15 October 1980). There may well be other factors to bear in mind; e.g. where the estate comprises one or two large assets only; where a partner personally is an executor. These could affect the value element of the charges so that clearly it is not always appropriate to apply the 1 per cent.

Clients often ask for an estimate of the charges that will be made for dealing with the administration of an estate, and giving a firm quotation is rarely possible, since many cases which appear straightforward at first are later found to be more complex. The difficulties where the final cost is in excess of a first estimate are obvious. However, it should be explained to the clients how charges are to be calculated.

A solicitor or a client has the right to have the solicitor's bill taxed under ss 70–72 Solicitors Act 1974, and if less than half of the bill is allowed on taxation, the Taxing Master must bring the matter to The Law Society's attention. However, if the bill has not been taxed, and is disputed, the solicitor must advise the client in writing of his right to require the solicitor to obtain a remuneration certificate from The Law Society, which certifies the amount to be fair and reasonable. The client is not entitled to require a remuneration certificate after the bill has been paid, or after the court has ordered a bill to be taxed, or for any matter in which court proceedings have been instituted.

Summary

- The personal representative should be advised to obtain tax clearance from the Inspector of Taxes before distributing the estate.

- Although it is not a fixed rule, the onus lies on the personal representative to provide reasons for delay in administering an estate after the so called 'executors year'.

- Although the personal representative is under no obligation to distribute the estate after one year, any persons interested in the estate may call upon the personal representative to give an account of his actions to date.

- The personal representative may make arrangements to carry on a business belonging to the deceased if in so doing he can preserve the estate assets. He may not, however, utilise the general assets of the estate to enable him to carry on the business. He may use only the business assets to do so.

- Distribution of the estate is in accordance with the terms of the will or in accordance with the intestacy rules.

- Personal representatives should obtain separate written values of any items or sets of items which have individual value in excess of £500. It is also advisable to obtain separate values for items which form specific legacies.

- Stocks and shares are valued at probate. If they are then transferred to a beneficiary, the beneficiary receives them at the probate value for the purposes of CGT. However, as far as the estate accounts and equal distribution of the estate is concerned, any stocks and shares transferred to a beneficiary are noted in the estate accounts as passing at the value on the date they are transferred.

- When shares are sold during the period of administration, a note of all capital gains or losses should be noted.

- Where there is an overall loss on shares which are sold within one year of the date of death, relief for inheritance tax may be claimed on Form SECT 5.

- A personal representative may not purchase any item from the estate of which he is the personal representative. This is because a trustee may not put himself in a position of conflict of interest. A personal representative is also prohibited from obtaining any property from the estate through a circuitous arrangement.

- Where an executor is also a legatee in a will, it is presumed that the legacy is given to him in consideration of his accepting the appointment.

- A legacy to an executor is liable to abatement the same as other legacies.

- Where there are insufficient assets to settle general legacies all of the legacies are liable to abate in equal proportions.

- If the charging clause in the will does not allow for legal fees to be paid in priority, those fees also abate in equal proportions.

- Legacies payable out of an estate are generally paid from the personalty with recourse to realty when there is insufficient personalty.

- Interest is payable on unpaid legacies after the period of one year from the date of death.

- A personal representative should not make any distribution of the estate while claims such as claims for family provision are pending. Where there is possibly a claim under the Inheritance (Provision for Family and Dependants) Act 1975 the personal representative should be advised not to make any distribution before the end of six months from the date of death.

- The Law Reform (Succession) Bill includes a recommendation to abolish the 'hotchpot' rules.

- Minor beneficiaries are unable to give the personal representative a valid receipt for their entitlement and therefore it should be invested in the name of the personal representative until the child attains the stated age or the age of majority. In an intestate's estate, minor children who marry under the age of 18 inherit their share without having to wait until they attain their age of majority.

- Where missing beneficiaries cannot be traced, the personal representative can either pay the sum into court or take out a missing beneficiary indemnity with one of the insurance companies.

- Where a woman dies intestate after 1 January 1927 leaving illegitimate children, those illegitimate children take the same interest as legitimate children. For deaths after 1 January 1970 illegitimate children of either parent have the same rights as legitimate children.

- If a beneficiary predeceases the testator any gift to that beneficiary will lapse unless there is provision to the contrary in the will. If the gift is of residue, that share will fall into residue. If the bequest is in the nature of a class gift it will pass to the other residuary beneficiaries. If it is not in the nature of a class gift it will be distributed as on intestacy.

- Personal representatives should obtain proof of the identity of beneficiaries before making payments to them.

- A copy of the clause in the will referring to the legacy can be given to a legatee. A copy of the estate accounts can be given to the residuary beneficiaries.

- Legatees receiving interest should be given a statement of that interest.

- If a personal representative cannot obtain a receipt because of the mental incapacity of a beneficiary, he may pay the fund into court.

- Personal representatives are entitled to an indemnity from the estate in respect of any costs and expenses incurred in the proper execution of their duties. Personal representatives must not make any unnecessary payments from the estate and, therefore, if separate personal representatives instruct separate solicitors they may be personally responsible for the solicitors' costs.

- A personal representative is not allowed to make any profit out of his office and is not entitled to remuneration for acting unless this is specifically provided for in the will.

- An administrator *pendente lite* may be granted remuneration by the court. Remuneration for solicitors is governed by the Solicitors Remuneration Order 1972 (SI 1972 No 1139).

- A solicitor or a client has the right to have the solicitor's bill taxed.

- If a bill has not been taxed and is disputed, the client should be advised of his right to require the solicitor to obtain a remuneration certificate.

Chapter 15

After completion of the administration

1. Trustees

The personal representative holds the estate in trust for the beneficiaries during the period of administration, and his trusteeship ends when the estate has been distributed. Where all or part of the estate cannot be distributed (perhaps because there are minor beneficiaries (see page 153) or because a life interest arises under the will or intestacy), the personal representative continues to hold the assets in trust.

(a) Settled land

Settled land is any immovable property either freehold or leasehold not held on an immediate trust for sale. The settlement may be created by a will or by a deed or trust instrument giving an interest to the tenant for his lifetime. It is not vested in the life tenant, but in the trustees of the settlement.

The trustees of a settlement at the date of death of the tenant for life qualify as special executors.

Trustees of a settlement are those with power of sale of the settled land, or with power of consent to the exercising of a power of sale, or those who are stated to be the trustees for the purposes of the Settled Land Act.

If for any reason there are no trustees of a settlement, the court may appoint trustees. Application to the court for such an appointment can be made by the tenant for life, or any other person with an interest in the settlement.

(b) Administrator trustee

After completing the administration of an estate the administrators become trustees for the beneficiaries and they have power under s 36 Trustee Act 1925 to appoint new trustees.

(c) Substituted trustees

On the death of a trustee, the surviving trustee or trustees may appoint a new trustee, which appointment must be made in writing.

Where one or more trustees wish to be discharged from the trusts, or are out of the United Kingdom for a period exceeding twelve months, or are incapable of acting, other trustees may be appointed in their place. The appointment may be made by the personal representative of a deceased trustee.

(d) Trustee mentally incapable

If a trustee becomes mentally incapable and has a beneficial interest in some or all of the trust property, no appointment of a trustee in his place can be made without agreement from the authority having jurisdiction under Part VII Mental Health Act 1983.

(e) Protection of trustees

A trustee is not under a duty to make enquiries to ascertain if a person is illegitimate or adopted if this could affect that person's entitlement, and he is not liable to anyone if he has distributed property, and he has not had notice of an illegitimacy or adoption before the distribution. This, however, will not prejudice any person's right to 'follow the property' in any other person's hands (i.e. claim it from the ultimate recipient) except those of a purchaser of such property.

(f) Trustee – party to proceedings

Unless it is ordered to the contrary, a trustee who is a party to any proceedings in his capacity as trustee is entitled to the cost of those proceedings from the trust fund, in so far as the costs are not recovered from another person, unless the trustee has acted unreasonably or has acted for his own benefit instead of that of the trust fund.

(g) Power to pay income

Where the trustees have power to pay income to the parent or guardian of any person, or to apply income towards a person's maintenance, education or benefit, and that person has attained the age of 18 years, then the trustees also have power to pay the income direct to that person.

When paying money for maintenance, education or benefit to a beneficiary from the trust funds, a certificate of deduction of income tax, and additional rate tax on Form R 185E should be given to that person to enable him to claim a refund of tax from his own tax district if he is eligible.

(h) Personal representative of deceased trustee

The personal representative of a sole or last surviving trustee exercises the powers of the trustee. The personal representative cannot be compelled to act, and he may be ousted if a new trustee is appointed.

2. Devastavit

Devastavit is a violation by the personal representative of his duties of administration of the estate assets, a misapplication of them for his own use, or acts of negligence or maladministration. Should such a personal representative die (and this includes an *executor de son tort*; see page 26) his own personal representatives become liable in respect of the wasting or conversion of those assets.

A devastavit is committed where a personal representative pays debts out of their due order, thereby prejudicing preferred creditors of whom he has knowledge, or pays out legacies without having allowed for the estate debts, even by reason of misinterpretation of the will.

(a) Collection of debts

A personal representative must collect in all debts owing to the estate (see Chapter 13), and where necessary he should sue for them. If any loss is suffered by the estate (e.g. the debt becomes statute barred or the debtor becomes bankrupt and the debt is lost due to the personal representative's negligent delay) he may become personally liable for the loss.

However, if the personal representative has reasonable grounds for believing that the estate will suffer further loss by pursuing a debt when there are reasonable grounds for believing that there is no hope of recovering it, he is not bound to pursue it. Under s 15 Trustee Act 1925, as long as the personal representative acts *bona fide* for the benefit of the estate he may abandon, accept security for payment of, submit to arbitration, or otherwise settle, any debts. (For beneficiaries' remedy, see page 165.)

(b) Advertising

When there may be creditors in various parts of the country, apart from advertising for claims in the London Gazette and a local newspaper (see page 131), the personal representative may decide to advertise also in a national newspaper. Where it is known that there are possibly creditors in other counties, the personal representative must also advertise in those counties. The cost of advertising is borne by the estate. These steps need to be taken to ensure the personal representative's responsibilities are fully discharged.

(c) Assets

Similarly, the personal representative is accountable for all of the deceased's estate which includes assets received after the death (e.g. interest, premium bond prizes) (see Chapter 7). It is not unusual for further assets to come to light long after the administration has been concluded, and if these are general assets they should be paid to, or divided among the residuary beneficiaries, and a receipt obtained.

(d) Investing estate assets

Where a personal representative neglects to invest money received by him into the estate during the administration period he may be charged with the lost interest, and may also be charged with the interest if he fails to pay debts on which interest is continuing to run as soon as there are sufficient assets in the estate.

(e) Beneficiaries' remedy for devastavit

An action may be commenced against the personal representative based upon a devastavit, and a beneficiary may also sue the personal representative for an unpaid legacy. It is no defence to a devastavit that the personal representative acted on his solicitor's advice (*Marsden v Regan* [1954] 1 All ER 475).

If the personal representative distributed the estate after having made every effort to trace creditors and beneficiaries as described above, he will not be liable for any claims against the estate of which he has not had notice.

To protect the interests of the residuary beneficiaries, a personal representative cannot purchase any assets (see page 151), but in the case of a surviving spouse acting as the, or one of the, personal representatives, the rules that trustees may not purchase property do not prevent the spouse from purchasing the dwelling in which he was resident at the time of the death.

Summary

- Personal representatives hold the estate in trust for the beneficiaries during the administration period, and when the estate has been distributed the trusteeship ends. Where administrators become trustees for the beneficiaries they have power under s 36 Trustee Act 1925 to appoint new trustees.

- A trustee is not under a duty to ascertain if a person is illegitimate or adopted if this could affect that person's entitlement. This will not prejudice any other person's right to 'follow the property' in any other person's hands except those of a purchaser of such property.

- Where a trustee is a party to any proceedings in his capacity as a trustee, he is entitled to the cost of those proceedings from the trust fund.

- The personal representative of a sole or last surviving trustee exercises the powers of that trustee. However, the personal representative cannot be compelled to act, and he may be ousted if a new trustee is appointed.

- Misapplication of the estate assets is a devastavit. The personal representative is liable in respect of the wasting or conversion of assets. If that personal representative dies, his own personal representatives become liable.

- Although the personal representative must collect in all debts owing to the estate and, where necessary, sue for them, he is not bound to pursue a debt if he believes the estate will suffer further loss by that pursuit. If a personal representative fails to pursue a debt and that debt becomes statute barred, the debtor becomes bankrupt, or the debt is lost in any other way due to negligence on the part of the personal representative, then the personal representative may become personally liable for the loss.

- The personal representatives should be advised to insert notices for claims in the London Gazette, and, if there is realty, in the local newspaper in the area where that realty is located.

- If a personal representative neglects to invest money received by him into the estate during the administration period, he may be charged with the lost interest.

- If he fails to pay debts on which interest is continuing to run, when there are sufficient assets in the estate to settle those debts, he may be liable for the loss.

Chapter 16

Modifying the provisions under the will or intestacy

1. The Inheritance (Provision for Family and Dependants) Act 1975

The Act applies to the estates of persons dying after 31 March 1976. Before 1 April 1976 the Inheritance (Family Provision) Act 1938 made slightly more limited provision.

Any of the persons listed below who consider that the terms of a will, or the intestacy rules, do not make reasonable financial provision for them may apply to the court under s 2 of the 1975 Act:

(i) the wife or husband of the deceased;

(ii) a former wife or husband of the deceased who has not remarried;

(iii) a child of the deceased;

(iv) any person (not being a child of the deceased) who in the case of any marriage to which the deceased was at any time a party was treated by the deceased as a child of the family in relation to that marriage;

(v) any person (not being a person included in the foregoing paragraphs of this subsection) who immediately before the death of the deceased was being maintained, either wholly of partly by the deceased;

(vi) The Law Reform (Succession) Bill (which has only received its second reading in Parliament at the time of writing) amends this Act to enable a cohabitant to apply for provision without having to prove actual dependence.

By virtue of s 1(a) of the Act, financial provision in the case of an application by the husband or widow of the deceased (except where the marriage with the deceased was the subject of a decree of judicial separation, and at the date of death the decree was in force, and the separation was continuing) means such financial provision as it would be reasonable in all the circumstances of the case for a husband or wife to receive whether or not that provision is required for his or her maintenance.

In the case of any other application made by virtue of subs (1) financial provision means such as would be reasonable in all the circumstances of the case for the applicant to receive for his maintenance.

For the purposes of subs (1)(e) a person is treated as being maintained by the deceased, either wholly or partly, as the case may be, if the deceased, otherwise than for full valuable consideration, was making a substantial contribution in money or money's worth towards the reasonable needs of that person.

The court has power to make orders for periodic payments, lump sum payments, transfer of property, acquisition of property, and may vary settlements. In making an order, the court will consider the financial resources and needs of any applicant, the size and nature of the estate, any disability of the applicant, the conduct of the applicant or any other person, etc.

This is merely a very brief synopsis of the Act, and the Act should be read as a whole before making a decision on a proposed claim.

It must be remembered that proceedings under this Act should be commenced within six months of the date of the original grant. Application is made by originating application to the High Court (Family or Chancery Division), or to the county court. By the High Court and County Courts Jurisdiction Order 1991 (SI 1991 No 724), and the County Courts Act 1984 (as amended) the courts have jurisdiction regardless of the estate value. A grant of representation must be obtained before an order can be made. (Inheritance Act 1975 s 19(3).)

For the purposes of this Act, the value of any nominated property (see page 69), after payment of any inheritance tax due on it, is treated as part of the deceased's net estate, but no-one will be liable for having paid over the property to the nominee. In addition, the court may order that the value of the severable share of the deceased's interest in joint property immediately before the death is to be treated as part of his net estate.

If a joint property was subject to a mortgage, and the mortgage was protected by an endowment policy, a half share of the sum payable on the endowment policy forms part of the estate. (*Powell v Osbourne* 1992.)

Note: where a surviving spouse applied for financial provision under the Inheritance (Provision for Family and Dependants) Act 1975 but died before the hearing date, her personal representatives were refused leave to continue the proceedings on behalf of her estate. Under the 1975 Act a surviving spouse is given the right to apply to the court for relief against the deceased's spouse's estate, but is given no enforceable right against the estate (*Whytte v Ticehurst* [1986] 2 WLR 700, [1986] 2 All ER 158).

Under the rules of intestacy, where the deceased leaves no relatives who are entitled to the estate (apart from claims under the 1975 Act), the estate passes *in bona vacantia* (see page 48).

2. Fatal accidents and rights to sue

If the deceased died in a fatal accident his family may have a claim under the Fatal Accidents Acts 1846, 1959 and 1976 for 'dependency or damages for themselves'. The persons who are entitled to claim are:

(i)   the spouse;

(ii)   the children;

(iii)   the grandchildren;

(iv)   the step-children;

(v)   the parents;

(vi)   the step-parents;

(vii)   the grandparents;

(viii) a brother or sister;

(ix)   an uncle or aunt.

A claim may be made by the personal representative under the Law Reform (Miscellaneous Provisions) Act 1934 on behalf of the estate for any tort committed against the deceased.

These rights of the personal representative to sue for benefit form part of the estate.

3. Modifying the intestacy rules

(a) Provision for the spouse where there are issue

With the higher values of matrimonial homes, the provisions under the Acts for the surviving spouse often leave the spouse with the personal chattels and the matrimonial home, the value of which uses up their entitlement, or worse, the value of the matrimonial home exceeds the amount of the statutory legacy. This leaves the spouse with the choice of either paying in the amount of the difference between the value of the home and the statutory legacy, or having the home sold. There are various other ways of dealing with this problem, if the issue and other beneficiaries agree:

(i)   the spouse and others can have the realty transferred to them as beneficial joint tenants, or tenants in common in various shares, giving the spouse continuing enjoyment of the dwelling plus an amount of cash;

(ii) the realty could be transferred to the issue with a provision for the spouse to continue living there, and the statutory legacy could then be in the form of cash;

(iii) the realty could be sold and a less expensive dwelling purchased (which is not always a welcome suggestion) and the cash balance paid to the spouse;

(iv) the spouse could capitalise his or her life interest in the remainder;

(v)   the distribution of the estate may be varied by deed by the beneficiaries (see forms).

(b) Capitalisation of the life interest

Under s 47A Administration of Estates Act 1925, where a surviving spouse is entitled to a life interest he or she may elect to have the life interest redeemed. Where the surviving spouse is the sole administrator he must give notice in writing in Form 6 of the Schedule to the Non-Contentious Probate Rules 1987 before the election becomes effective. The election must be made within twelve months of the issue of the grant. The notice must be filed either in the Principal Registry, or in duplicate in the registry from which the grant issued. The other beneficiaries sharing in the estate must be advised of the election.

If the surviving spouse has a co-administrator, he does not have to give notice as above, but he should give notice of his intention to the co-administrators, and advise the other beneficiaries.

The right of the surviving spouse to capitalise the life interest cannot be exercised until the personal representative is constituted, i.e. until a grant has issued.

With this action the surviving spouse will benefit as shown below, and the issue or other beneficiaries will benefit by receiving the remainder of the capital of the life interest immediately instead of waiting until the death of the life tenant. See r 2 Intestate Succession (Interest and Capitalisation) Order 1983.

To prepare the calculation of the amount due to the surviving spouse the actuary will require the date of birth of the spouse, whether male or female, and the value of the estate, and will calculate the yield as a percentage of the life interest, and this will be in addition to the chattels and the statutory legacy as follows:

Spouse receives:	*Other beneficiaries receive:*
Before capitalisation:	
Chattels	Half the remainder immediately (if
Statutory legacy	of age), the balance on the death of
Life interest in half the remainder.	the spouse.
After capitalisation:	
Spouse receives:	*Other beneficiaries receive:*
Chattels	The remainder.
Statutory legacy	
Percentage yield of the life interest.	

The statutory legacy to the surviving spouse is also entitled to interest from the date of death until it is paid over to the person entitled. The interest must be paid 'gross' and if resort must be made to capital to fulfil this requirement, the Inland Revenue may tax the capital element as if it were income.

4. Deeds of variation and disclaimers

Beneficiaries under a will or intestacy are not compelled to accept the property that is given to them. It is open to any beneficiary or group of beneficiaries to arrange to redirect that property as they wish.

It is common for the redirection to be made by means of a deed of variation (in the past often called a deed of family arrangement). Provided the deed of variation is made within two years of the date of death, and appropriate elections are given to the Inland Revenue within six months of the date of the deed, the provisions of the deed are treated for both inheritance tax and capital gains tax purposes as if they had been incorporated in the deceased's will.

It is important to note that the provisions for 'writing back' the effect of a deed of variation into the will do *not* apply for income tax purposes. As a result, the beneficiary making the variation will always be liable to tax on any income he has received from property which he has subsequently redirected. If any kind of settlement is created, the deceased is treated as the settlor for inheritance tax purposes, but the beneficiary making the variation is the settlor for the purposes of both capital gains tax and income tax.

It is very common for deeds of variation to redirect all, or almost all, of the deceased's property to his spouse, so taking advantage of the inheritance tax surviving spouse exemption. Often the intention of the parties making such a variation is that the spouse should, shortly after the variation has been executed, make gifts of property which will qualify as potentially exempt transfers. The Inland Revenue always investigates variations of this kind. Section 142(3) Inheritance Tax Act 1984 provides that the deed of variation cannot be accepted as writing back provisions into the will if there is any consideration for making the deed, outside the deed itself. Any arrangement for the surviving spouse to make subsequent gifts is treated by the Inland Revenue as consideration. It is essential that, should any such arrangements be contemplated, there is a clear record that the surviving spouse was under no obligation of any kind to make any further gifts.

The freedom for beneficiaries to redirect assets which they inherit to others only became fully effective for inheritance tax purposes in 1978. Disclaimers have a much longer history.

A disclaimer gives the beneficiary no opportunity to direct who will receive the property which he says he does not want to receive. As a result, the other provisions of the will or intestacy must be consulted and very careful note taken of exactly what will happen.

Under intestacy, if one member of a class of beneficiaries disclaims the other members of that class will receive an increased share.

One major advantage of disclaimers over deeds of variation is that the variation effected by a disclaimer is fully effective for income tax purposes. The disclaiming beneficiary is not liable to tax, nor is he likely to be treated as the settlor of any gift which may result, for example to his minor children.

There is no technical requirement for the parties to a disclaimer to elect for the disclaimer to be written back into the will for tax purposes, since this happens in any event. It is, of course, advisable for the personal representatives to ensure that the Inland Revenue is fully aware of the provision.

There is no longer any stamp duty payable on either deeds of variation or disclaimers.

Joint tenancies mean that the surviving joint owner automatically becomes the owner at the death. Therefore he cannot disclaim the deceased's interest in the joint ownership. He can, however, deal with that share by way of a deed of variation.

Summary

- Any of the persons listed in the Inheritance (Provision for Family and Dependants) Act 1975 may make a claim for reasonable financial provision if they consider the terms of a will or intestacy laws do not make reasonable provision for them. The Law Reform (Succession) Bill recommends amendments to this Act to enable a cohabitant to apply for provision without having to prove actual dependency.

- Under the Fatal Accidents Acts 1846, 1959 and 1976, the family of a deceased who died in a fatal accident may have a claim for dependency. The persons entitled to claim are listed in the Act. Personal representatives may also make a claim on behalf of the estate for any tort committed against the deceased.

- Where it is considered that the provisions under the intestacy rules give insufficient provision to the surviving spouse, the distribution of the estate may be varied by a deed by all of the beneficiaries.

- Where the surviving spouse, under intestacy, receives an entitlement to a life interest, the surviving spouse may elect to have that life interest redeemed. Election must be made within twelve months of the issue of the grant. The right to capitalise a life interest cannot be exercised until after the grant is issued.

- It is open to beneficiaries under a will or intestacy to rearrange the distribution of estates by way of Deeds of Variation and Disclaimers.

- The surviving owner of a joint tenancy cannot disclaim the deceased's interest in the joint ownership because the survivor automatically becomes the owner at death. However, he may deal with the deceased's share by way of a deed of variation.

Chapter 17

Caveats and warnings

1. Caveats

The procedure relating to caveats is contained in r 44 Non-Contentious Probate Rules 1987. See Appendix 5 for examples of forms relevant to this chapter.

Where a person wishes to be given notice of an application for a grant of representation, he may enter a caveat (on Form 3) in *any registry* on payment of the appropriate fee (currently £4.00).

By entering a caveat, a person ensures that while the caveat remains effective no grant of representation is issued to anyone without the caveator first being notified of the application. The duration of the caveat is six months; it can be extended for further periods of six months on written application to the registry at which the caveat was first entered and on payment of a further fee of £4.00. Applications for the extension of a caveat must be made in the last month before the expiry of the existing caveat.

If an application for an extension of the caveat has not been entered before that caveat expires, the caveator may enter a new caveat. It is advisable, however, to confirm that the grant has not issued since the expiry. Where a warning has been issued against the first caveat, which has then been removed by a district judge or a registrar's order, the caveator may not enter a further caveat.

A caveat may be entered by personal attendance at the registry where the caveat book will be completed. Alternatively, the caveat may be entered by sending by post a typed copy to the registry with the appropriate fee. A caveat received on the same day on which a grant is to be sealed will not prevent the issue of the grant.

An index of caveats is held in the registry at which the index of pending grant applications is maintained, and the caveat index is searched when an application for a grant is received. Where a caveat has been entered, the person applying for a grant is advised that his application has been stopped. Both indexes are currently held at the Leeds District Probate Registry.

A caveat may be withdrawn by cancellation, by giving notice to the registry at which the caveat was entered. The receipt for the caveat, issued when it is entered, should be sent to the registry with the notice of withdrawal. If a warning has been issued, the caveat may be withdrawn by giving notice to the registry and also to the person who has warned the caveat, so long as the caveator has not entered an appearance to that warning.

If the caveator has entered an appearance to a warning, he cannot then withdraw the caveat until the probate action has commenced, unless a district judge directs otherwise. In cases where the application to discontinue the caveat has been made by consent, a district judge or a registrar may direct that the caveat can be withdrawn.

2. Warnings

When a person applies for a grant of representation, he will be advised by the registry of the existing caveat. He may then warn the caveator by issuing a warning in Form 4. The person warning a caveat must show his interest in the deceased's estate, and require the caveator to give details of any contrary interest in the estate. The warning should be served on the caveator immediately it has issued. Warnings are now issued only from the Leeds District Probate Registry (r 44(5) Non-Contentious Probate Rules 1987). Form 4 may be lodged personally or by post.

3. Appearance

Where the caveator has a contrary interest to that of the person issuing the warning, he should enter an appearance in the registry in Form 5 within eight days of service of the warning on him. A sealed copy of Form 5 should then be served immediately on the person issuing the warning.

An appearance to a warning may be made (on Form 5) only at the Leeds District Probate Registry and only by personal attendance (r 44(10) Non-Contentious Probate Rules 1987). One of the many firms of solicitors in Leeds can be instructed to act as agents to enter an appearance.

4. Summons for directions

If the caveator (having no contrary interest in the grant) wishes to show cause why a grant should not be issued to the person applying, he should, within eight days of receiving the warning, apply for the issue of a summons for directions and serve a copy on the person warning. The caveat remains in force until the summons has been dealt with, unless a district judge or a registrar has directed that the caveat should cease to have effect, or until it has been withdrawn by the caveator by giving notice at the registry. The caveator may withdraw his caveat so long as he has not entered an appearance to a warning.

5. Summons for an order of discontinuance

If, after an appearance to a warning, agreement is reached between the parties concerned, a summons for an order of discontinuance may be issued and will be heard by a district judge or a registrar. Where the parties do not reach agreement, a writ of summons is issued to commence an action. The writ is issued in the Chancery Division.

6. Affidavit of service

Where a warning to a caveat has been issued, and eight days after service of the warning the other party has not entered an appearance or issued a summons for directions, the person applying for the grant should file an affidavit of service of warning. The caveat can then be removed and the grant application can continue.

The address of the Leeds District Probate Registry is:

> Third Floor
> Coronet House
> Queen Street
> Leeds LS1 2BA
> or DX 26451 Leeds Park Square
> (Tel: (0113) 243 1505)

Summary

- Any person may enter a caveat, in any Probate Registry on payment of the appropriate fee. A caveat ensures that no grant of representation can be issued to anyone without the caveator first being notified of the application.

- A caveat remains in force for six months and can be extended for further periods of six months. An application to extend the caveat must be made in the last month before the expiry date.

- When a person applies for a grant of representation, he will be advised if a caveat has been registered.

- The caveat may be withdrawn by cancellation just so long as an appearance has not been entered.

- If the person applying for a grant is advised of the existence of a caveat he may warn the caveator in Form 4.

- When the warning has been issued the caveator should enter an appearance in the Probate Registry in Form 5 within eight days of service of the warning on him. Within eight days of receiving a warning the person warned should apply for the issue of a Summons for Directions.

- If agreement is reached between the parties after an appearance to a warning has been entered, a Summons for an Order of Discontinuance may be issued.

- Where the parties do not reach agreement, a Writ of Summons is issued in the Chancery Division to commence an action.

- If, eight days after the service of a warning, the other party named has not entered an appearance or issued a Summons for Directions, the person applying for the grant should file an Affidavit of Service of Warning. The caveat can then be removed.

Chapter 18

Enduring powers of attorney

The Court of Protection Rules 1994 and Court of Protection (Enduring Powers of Attorney) Rules 1994 formalise the changes in practice which have developed since 1986. The judicial powers of the Court of Protection are exercised by the Master, Assistant Master, and nominated officers, but the administration is carried out by the Public Trustee and the Public Trust Office.

These rules have also been utilised to revise the various fees and to introduce procedural amendments.

The Public Trustee may now:

(a) Register (or refuse to register) or cancel an enduring power of attorney.

(b) Give directions, dispense with the requirement to give notice, and receive notices of disclaimer.

These rules do not prevent the court from exercising these functions.

The time limits and procedures relating to reviews and appeals have been brought into line with the Court of Protection Rules 1994 and the same procedures and limits apply to receivership and to enduring power of attorney matters.

New forms now refer both to the Court of Protection and the Public Trust Office.

Practitioners should seriously consider using the standard printed forms in preference to forms drafted in their own offices. The forms can be amended to include restrictions and additional powers.

1. Instructions

The possible advantages of having an enduring power of attorney prepared should be brought to the attention of all clients over the age of fifty.

When receiving instructions, practitioners should consider whether an enduring power of attorney (EPA) is the appropriate form needed, or if an ordinary power of attorney, or the appointment of a receiver is more relevant.

2. The donor

Consider, at the outset, if the donor is capable of giving instructions for the EPA, and if the donor understands the consequences of doing so.

The donor must be capable of understanding the effect of the EPA but does not have to be capable of managing his affairs at the time of signing it, for the power to be valid. The donor must understand that the appointed attorney can deal with the donor's property and can take complete control over it. That the appointment of the attorney will continue even in the event of the donor becoming mentally incapable and, if he becomes incapable, then the appointment cannot be revoked unless and until the court intervenes.

The power can be revoked by the donor at any time if he has not become mentally incapable.

If there is any doubt about the donor's capacity to appoint an attorney, practitioners should consider whether the donor's doctor should be consulted, and if the doctor should be invited to be the donor's witness.

3. The attorney

Is there any suspicion that the proposed attorney is using undue pressure on the donor?

Is the attorney a member of the donor's family; if not, are the donor's family aware of the proposed appointment?

Is the attorney bankrupt or is there any possibility of him becoming bankrupt?

How old is the attorney? Is he as old as, or older than the donor? If so, could he become mentally or physically incapable of carrying out an attorney's duties?

Does the proposed attorney reside close to the donor, if not, will he be able to attend to the donor's needs?

Does the proposed attorney know everything about the donor's affairs?

If there are two or more attorneys, is the power to be joint, or joint and several?

If the proposed attorney is a professional, it is recommended that a charging clause be included in the EPA.

4. Essential information

(1)   The full names including any aliases, the date of birth, and the address of the donor.

(2)   Details of the donor's assets (including a will) and their whereabouts.

(3)   If the donor is disabled (for example, blind) a special attestation clause will have to be used.

(4)   Does the donor's doctor need to be consulted? Note his name and address.

178

(5) Does the donor's social worker need to be consulted? Note his name and address.

(6) Obtain full details of the donor's relatives including their relationship, ages, full names and addresses.

(7) Advise the donor that the appointment may be revoked at any time before it has to be registered, otherwise the appointment continues, even if the donor becomes incapable.

(8) The full names and addresses of the attorneys and, if possible, their occupations.

(9) Is the appointment to be joint, or joint and several?

(10) What powers are to be given, and what are to be excluded?

(11) Advise the attorney of his duty to register the EPA as soon as he believes the donor is becoming mentally incapable.

(12) Make certain the EPA form is the current version.

(13) Advise both the donor and the attorney that the power is revoked by the attorney becoming bankrupt.

(14) Advise the attorney to use certified copies of the document and not the original.

(15) Banks require copies of the EPA to be certified on every page, not just on the front page.

(16) If the power has to be registered, the original document must be produced to the court.

(17) The cost of registration is currently £50.

5. Revocation of enduring power

This deed

made this   day of   One thousand nine hundred and
BY

1. Whereas I granted an enduring power of attorney dated   day
    of One thousand nine hundred and

    (the enduring power of attorney) to
    (jointly) and (severally) to be my attorney(s) for the purpose of the
    Enduring Powers of Attorney Act 1985.

2. I declare that the enduring power of attorney has not been registered by the Court of Protection.

3. I revoke the enduring power of attorney and the authority granted by it.

Signed as a deed and delivered by
In the presence of

6. Registration

Where there are joint attorneys only one of them needs to apply to register the power but he must give notice to the other joint attorney of his intention.

When the attorneys are joint and several, all of them must apply to register the power.

Objections to a proposal to register must be made in writing.

7. Dispensation

The need to give notice to the donor may be dispensed with on production of medical evidence. The medical evidence should be produced with a request to dispense with a notice, before the application to register is submitted.

EP1 – Notice of intention to apply for registration must be given to the donor (save where dispensation is given), and to the donor's family.

8. Family

Notice should be given to at least three relatives (attorneys who are family are counted in the three family members).

Notice may be handed to relatives personally or sent by first class post.

The Act sets out the order of priority of relatives to be informed:

(1) The donor's spouse.

(2) The donor's children.

(3) The donor's parents.

(4) The donor's brothers and sisters of the whole or half blood.

(5) The widow or widower of a child of the donor.

(6) The donor's grandchildren.

(7) The children of the donor's brothers or sisters of the whole blood.

(8) The children of the donor's brothers or sisters of the half blood.

(9) The donor's uncles or aunts of the whole blood.

(10) Children of the donor's uncles or aunts of the whole blood.

Where there are several persons in a particular class, then all persons in that class must receive notice, even if there are more than three.

Notice need not be given to persons under the age of eighteen years, or to persons who are mentally incapable, or to a person whose address cannot be ascertained.

Where there are less than three relatives, or none at all, this fact should be stated on the application.

The application must be made in Form EP2 to Protection Division, The

Public Trust Office, Stewart House, 24 Kingsway, London, WC2B 6JX or DX:37965 Kingsway. Tel (0171) 269 7300.

The application must be made within ten days of serving the notice of intention to apply for registration.

The original EPA and the registration fee of £50 must be sent with the application.

The court will hold the application for 35 days (from the date of the last EP1) and if no written objections are received, the EPA will be registered, and the document returned.

EP2 – Application to register the enduring power of attorney

Form EP2 should be completed showing:

- the full details of the attorney(s) applying to register the EPA;

- the donor's full details;

- the date of the EPA;

- the place and date of giving notice to the donor;

- the names, relationships, and addresses of the relatives who have been notified and the date of the notification;

- the form should then be signed by those applying for registration, dated, and the address where notices are to be sent must be included.

9. Death of the patient

If the EPA was registered at the Court of Protection during the patient's lifetime, the personal representative must advise that court of the patient's death.

Summary

- The judicial powers of the Court of Protection are now excercised by the Master Assistant, Master and nominated officers. The administration is dealt with by the Public Trustees. The Court of Protection Rules 1994 and the Court of Protection (Enduring Powers of Attorney) Rules 1994 formalise changes in practice.

- The correct form, whether a standard printed form or a practitioner's version, must be used to make absolutely certain that an enduring power of attorney (EPA) is not declared invalid.

- The availability and advisability of issuing an EPA ought to be brought to the attention of all clients, but especially those aged 50 or above.

- It is most important that the person preparing an EPA is certain that the donor is capable of understanding the purpose and effect of the document.

In some cases it would be advisable to consult the person's medical practitioner.

- Equally important is the need to be sure that the proposed attorney is a person of discretion and that the donor's family are aware of the proposed appointment.

- If the proposed attorney is a professional person, include a charging clause in the power.

- Full details of the donor, the attorney, the donor's family and estate should be obtained. These may be useful to the personal representatives if the donor dies.

- When the donor is becoming or has become incapable the power must be registered.

- The power can be revoked at any time before the donor becomes incapable.

- Notice of intention to register a power must be given to at least three relatives.

Chapter 19

The Court of Protection

The Court of Protection Rules 1984 and the Court of Protection (Amendment) Rules 1992 were revoked and replaced by the Court of Protection Rules 1994 which came into force on 22 December 1994. The major change is the introduction of directions which are given under the authority of the seal of the Public Trust Office and the introduction of the authority of the Public Trustee. The changes also take into account the Children Act 1989.

When a person becomes mentally incapable of managing his affairs, and has not appointed an enduring power of attorney, application should be made to the Court of Protection for a receiver to be appointed.

The application may be made personally or the applicant can instruct solicitors. In both cases the following forms are required:

(1) Two copies of Form CP1 (the originating application).

(2) Form CP3 (the medical certificate).

(3) Form CP5 (the certificate of family and fortune).

(4) The patient's will, or a copy.

(5) The commencement fee of £100.

(6) If the Public Trustee is appointed, an additional fee of £150 is payable.

Cheques are payable to the Public Trust Office.

1. Short procedure

The Short Procedure Orders which were previously dealt with by the Court of Protection are no longer available.

When a patient has less than £5,000 capital, an application for directions is made to the Public Trustee.

When a patient has more than £5,000 the full receivership order must be applied for as above.

2. The hearing

One copy of the Form CP1 showing the date and time of the hearing will be returned to the applicant, and the hearing date will be approximately four weeks from the date of the notice.

3. Notifying the patient

In addition, a letter and details of the proposed hearing, addressed to the patient, will be sent to the applicant. This letter has to be delivered to the patient, in person, at least ten days before the hearing date, and a certificate of service (with a copy of the letter attached) must be completed by the person delivering the letter to the patient, and returned to the court.

4. Dispensing with the notice

If a doctor believes the patient would be distressed or harmed if the notice is served on him, the doctor should give medical evidence to this effect. The court has power to dispense with notice.

(a) Attendance

No attendance is required unless the court indicates otherwise.

5. Interim directions

If urgent directions are required pending hearing of an application, a written request should be made to the court stating the reason for the urgency, and the relief required. Interim directions are usually sought if the patient's house is being sold, or if money is needed urgently.

Interim directions cannot be given until the medical evidence has been received by the court.

(a) Receiver's security

The receiver is required to give security (in most cases) for the assets he is handling on behalf of the patient. The court fixes the amount of the security and will supply a list of recommended companies. The security must be arranged before the order will be completed. The security is renewable annually.

6. Draft order

After the hearing of the application, a draft first general order will be issued (in duplicate) listing any further information required to perfect the order. This further information (if any) should be noted on the draft order, and one copy returned to the court. Thereafter the general order will be issued together with the number of office copies requested.

(a) Bank account

A receiver's bank account will have to be opened in the name of the patient 'by his receiver'.

7. Annual accounts

The court may direct that annual accounts are prepared by the receiver, and submitted to the court. These accounts are a record of the patient's money which has been received by the receiver, and money paid out during the year. The first annual account is usually prepared up to the first anniversary of the issue of the general order, and annually thereafter.

(a) Deeds – approval

The new rules abolished the need for the court to settle and approve deeds.

8. Fixed costs

On 22 December 1994 a practice direction was issued which increased the amounts of fixed costs.

(1) For work up to and including the date of the first general order: £425 plus VAT.

(2a) For preparing and lodging a receivership account: £117 plus VAT.

(2b) For preparing and lodging a receivership account which has been certified by a solicitor under the provisions of the practice notes of 13 September 1984, and 5 March 1985:   £133 plus VAT.

(3) For general management work in the second and subsequent years:

(3a) Where there are lay receivers   £330 plus VAT;

(3b) Where there are solicitor receivers   £384 plus VAT.

(4) Appointments under Trustee Act 1925 s 36 – the appointment of a new trustee in the place of the patient for the purposes of making title to land: £247 plus VAT.

(5) Conveyancing – two elements are allowable.

   (a) Correspondence with Court of Protection, preparing a certificate of value, arranging for the documents to be sealed by the court, and including all other work attributable solely to the Court of Protection: £137 plus VAT.

   (b) A value element:

      (i) up to £400,000 at 0.5%;

      (ii) in excess of £400,000 at 0.25%.

With a minimum sum of £273 plus VAT.

(a) Taxation of costs

The option for solicitors to have their costs taxed remains, if they do not wish to accept fixed costs.

(b) Death of patient

The receiver is automatically discharged when the patient dies, but he remains liable to account up to the date of death. The court can direct the termination of proceedings by the receiver but has no further jurisdiction, and cannot give formal directions.

The receiver can no longer deal with the patient's money.

The court will issue final directions for preparation of final receivership accounts, unless the deceased's personal representative agrees to dispense with final accounts.

9. Final directions

Written application should be made to the Public Trust Office for final directions, and the original or office copy grant of representation with a certified copy of the will should be sent.

1. The personal representative should request that the final receivership accounts be passed or that they be dispensed with.

2. For any funds in court to be transferred.

3. If solicitor's final costs are not agreed, the personal representative should ask for them to be taxed.

10. Estate under £5,000

If no grant of representation is needed, and the net estate is less than £5,000, the following should be sent to the Public Trust Office:

(i) the death certificate;

(ii) a schedule of assets and liabilities;

(iii) the names, addresses, and relationships to the deceased of all persons entitled to the estate.

11. Funds in court

Correspondence concerning any funds in court should be addressed to:

The Principal
Court Funds Office
22 Kingsway
London WC2B 6LE

All correspondence should quote the case number and the patient's name.

12. Supreme Court Taxing Office

All correspondence concerning taxation should be addressed to:

The Supreme Court Taxing Office
Court of Protection Branch
Room 271
Royal Courts of Justice
The Strand
London WC2A 2LL

Summary

- When a person becomes incapable of managing his affairs and has not appointed an attorney under an enduring power of attorney, application should be made to appoint.

- The application may be made personally or through a solicitor.

- The commencement fee is £100 but if the Public Trustee is appointed an additional fee of £150 is payable.

- When a patient has less than £5,000, directions should be sought from the Public Trustee. In all other cases a full receivership order is required. The short procedure order is no longer available.

- The date and time of the hearing of the application will be advised four weeks before the hearing. The patient must be advised except in special circumstances.

- A written request should be made to the court if urgent interim directions are needed.

- The receiver will be required to give security for the patient's assets.

- A receiver's bank account will be required.

- Annual receivership accounts must be submitted to the court.

- Fixed costs are available for dealing with the application. If fixed costs are considered to be insufficient, costs may be taxed.

- On the death of the patient the receiver is automatically discharged but remains liable to account up to the date of death.

- A written application for final directions should be made to the court.

Appendix 1

Probate and administration questionnaire

A. Personal details

Full Name:

Any other name in which the deceased's assets are registered:

Address:

Former Address:

Obtain death certificate. If not ask:

1. Date of Death:
2. Date of Birth:
   (or approximate age if not known)
3. Place of Birth:
4. Occupation:

Surviving relatives: Husband/Wife
                                        ..... Child(ren)
                                        ..... (number)
                                        ..... Parent(s)

Marital Status:

Domicile (if not in England and Wales):

B. Preliminary arrangements

(a) Death Certificate (see above)

Have arrangements been made to register the death?

Obtain copy of death certificate and Certificate of Registration of Death

(b) Will

Did the deceased make a will?

Ascertain the whereabouts of the will and obtain a copy.

Names addresses occupations and telephone numbers of executors named in the will.

(c) Funeral

Are there any funeral wishes in the will?

Are the funeral arrangements in hand?

If so, who is making the arrangements?

Date and place of funeral.

Name, address and telephone number of the undertakers.

Are we to write to anyone?

(i) to advise them of the death

(ii) to advise of funeral arrangements

(iii) letters of condolence

Is an obituary notice needed?

C. Details of family and will

Date of will:

Date of Codicil(s):

Are names and addresses as shown in the will correct?

(If not obtain up to date information.)

Are all beneficiaries alive?

Are all beneficiaries of age?

(If not obtain dates of birth (and copy of birth certificates).)

If the deceased died intestate supply names and addresses of those of the following who survived:

Husband/Wife
Child(ren)
Grandchild(ren)
Parent(s)
Grandparent(s)
Brothers and/or Sisters
Nephews and/or Nieces

Supply details of any former spouse or other dependants i.e. any other person treated as a child of the family or any person maintained by the deceased.

Do all named executors or possible administrators wish to apply for the grant?

Are there any urgent short-term financial problems or requirements?

D. Agents

Supply names, addresses and references of the following:

> Accountant or other tax adviser
>
> If no advisers the Tax District to which Returns were submitted
>
> Estate agents
>
> Stockbrokers

E. Details of assets

Cash: Amount
> Where held
>
> Any needed for urgent requirements

Uncashed cheques or dividend warrants

Stock Exchange securities

Banking account

National Savings Bank

Trustee Savings Bank

Building Societies

Co-operative & Friendly Society Accounts

National Savings Certificates

Premium Savings Bonds

Life or Endowment Policies

Money lent or mortgage

Money lent without security

Debts owing to the deceased

Pensions or lump sum payments

Television licence refund

Directorships, salaries or other remuneration

Interest in any business, trade or profession as sole proprietor or partner

Private Company shares

Annuities

Motor vehicles (obtain registration document, insurance details, insurance certificate and MOT). NB VEHICLE IS NOT TO BE DRIVEN UNTIL PROPER INSURANCE COVER IS ARRANGED.

Refund unused car insurance premium

Boats

Jewellery and Furniture – are these adequately insured and in a safe place?

Name and address of insurance company and policy number. Ask insurance company for details of cover.

Are assets to be sold, if so how?

Are any specifically given by the will?

If they are to be retained is a Probate valuation necessary and if so by whom?

(What is the approximate value?)

Are any special security arrangements needed?

Any miscellaneous assets (including foreign property).

F. Property (freehold or leasehold)

Did the deceased own any property?

If so deal with the following:

Freehold or leasehold.

Description of the property.

Name and address of the insurance company and policy number.

Is it adequately insured?

Who is checking this?

Have the insurance company and police been advised if it is vacant?

Notification of death?

Ask for details of cover and whether this is being maintained.

Who is holding the keys?

Where are the deeds?

Is the property to be sold?

If it is to be retained is a probate valuation necessary?

What is the approximate value?

Which valuers are to be used?

Is the property let?

If so who collects the rent?

Give details of rent and other terms of tenancy.

G. Liabilities

Estimate of funeral expenses.

Loans.

Mortgages.

Items on Hire Purchase or other arrangement.

Credit cards (obtain cards).

Services:

  Are they to be transferred?

  Are final readings required?

  Gas

  Electricity

  Telephone

  Local authority charges

  Water Rates

  Water Service Charges.

Other debts.

H. Miscellaneous

Did the deceased act as guarantor?

Did the deceased have a bankers card?

(If so obtain card.)

Did the deceased benefit from an estate in the last five years?

Was the deceased an executor or trustee?

Had the deceased made any settlements?

Was the deceased a beneficiary under any settlement or will trust? If so who are the trustees and/or their solicitors?

Did the deceased make any gift other than to his/her spouse within the last seven years except the usual birthday and Christmas presents?

Did the deceased at any time make any gift, reserving to himself some interest or benefit?

Was the deceased the recipient of any gifts which could be chargeable to tax on death of donor?

Did the deceased pay any premiums on a life or endowment policy? (Details not needed in respect of monies payable to the estate.)

Did the deceased nominate any savings bank account, Savings Certificates or other monies in favour of any person?

Was any money held on a joint account in the name of the deceased and any other persons: if so, supply full details and in particular by whom and in what shares the money was provided?

Did the deceased transfer any property into the joint names of himself and any other persons or buy any other property in their joint names?

If so, supply full details including the date of the transaction if any contribution was made by anyone other than the deceased and how any income, if any, was dealt with and enjoyed.

Are there any animals to be attended to?

Were there any employees, if so who and what were the terms of their employment?

Is mail to be redirected?

Are Statutory Notices to claimants to be inserted? (Care if property vacant.)

Are we to inform beneficiaries of their interests?

Was the deceased a member of BUPA or any similar scheme?

Appendix 2

Standard probate letters

1. Letter to London Gazette

HMSO Publications Centre
Gazette Office
Room 410
Nine Elms Lane
LONDON
SW8 5DR

Dear Sir

DECEASED

We enclose an advertisement under section 27 Trustee Act 1925 for publication in the next edition of the London Gazette.
We enclose our cheque for £39.05 in payment of your charges.
Please let us have a copy of the page containing the advertisement.

Yours faithfully

Encs

Note: Fee at 1/3/1995 £32.00 plus VAT plus £1.45 for a copy of the gazette.

2. Gazette advertisement

DECEASED

UNDER SECTION 27 TRUSTEE ACT 1925

Name of Deceased:
(Surname first)

Address:

Description:

Date of death:

Name and address of persons to whom Notices of Claim are to be given:	Messrs Solicitors

Name of Personal Representatives:

Date on or before which Notice
of Claims must be given

Solicitors for the

Note: The advertisement must be signed personally by a solicitor; *not* in
the firm's name.
Cost: £32.00 plus VAT plus £1.45 for a copy of the gazette.

3. Letter to local newspaper

The Advertising Manager
Local Newspaper

Dear Sir

DECEASED

We enclose a notice under section 27 Trustee Act 1925. Please arrange for this to be published in the Legal and Public Classified section in the next edition of your newspaper.

Please send us a copy of the advertisement, together with a note of your charges.

Yours faithfully

Encs

4. Local newspaper advertisement

IN THE ESTATE OF

(DECEASED)

NOTICE PURSUANT TO
SECTION 27
TRUSTEE ACT 1925

Any person having a claim against or an interest in the Estate of (the deceased) late of   who died on the   day of   199
is required to send particulars thereof to the undernamed Solicitors no later than 2 calendar months from the date of publication of this notice after which date the Executor will proceed to distribute the Estate having regard only to valid claims and interests of which he has had notice, and will not, as respects the property so distributed, be liable to any person of whose claim he shall not then have had notice.

Dated this   day of   199

Messrs

and address

Solicitors for the Executors

5. Letter to bank

The Manager
  Bank Plc

Dear Sir

DECEASED

DATE OF DEATH:

We act for the personal representatives of the above. We understand the deceased held accounts with you and we enclose a copy of the death certificate.

Please will you let us have:

1. A full description of all accounts in which the deceased had any interest. Please advise us of the full name of the joint-holder and the date when the account was opened, in the case of any joint accounts.

2. A note of the date of death balance on all accounts in which the deceased was interested, and of any interest accrued but not yet paid at that date.

3. A statement of what interest, if any, has been paid to the deceased since 5th April 19 .

4. A list of any existing standing orders or direct debit arrangements and your confirmation that these are now cancelled.

5. Up-to-date statements of all the deceased's accounts. Please arrange for us to be sent future statements at monthly intervals until further notice.

6. A full list of any valuables, securities or documents which you hold on behalf of the deceased (or jointly with anyone else). Please indicate if any items are held by way of security.

7. Any counterfoils for interest or dividends which you hold. Please send to us all further counterfoils received, with the statements in which the relevant items appear.

8. Confirmation that you have no outstanding charges.

Please transfer all funds held on current account to a deposit account, pending registration of a grant of representation, and credit any further payments received to this deposit account.

Please provide full details and copies of any relevant documents of any guarantee in which the deceased was involved. Please advise to what extent any guarantees are relied on, and their position generally.

Yours faithfully

Enc

6. Personal representative's authority for transfer of current account to deposit account

The Manager
Bank Plc

Dear Sir

Re: DECEASED
    DATE OF DEATH:

I/we, the undersigned, as personal representative of the above named request you to transfer the balance in the deceased's current account to a deposit account pending receipt of the grant of representation.

Yours faithfully

7. Building society

The Manager
Building Society

Dear Sir

DECEASED
DATE OF DEATH:
ACCOUNT NUMBER:

We act for the personal representatives of the above, and enclose a copy of the death certificate and the passbook of the above account showing a balance of £

Please will you let us have:

(1) A full description of all accounts in which the deceased had any interests, and in the case of any joint accounts, please advise us of the full names of the joint-holder and the date when the accounts were opened.

(2) A note of the date of death balance on all accounts in which the deceased was interested, and of any interest accrued but not yet paid at that date.

(3) A statement of what interest, if any, has been paid to the deceased since 5th April 19

(4) Withdrawal forms to close all accounts, once a grant of representation is obtained. Please advise us if there will be any penalty or restriction on withdrawals.

Yours faithfully

Encs

8. National Savings Bank

Director of Savings
National Savings Bank
GLASGOW
G58 1SB

Dear Sirs

DECEASED
DATE OF DEATH:
ORDINARY OR INVESTMENT ACCOUNT NUMBER:

We act for the personal representatives of the above, and enclose a copy of the death certificate and the passbook of the above account showing a balance of £

Please let us have:

(1) A full description of any accounts in which the deceased had any interest, and in the case of any joint accounts, please advise us of the full names of the joint-holder and the date when the accounts were opened.

(2) A note of the date of death balance on all accounts in which the deceased was interested, and of any interest accrued but not yet paid at that date.

(3) A statement of what interest, if any, has been paid to the deceased since 5th April 19 .

(4) Withdrawal forms to close all accounts once a grant of representation is obtained. Please advise us if there will be any penalty or restriction on withdrawals.

(5) Details of any regular credits to any accounts from any other form of National Savings.

(6) Copies of any nominations affecting any accounts.

Yours faithfully

Encs

9. Savings certificates

Director of Savings
Savings Certificate and SAYE Office
DURHAM
DH99 1NS

Dear Sir

DECEASED
DATE OF DEATH:
HOLDER'S NUMBER:

We act for the personal representatives of the above and enclose a copy of the death certificate.

We also enclose a list of National Savings Certificates held by the deceased [or] We enclose the National Savings Certificates set out on the enclosed list; please advise us of their value at the date of death. Please let us know if there are any other Certificates in the deceased's name, either solely or jointly with another.

When replying, please let us have forms to encash or transfer the certificates and let us know whether or not you require to see a grant of representation.

Yours faithfully

Enc

10. Premium bonds

Director of Savings
Bonds & Stock Office
BLACKPOOL
Lancashire
FY3 9YP

Dear Sir

DECEASED
DATE OF DEATH:
HOLDER'S NUMBER:

We act for the personal representatives of the above and enclose a copy of the death certificate.

We also enclose a list of the Premium Savings Bonds [or] We also enclose the Premium Savings Bonds set out on the enclosed list, please confirm that these are the only Bonds registered in the deceased's name and advise us if there are any unclaimed prizes.

Please let us have a repayment application form, and let us know if you require to see a grant of representation.

Yours faithfully

Enc

11. Bonds and Stock Office – other investments

Director of Savings
Bonds & Stock Office
BLACKPOOL
Lancashire
FY3 9YP

Dear Sir

DECEASED

DATE OF DEATH:

We act for the personal representatives of the above and enclose a copy of the death certificate.

A grant of representation will be registered with you as soon as it is available.

We understand that the deceased held [Income Bonds/Deposit Bonds/ Defence Bonds/Securities/National Development Bonds/British Savings Bonds/Stocks on the National Savings Register] as detailed in the accompanying list. Please confirm that this is the only holding registered in the deceased's name either solely or jointly with another.

Please provide Probate valuations of the holding(s) and provide details of any income accrued, but not yet paid at the date of death. Also, please let us have forms to enable the holdings to be encashed or transferred.

Please let us know if any dividends are mandated direct to a National Savings Bank Savings Account, and if so, the account number.

Yours faithfully

Enc

12. Life insurance policies

Insurance Company

Dear Sirs

DECEASED
DATE OF DEATH:
POLICY NO(S):

We act for the personal representative(s) of the above and enclose a registrar's copy death certificate, and the policy document.

A grant of representation will be registered with you as soon as possible.

Please let us know the amount payable on the policy as at the date of death, including bonuses, and let us have claim forms for completion.

Please confirm that no other policy(ies) became payable in consequence of the deceased's death. Alternatively, please supply details.

Yours faithfully

Enc

Note: If unable to trace the address of an insurance company, or to resolve other queries contact: The Registrar of Friendly Societies, 15 Great Marlborough Street, London W1V 2LL (tel: (0171) 437 9992); The Association of British Insurers, 51 Gresham Street, London EC2V 7HQ (tel. (0171) 600 3333); The Insurance Brokers Registration Council, 15 St Helens Place, London EC3A 6DS (tel: (0171) 588 4387).

In the case of a dispute, contact: The Insurance Ombudsman Bureau, City Gate 1, 135 Park Street, London SE1 9EA.

13. Request for valuation of securities

Stockbrokers

Dear Sirs

DECEASED
DATE OF DEATH:

We act for the personal representatives of the above.

We enclose a list of the deceased's investments. Please prepare a Probate valuation and let us have this as soon as possible, together with a note of your fees.

Yours faithfully

Enc

Note: • give separate lists of holdings in the deceased's sole name, and those in joint names;
  • ask brokers to check holdings where there is any uncertainty;
  • The Unit Trust Association, 65 Kingsway, London WC2B 6TD (tel: (0171) 831 0898) will provide details of funds which have changed names or ownership.

14. Creditors

Creditor

Dear Sirs

DECEASED
DATE OF DEATH:

We act for the personal representatives of the above.

We have been handed your account dated   for £   . We regret no funds are available to settle this at present. Your account will receive further attention as soon as a grant of representation has been obtained and funds are available.

Yours faithfully

15. Personal representative's authority to bank to release deeds and securities

The Manager
  Bank Plc

We confirm that we are the personal representatives of   deceased and we have instructed Messrs   , our solicitors, to obtain a grant of representation on our behalf. We request that you deliver the deeds and securities held by you for the deceased to our solicitors forthwith.

Dated ....

Signed ....

16. Lloyds Bank – deeds and securities

The Manager
  Lloyds Bank Plc

Dear Sirs

Re: DECEASED

We enclose a copy of the last will of the deceased and we confirm that we have been instructed by   ('the personal representatives') to obtain a grant of representation on their behalf.

The personal representatives have requested that the deeds and securities held by you for the deceased should be delivered to this firm.

In consideration of your supplying to us such deeds and securities without the personal representatives having obtained a grant of representation to the estate of the deceased, we undertake to:

(a) hold them in safe custody pending production of the grant and, to return these items to you on demand,

(b) produce the grant to you or a sealed copy thereof as soon as this is available in discharge of this undertaking.

We confirm that we are not aware of any dispute concerning the validity of the will or any event which may delay the obtaining of a grant of probate/letters of administration or the handling of the estate of the deceased.

We enclose the death certificate for registration and return.

Yours faithfully

Enc

17. Midland Bank or National Westminster Bank – deeds and securities

The Manager
[Midland Bank Plc] [National Westminster Bank Plc]

Dear Sirs

Re: DECEASED

We have been instructed by the personal representatives of the deceased.

In consideration of your sending us the securities and other property, which you have been holding on behalf of the above we hereby undertake and confirm:

(a) to hold them in safe custody pending the issue to our clients of a grant of representation to the estate of the deceased and until the issue of such a grant to return these items to you on demand; and

(b) to produce to you the grant or a sealed copy thereof as soon as this is in our possession; and

(c) that we are not aware of any dispute concerning the validity of the will or any event which may delay the obtaining of the grant of probate/letters or administration or the handling of the estate of the deceased.

We enclose the death certificate for registration and return.

Yours faithfully

18. Barclays Bank – securities

The Manager
  Barclays Bank Plc

Dear Sir

Re: DECEASED

In consideration of your sending us the securities and other property which
you have been holding on behalf of the deceased we hereby undertake (a)
to hold them in safe custody pending the issue to our client(s) of a grant
of representation to the estate of the deceased and, until the issue of such
a grant, to return these items to you on demand, and (b) to produce to
you the grant or a sealed copy thereof in discharge of this undertaking as
soon as this is in our possession.

Yours faithfully

19. HM Inspector of Taxes

HM Inspector of Taxes

Dear Sir

                        DECEASED
REFERENCE:
NATIONAL INSURANCE NUMBER:

We act for the personal representatives of the above. We enclose a copy
of the death certificate.

We understand the deceased's tax affairs were dealt with by your office,
under the above reference.

Please let us have the necessary tax returns or claim forms to finalise the
tax position to the date of death, or if you have no further requirement,
please confirm this in writing. It will be helpful if you can provide us with
a copy of the deceased's most recent return.

We confirm we shall register the grant of representation with you as soon
as it is obtained.

Yours faithfully

20. Accountants

Messrs
Accountants

Dear Sirs

DECEASED

We have been instructed by   , the personal representatives of the above, and we enclose a copy of the death certificate.

We understand you dealt with the deceased's tax affairs. The personal representatives would like you to deal with the final tax returns or claims to the date of death. Please confirm that you will deal with this.

Please can you let us have a copy of the deceased's most recent tax return, to assist us in checking the assets of the estate. If it is not clear from the copy return, please let us know the deceased's tax district and reference number.

If further tax is likely to be payable by the estate, or if a repayment is due, can you please provide us with an estimate of this, within the next two weeks, for inclusion in the Inland Revenue Account.

Finally, please let us know what charges (if any) you have outstanding for work done prior to the date of death.

Yours faithfully

Enc

21. Redirection of mail where solicitors are the executors

District Head Postmaster

Dear Sir

DECEASED
LATE OF
DATE OF DEATH:

The executors wish to have all mail addressed to the above redirected to this firm for a period of twelve months beginning immediately. We enclose a cheque for £30.00, payable to 'Royal Mail', being the annual fee for redirection, a completed redirection form, and a certified copy of the death certificate.

We confirm that [one of] the partners in this firm is an/are the executors named in the will of the deceased; that we know no reason why the will should not be admitted to probate, and that we will inform you immediately if we believe that a grant will not be made to the executors.

Yours faithfully

Enc

Note: Fees are:
1 month   £6.00
3 months   £13.00
12 months   £30.00

22. IR Account (and cheque) to Capital Taxes Office

Inland Revenue
Finance Division (Cashier)
Barrington Road
WORTHING
West Sussex
BN12 4XH

(or DX: 90951 WORTHING 3)

Dear Sirs

Re: DECEASED

We enclose the Inland Revenue Account in respect of the above, together with a cheque for £   in respect of inheritance tax now due.
We look forward to receiving the Inland Revenue Account duly receipted.

Yours faithfully

Enc

23. Application for grant of probate

The District Registrar
District Probate Registry

Dear Sir

DECEASED

We enclose:

1. Will of the above (with [ ] codicils).

2. Executors' oath.

3. Inland Revenue Account.

4. Cheque for £[ ] for your fees.

We look forward to receiving the grant with [ ] office copies.

Yours faithfully

Encs

Note: All cheques to HMPG should be endorsed on the reverse with the full names of the deceased in BLOCK CAPITALS.

24. National Savings Bank encashment

The Director of Savings
National Savings Bank
GLASGOW
G58 1SB

Dear Sirs

DECEASED

ORDINARY SAVINGS BANK ACCOUNT NO:
INVESTMENT ACCOUNT NO:

Further to our previous correspondence we enclose:

1. The pass book(s) of the above account(s).

2. A withdrawal form requesting closure of the account.

3. An office copy grant for registration and return.

Please let us have a cheque, together with a note of the closing interest.

Yours faithfully

Encs

25. Savings certificates repayment/new certificates

The Director of Savings
Savings Certificate and SAYE Office
DURHAM
DH99 1NS

Dear Sirs

DECEASED

Further to our previous correspondence, we enclose:

1. Completed repayment form, or

2. completed transfer form.

3. The certificates as set out on (the enclosed list/the reverse of the repayment/transfer form).

4. Office copy grant for registration and return.

Please let us have (a repayment cheque/the new certificates) as soon as possible.

Yours faithfully

Encs

26. Repayment of premium bonds

The Director of Savings
Bonds & Stock Office
BLACKPOOL
Lancashire
FY3 9YP

Dear Sirs

DECEASED

Further to our previous correspondence, we enclose:

1. Office copy grant for registration and return.

2. The bonds as set out in [the enclosed list/list already supplied/ reverse of the repayment form].

3. Form for repayment of the deceased's premium bonds.

We look forward to hearing from you with the repayment cheque as soon as possible.

Yours faithfully

Encs

Note: Premium bonds cannot be transferred but may be kept in the prize draw up to the first anniversary of the death. Thereafter they are no longer eligible to remain in the prize draw, and should be encashed.

27. Building societies

The Manager
 Building Society

Dear Sirs

DECEASED

ACCOUNT NUMBER:

Further to our previous correspondence we enclose:

1. A withdrawal form requesting closure of the account.

2. The pass book(s) of the above account(s).

3. Office copy grant for registration and return.

We look forward to hearing from you with the closing cheque, together with the cancelled pass book, and office copy grant as soon as possible. Please provide a certificate of deduction of tax.

Yours faithfully

Encs

28. Repayment of insurance policies

Insurance Company

Dear Sirs

DECEASED

POLICY NO(S):

Further to our previous correspondence we enclose:

1. The policy document.

2. The completed claim form.

3. Office copy grant for registration and return.

4. The deceased's birth certificate for registration and return.

We look forward to hearing from you as soon as possible with a cheque for the amount due together with interest for the period from the date of death to the date of payment. If tax is deducted from the interest please provide a certificate of deduction of tax.

Yours faithfully

Encs

29. Closure of bank accounts

The Manager
  Bank Plc

Dear Sirs

DECEASED

Further to our previous correspondence, we enclose:

1. Office copy grant for registration and return.

2. The authority of the personal representatives to close all the deceased's accounts and to send the balance together with all other items held by you to this office.

We look forward to hearing from you as soon as possible. When writing with the items requested, please confirm that you then hold nothing either in the sole name of the deceased or jointly with anyone else.

Please let us have closing statements and a certificate of deduction of tax.

Yours faithfully

Encs

30. Personal representative's authority for closure of bank accounts

The Manager
Bank Plc

Dear Sirs

DECEASED

As personal representatives of the above, we hereby authorise and request you:

1. to close all accounts held by you in the name of the deceased or in our names on behalf of the deceased's estate;

2. to send the balance of such accounts by cheque payable to our Solicitors Messrs   (together with closing statements);

3. to send to Messrs   any deeds, documents, securities, counterfoils or other items which you hold or may receive on behalf of the deceased;

4. to accept the receipt of our solicitors as a full discharge to you in every respect.

Please provide a certificate of deduction of tax.

Yours faithfully

31. Company Registrar

The Registrar
  Plc

Dear Sirs

PLC
DECEASED

We act for the personal representatives of the above. We enclose:

1. Office copy grant for registration and return.

2. The certificate(s) set out below for a holding of

3. A transfer of the holding into the names of

4. Dividend instructions.

We look forward to receiving the certificate(s) duly endorsed in favour of the personal representatives as soon as possible.
[or]

We look forward to receiving a new certificate(s) as soon as possible.

Yours faithfully

Encs

32. Paying creditors

Creditor

Dear Sirs

DECEASED

We are now able to let you have the enclosed cheque for £   in payment of your attached account. Please receipt and return this to us.

Yours faithfully

Enc

33. Building Society – adding to existing account

The Manager
  Building Society

Dear Sirs

RE:
ACCOUNT NO:

We enclose the passbook of the above account together with a cheque for
£   .
Please place this cheque to the credit of the account and return the amended passbook to us.

Yours faithfully

Encs

34. Building Society part-withdrawal

The Manager
   Building Society

Dear Sirs

RE:
ACCOUNT NO:

We enclose the passbook of the above account together with a completed withdrawal form for £   .
Please let us have your cheque for this amount together with the amended passbook as soon as possible.

Yours faithfully

Encs

35. Building Society – closure of account

The Manager
   Building Society

Dear Sirs

RE:
ACCOUNT NO:

We enclose the passbook of the above account together with a completed withdrawal form. Please let us have your cheque closing this account as soon as possible.

Yours faithfully

Encs

36. Receipt for estate accounts
THE LATE

I hereby confirm receipt of the final estate accounts which I have read and approve.

Dated this   day of   19

....

(reference   )

37. Receipt of money on account
THE LATE

I acknowledge receipt of a cheque for £   on account of my entitlement under the will/estate of the above.

Dated this   day of   19

....

(reference   )

38. Receipt of final payment

THE LATE

I hereby acknowledge receipt of a cheque for £ being the final sum due to me under the will/estate of the above.

Dated this   day of   19

....

(reference   )

39. Receipt of legacy payment

THE LATE

I acknowledge receipt of a cheque for £ representing the legacy given to me in the will of the above.

Dated this   day of   19

....

(reference   )

40. Receipt of final payment and approval of estate accounts

THE LATE

I acknowledge receipt of a cheque for £   being the final sum due to me under the will/estate of the above and I hereby confirm receipt of the final estate accounts which I have read and approve.

Dated this   day of   19

....

(reference   )

41. Approval of estate accounts and indemnity

THE LATE

I, the undersigned, hereby confirm receipt and approval of the final estate accounts.

I agree to accept the balance of £   shown to be due to me and indemnify the personal representatives against all and any claims against the estate for an amount not exceeding the total received by me.

Yours faithfully

Appendix 3

Specimen schedule of assets and liabilities

Assets	P*	R*	Balance	Accrued interest	Totals
Dwelling-house, 1 King Road, Smithtown (estimate or valuation)	...	...	£......	£......	£......
Personal chattels (estimate or valuation)	...	...	£......	£......	£......
Current account at A Bank plc	...	...	£......	£......	£......
Deposit account at A Bank plc	...	...	£......	£......	£......
Share account at B Building Society	...	...	£......	£......	£......
Investment account at B Building Society	...	...	£......	£......	£......
Term account at C Building Society	...	...	£......	£......	£......
Stocks and shares per list attached	...	...	£......	£......	£......
National Savings Certificates	...	...	£......	£......	£......
Premium Savings Bonds	...	...	£......	£......	£......
Life insurance policy – D Insurance Co	...	...	£......	£......	£......
Life insurance policy – E Insurance Co	...	...	£......	£......	£......
Life insurance policy – F Insurance Co	...	...	£......	£......	£......
Salary/holiday pay – G Employers Ltd	...	...	£......	£......	£......
Pension arrears – G Employers Ltd	...	...	£......	£......	£......
DSS retirement pension arrears	...	...	£......	£......	£......
TOTAL (A)					£......(A)

Liabilities					
Funeral account	...	...	£......	£......	£......
Mortgage	...	...	£......	£......	£......
Hire purchase – A Company	...	...	£......	£......	£......
Personal loan – B Company	...	...	£......	£......	£......
Gas bill	...	...	£......	£......	£......
Electricity bill	...	...	£......	£......	£......
Telephone bill	...	...	£......	£......	£......
Local authority and water charges	...	...	£......	£......	£......
Credit card – A Bank plc	...	...	£......	£......	£......
TOTAL (B)					£......(B)
NET ESTATE (C)					£......(C)

*Tick columns P & R as the death certificate is produced and returned

Appendix 4

Specimen estate accounts

MRS ANNE JOYCE BLOGGS DECEASED

ESTATE ACCOUNTS

Date of Death: 1st August 1990

In her Will dated 5th July 1988 the testatrix appointed her brother John Smith sole executor. She gave a legacy of £5,000.00 to Mrs Hilda Jones, and the residue to her brother absolutely.

MRS ANNE JOYCE BLOGGS DECEASED

ESTATE ACCOUNTS

SUMMARY

Net Capital of Estate			252,968.99
Net Income of Estate			1,246.95
			254,215.94
Legacy to Mrs H Jones		5,000.00	
Balance to Mr Smith:			
Dwelling-house	100,000.00		
Personal chattels	12,850.00		
Shares	12,297.61		
Cash balance	124,068.33	249,215.94	
		254,215.94	254,215.94

MRS ANNE JOYCE BLOGGS DECEASED

ESTATE ACCOUNTS

Assets at (date of death)

Dwelling-house – 18 The Crescent		100,000.00
Stocks & Shares per Schedule		149,359.99
dividends & interest due		320.00
A Bank Current Account		854.22
A Bank Deposit Account	7,049.00	
accrued interest	67.21	7,116.21
B Bank Current Account		754.10
B Bank Deposit Account	15,795.42	
accrued interest	459.20	16,254.62
A Building Society	29,500.00	
accrued interest	750.20	30,250.20
B Building Society	14,795.00	
accrued interest	620.00	15,415.00
National Savings Certificates	7,850.00	
accrued interest	420.20	8,270.20
Premium Bonds		950.00
Personal chattels – valuation		12,850.00
		342,394.54

Liabilities at (date of death)

A Funeral Director	868.00	
British Gas	37.20	
Electricity	42.10	
British Telecom	64.84	
A Accountant – fees outstanding	600.00	1,612.14
Net Estate carried forward		340,782.40

MRS ANNE JOYCE BLOGGS DECEASED

ESTATE ACCOUNTS

Brought forward		340,782.40
Premium bond prize		50.00
Net gain on shares sold		1,572.62
		342,405.02
LESS Administration expenses:		
A Estate Agent – valuation of dwelling house	1,500.00	
A Accountant – final fees	780.00	
A Stockbroker – valuation of shares	87.00	
Inland Revenue – Income tax	72.00	
Commissioner's fees	7.50	
Probate Registry fees inc. 23 copies	400.00	
Inheritance Tax	85,112.96	
London Gazette notice for claims	34.07	
A Newspaper – notice for claims	62.50	
A Solicitor & Co – costs for acting in the administration	1,200.00	
VAT thereon	180.00	89,436.03
To Summary		252,968.99

MRS ANNE JOYCE BLOGGS DECEASED

INCOME ACCOUNT

TAX YEAR 1990/91

10,000	Treasury 11% stock		385.00
2,000	Shoes Co 25p 'o' shares		118.00
2,600	KGG £1 'o' shares		65.00
A Bank	Closing interest		372.00
B Bank	Closing interest		120.60
A Building Society	Closing interest		16.20
B Building Society	Closing interest		95.15
Gross income from A Solicitors		100.00	
Less Income Tax 25% × 100.00		25.00	75.00
Carried to Summary			1,246.95

Schedule of Stocks and Shares

No.	Item	Probate Value	Sales Net receipt	Transferred to	Gain	Loss
10,000	11% Treasury Stock 1991 + 55 days interest	10,125.00 187.70	9,860.20			452.50
10,000	11.5% Treasury Stock 1989 + 42 days interest	10,250.00 132.30		Mr Smith 10,382.30		
7,549	Barford plc Ordinary 25p Shares	45,067.53	45,072.00		4.47	
2,000	Shoes Co plc Ordinary 25p Shares	3,546.00	3,217.10			328.90
218,000	European Cars Group plc Ordinary 25p Shares	23,850.00	24,790.60		940.60	
2,600	KGG plc Ordinary £1.00 Shares	5,954.00	5,420.10			533.90
11,700	A Bank Ltd £1.00 Shares	47,802.15	49,800.00		1,997.85	
2,400	Kings House plc Ordinary 5p Shares	1,212.00		Mr Smith 1,212.00		
1,000	Torse Ltd Ordinary 10p Shares	850.00	795.00			55.00
825	Tragon House plc 9% Unsecured Loan Stock 1990/2005	703.31		Mr Smith 703.31		
		149,679.99	138,955.00	12,297.61	2,942.92	1,370.30

239

Appendix 5

Forms

Contents

1. Oath for executor(s)

Extracted by
of   Solicitors
DX:

IN THE HIGH COURT OF JUSTICE
Family Division
[Principal] [....District] Probate Registry
In the estate of...Deceased
[I] [We] (1)
Make oath and say (2) as follows:

1. [I] [We] believe the paper writing now produced to and marked (3) by [me] [us] to contain the true and original last will and testament(4)

2. of (5)

   of   deceased

   formerly of (6)

   who died on the   day of   19   domiciled in England and Wales (7)

   aged (8)

3. To the best of [my] [our] knowledge information and belief there was [no] land vested in the deceased which was settled previously to the death [and not by the will (4)   ] of the deceased and which remained settled land notwithstanding such death.(9)

   '*When a firm of solicitors is named as executors insert*: 'And we further make oath and say that we are two; three; four of the partners at the date (normally 'at the date of the will' unless the will states otherwise) (of death/of the will) of the said deceased in the firm of (firm's name) of (address) (which has succeeded to the practice of the firm known as).']

4. And I/we further make oath and say (2) that notice of this application has been given to the executor(s) to whom power is to be reserved (save) (14)

5. [I am] [We are] (10)

   named in the said will.

6. [I] [We] will

   (a) collect, get in and administer according to the law the real and personal estate (11)   of the above-named deceased;

   (b) when required to do so by the court exhibit in the court a full inventory of the said estate of the deceased and render an account thereof to the court; and

   (c) when required to do so by the High Court, deliver up to that court the grant of probate.

7. To the best of [my] [our] knowledge information and belief the gross

value of the estate (11)(12)   passing under the grant
[does not exceed] [amounts to] (13) £   and that the net value of
the estate (11)(12) [does not exceed] [amounts to] (13) £   [and that
this is not a case in which an Inland Revenue Account is required
to be delivered].

Power reserved to (full names) the other executors.

[*When a firm is appointed*: Power reserved to the remaining partners at the date of death in the firm of (firm's name) the other executors.](14)

Sworn by the above-named deponent[s]

at

in the County of

This   day of   19

Before me,   A commissioner for oaths/solicitor

Notes

(1)   Insert full name(s), address(es) and occupation(s) or description(s) of executor(s)
        applying.

(2)   If affirmation made, substitute 'do solemnly and sincerely affirm'.

(3)   Each testamentary document must be signed by each deponent and the person admin-
        istering the oath.

(4)   Insert 'and codicil[s]' and number thereof.

(5)   Insert full name, address and occupation or description of deceased.

(6)   Insert any previous address(es).

(7)   If deceased died domiciled outside England and Wales, delete 'England and Wales'
        and insert the state, province or country within whose jurisdiction the deceased died
        domiciled.

(8)   Insert the deceased's age in years. If the exact age is not known, state the approxi-
        mate age, e.g. 'over 65'.

(9)   Where land remains settled and these applicants are also entitled to the grant in
        respect of such land the grant will issue 'including settled land'. Where these appli-
        cants are not so entitled the grant will issue 'save and except settled land'; a sepa-
        rate grant will be necessary to administer such land.

(10)   Insert capacity of executor(s).

(11)   Insert 'save and except settled land' if appropriate.

(12)   Where the deceased died domiciled outside England and Wales, insert after 'estate'
        'in England and Wales'.

(13)   Where an Inland Revenue Account is filed the actual gross and net values of the
        estate as taken from the Inland Revenue Account must be inserted; where an account
        is not required, insert the gross and net values the estate does not exceed, e.g. gross
        value £145,000 where the death occurred on or after 6 April 1995 (see page 88).
        The net value should be stated as 'does not exceed £10,000, £25,000, £40,000,
        £70,000, or £100,000' as appropriate (see scale of Probate Court Fees).

(14)   Notice must be served on all executors to whom power is to be reserved unless pre-
        viously dispensed with by a district judge or a registrar under rule 27(3) (see Form
        31 on page 289).
        Where one of the partners in a firm who have been appointed by reference to their
        being partners (and not by their names) has applied for probate, notice need not be
        given to the non-acting partners.

2. Double probate – not more than four executors

IN THE HIGH COURT OF JUSTICE
Family Division
[Principal] [....District] Probate Registry
I, AB of   make oath and say that I believe the paper writing
now produced to and marked by me to contain the true and original [or
an official copy of the true and original] last will and testament of CD
          of   deceased, who died on the   aged   years,
domiciled in England and Wales [add statement as to settled land]; that
on the   day of   19   probate of the said will was
granted at the   Probate Registry to EF one of the executors named
in the said will, power being reserved to (name(s)) the other executor; that
I am the other executor named in the said will; and that I will

(i)   collect, get in and administer according to law the real and personal estate of the said deceased;

(ii) when required to do so by the court, exhibit in the court a full inventory of the said estate and render an account thereof to the court; and

(iii) when required to do so by the High Court, deliver up to that court the grant of double probate:

To the best of my [our] knowledge, information and belief the gross estate
passing under the grant [does not exceed/amounts to] £   and that
the net estate [does not exceed/amounts to/] £   [and that this is
not a case in which an Inland Revenue Account is required to be
delivered].

Sworn by the
above-named deponent(s)
at
this   day of   19
Before me,

a commissioner for oaths/solicitor.

3. Double probate – more than four executors

IN THE HIGH COURT OF JUSTICE
Family Division
[Principal] [....District] Probate Registry
I, AB of   make oath and say that I believe the paper writing now produced to and marked by me to contain the true and original [or an official copy of the true and original, as the case may be] last will and testament of CD of   formerly of   deceased, who died on the   day of   19   aged   years, domiciled in England and Wales [add statement as to settled land]; that on the   day of   19   probate of the said will was granted at the   Probate Registry to   and   , four of the executors named therein, power being reserved to (name(s)) the other executor(s) that the said   died on the   day of   19   ; and that I am the other executor (or one of the other executors) named in the said will, and will

(i)   collect, get in and administer according to law the real and personal estate of the said deceased;

(ii)   when required to do so by the court, exhibit in the court a full inventory of the said estate and render an account thereof to the court; and

(iii)   when required to do so by the High Court, deliver up to that court the grant of double probate.

To the best of my [our] knowledge, information and belief the gross estate passing under the grant [does not exceed/amounts to] £

and that the net estate [does not exceed/amounts to] £

[and that this is not a case in which an Inland Revenue Account is required to be delivered].

Sworn by the
above-named deponent(s)
at
this   day of   19
Before me,

a commissioner for oaths/solicitor.

4. Oath for executors – a trust corporation

IN THE HIGH COURT OF JUSTICE
Family Division
The Principal [.....................................District] Probate Registry
In the estate of (deceased's full name and alias) Deceased
I, (full names) (description) of (full address) in the employ of (full title of trust corporation) whose registered office is situated at (full address) make oath and say as follows:

1. That I believe the paper writing(s) now produced to and marked by me to contain the true and original last will and testament (with codicil(s)) of (full names of deceased) of (full address (the last permanent address) of the deceased) formerly of (address in the will) deceased who died on the   day of   199 , domiciled in England and Wales.

2. That in his said will (or codicil) the deceased appointed (name of trust corporation) to be his executor(s).

3. That the said (name of trust corporation) is a trust corporation as defined by rule 36 Non-Contentious Probate Rules 1987 and has power under its constitution to accept the grant now applied for and that the said (name of trust corporation) by a resolution dated the   day of   199 , (a certified copy of which is annexed hereto) appointed me for the purpose of applying for probate of the said will on its behalf

    or

    a certified copy of which has been lodged with the Senior Registrar and is still in force which authorises persons holding my position to apply for grants of probate on its behalf.

4. That the said (name of trust corporation) is the sole executor named in the said will (with   codicil(s)).

5. That to the best of my knowledge, information and belief there was no land vested in the said deceased immediately before his death which was settled previously to his death (and not by the will and codicil(s)) and which remained settled land notwithstanding his death.

6. That the said (name of trust corporation) will:

    (a) collect, get in and administer according to law the real and personal estate of the said deceased;

    (b) when required to do so by the court, exhibit in the court a full inventory of the said estate and render an account thereof to the court; and

    (c) when required to do so by the High Court, deliver up to that court the grant of probate.

7. That to the best of my knowledge, information and belief the gross estate passing under the grant (does not exceed) (amounts to) £   and the net estate (does not exceed) (amounts to) £   and

that this is not a case in which an Inland Revenue account is required to be delivered.

Sworn by the above named

(Full names)

this

day of

Before me,

a solicitor/a commissioner for oaths

5. Oath for administrators (with will annexed)

Extracted by

of   Solicitors

DX:

IN THE HIGH COURT OF JUSTICE
Family Division
[Principal] [....District] Probate Registry
In the estate of ....Deceased
[I] [We] (1)
make oath and say (2) as follows:

1. [I] [We] believe the paper writing now produced to and marked (3) by [me] [us] to contain the true and original last will and testament (4).

2. of (5)

   of   deceased

   formerly of (6)

   who died on the   day of   19   domiciled in England and Wales (7) aged (8).

3. No minority or life interest arises in the estate (9).

4. To the best of [my] [our] knowledge information and belief there was [no] land vested in the deceased which was settled previously to the death [and not by the will (10)   ] of the deceased and which remained settled land notwithstanding such death(11).

5. (12)

6. [I am] [We are] (13)

7. [I] [We] will

   (a) collect, get in and administer according to the law the real and personal estate(14)   of the above-named deceased;

   (b) when required to do so by the court exhibit in the court a full inventory of the said estate of the deceased and render an account thereof to the court; and

   (c) when required to do so by the High Court, deliver up to that court the grant of letters of administration (with will annexed).

8. To the best of [my] [our] knowledge information and belief the gross value of the estate(14)(15)   passing under the grant [does not exceed] [amounts to] (16) £   and that the net value of the estate (14)(15) [does not exceed] [amounts to] (16) £   [and that this is not a case in which an Inland Revenue Account is required to be delivered].

   Sworn etc.

Notes

(1) Insert full name(s), address(es) and occupation(s) or description(s) of administrator(s) applying.

(2)   If affirmation made, substitute 'do solemnly and sincerely affirm'.

(3)   Each testamentary document must be signed by each deponent and the person administering the oath.

(4)   Insert 'and codicil[s]' and number thereof.

(5)   Insert full name, address and occupation or description of deceased.

(6)   Insert any previous address(es).

(7)   If deceased died domiciled outside England and Wales, delete 'England and Wales' and insert the state, province or country within whose jurisdiction the deceased died domiciled.

(8)   Insert the deceased's age in years. If the exact age is not known, state the approximate age, e.g. 'over 65'.

(9)   If a life or minority interest does arise, delete the word 'no' and insert 'A'; there must be at least two applicants for the grant.

(10)   Insert 'and codicil[s]' if any.

(11)   Where land remains settled and these applicants are also entitled to the grant in respect of such land the grant will issue 'including settled land'. Where these applicants are not so entitled the grant will issue 'save and except settled land'; a separate grant will be necessary to administer such land.

(12)   Insert the names and capacity to take the grant of persons with a prior right to the grant and the manner in which they have been cleared off.

(13)   Insert capacity of administrator(s) (see page 32).

(14)   Insert 'save and except settled land' if appropriate.

(15)   Where the deceased died domiciled outside England and Wales, insert after 'estate' 'in England and Wales'.

(16)   Where an Inland Revenue Account is required the actual gross and net values of the estate must be inserted; where an account is not required, insert the gross and net values the estate does not exceed, e.g. gross value £145,000 where the death occurred on or after 6 April 1995 (see page 88). The net value should be stated as 'does not exceed £10,000, £25,000, £40,000, £70,000 or £100,000' as appropriate (see scale of Probate Court Fees).

6. Oath for administrator (with will annexed) to attorney of executor

Extracted by
of   Solicitors
DX:

Family Division
[Principal] [....District] Probate Registry
In the estate of..Deceased
[I] [We] (1)
of
and
of
respectively make oath and say as follows:

1. That (2)

    of

    deceased, died on the   day of   19   domiciled in
    England and Wales (3) aged   years having duly made and exe-
    cuted [his] [her] last will and testament [and codicil[s] (4)] wherein
    [he] [she] appointed (5)   the [sole] executor.

2. That [no] [a] life or [but] [a] minority interest arises in the estate
   of the deceased (6).

3. That there was no land vested in the deceased which was settled
   previously to [his] [her] death and not by [his] [her] will and which
   remained settled land notwithstanding [his] [her] death.

4. That [I am] [we are] the lawful attorney[s] of the said (5).

5. That [I] [we] believe the paper writing now produced to and marked
   by [me] [us] to contain the true and original last will and testament
   [and   codicil[s] (4)] of the said deceased.

6. That [I] [we] will:

    (a) collect, get in and administer according to law the real and per-
        sonal estate of the said deceased for the use and benefit of (5)
        until further representation be granted;

    (b) when required to do so by the court, exhibit in the court a full
        inventory of the said estate and render an account thereof to the
        court; and

    (c) when required to do so by the High Court, deliver up to that
        court the grant of letters of administration.

7. That to the best of [my] [our] knowledge, information and belief the
   gross estate passing under the grant [does not exceed] [amounts to]
   £   and the net estate [does not exceed] [amounts to]
   £   [and that this is not a case in which an Inland Revenue
   Account is required to be delivered] (7).

Sworn etc.

Notes

(1)   Insert full name(s) and address(es) of the attorneys.

(2)   Insert full name and last permanent address of the deceased.

(3)   If the deceased did not die domiciled in England and Wales insert the state, province and country of domicile.

(4)   Insert number of codicil(s) (if any).

(5)   Insert full name of executor.

(6)   If a life or minority interest arises at least two applicants to the grant are required, but a district judge or a registrar has power to dispose with this requirement in exceptional circumstances (his prior agreement should be obtained before the oath is sworn).

(7)   Where an Inland Revenue Account is required the actual gross and net values of the estate must be inserted; where an account is not required, insert the gross and net values the estate does not exceed, e.g. gross value £145,000 where the death occurred on or after 6 April 1995 (see page 88). The net value should be stated as 'does not exceed £10,000, £25,000, £40,000, £70,000 or £100,000' as appropriate (see scale of Probate Court Fees).

7. Oath for administrator(s) (with will annexed) *de bonis non*

Extracted by

of   Solicitors

DX:

IN THE HIGH COURT OF JUSTICE

Family Division

[Principal] [....District] Probate Registry

In the estate of...Deceased

[I] [We] (1)

of

and

of

respectively make oath and say as follows:

1. That (2)

    of

    deceased, died on the   day of   19   aged   .
    domiciled in England and Wales having made and duly executed
    [his] [her] last will and testament [and (3) codicil[s]] wherein [he]
    [she] named (4)   executor(s) and
    residuary legatee and devisee.

2. That on the   day of   19   [probate of the said
    will] [letters of administration (with will annexed)] [and
    codicils] (6) [was] [were] granted out of the [Principal]
    [District Probate] Registry to (7).

3. That the said (8)   (survived his [co-executor]) [co-adminis-
    trator] but died on the   day of   19   intestate (9)
    leaving part of the estate of the deceased unadministered.

4. That no minority or life interest arises in the estate of the deceased.

5. That there was no land vested in the deceased settled previously to
    [his] [her] death which remained settled land notwithstanding [his]
    [her] death.

6. That [I] [we] believe the paper writing now produced to and marked
    by [me] [us] to contain [an official copy of] the true and original
    last will and testament of the said deceased.

7. That [I am] [we are] the administrators [with will annexed] of the
    estate of (10)   deceased, under a grant of adminis-
    tration made to [me] [us] at the   Registry on the
        day of   19   .

8. That [I] [we] will:

    (a) collect, get in and administer according to law the unadminis-
    tered real and personal estate of the said deceased;

    (b) when required to do so by the court, exhibit in the court a full
    inventory of the said estate and render an account thereof to the

court; and

(c) when required to do so by the High Court, deliver up to that court the letters of administration.

9. That to the best of [my] [our] knowledge, information and belief the gross value of the unadministered estate amounts to £ .

Sworn etc.

Notes

(1)   Insert full name(s) and address(es) of the applicant(s).

(2)   Insert full name and last permanent address of the deceased.

(3)   Insert number of codicil(s) (if any).

(4)   Insert name(s) of executor(s).

(6)   Delete as appropriate.

(7)   Insert name of executors or residuary legatees and devisees who proved the will.

(8)   Insert name of the last surviving grantee.

(9)   If the person named above (in (7)) did *not* die intestate state how the chain of executorship (if there was a chain) was broken.

(10) Name of the residuary beneficiary through whom title is derived.

Note: An Inland Revenue Account is required in Form A5, this being an application for a second or subsequent grant, unless the first grant issued as an excepted case and the value of the unadministered estate does not now exceed the threshold appropriate to the case.

8. Oath for administrator(s) (with will annexed): To personal representative of a residuary beneficiary who died before taking out a grant

Extracted by
of   Solicitors
DX:

IN THE HIGH COURT OF JUSTICE
Family Division
[Principal] [....District] Probate Registry
In the estate of...Deceased
[I] [We] (1)
make oath and say (2) as follows:

1. [I] [We] believe the paper writing now produced to and marked (3) by [me] [us] to contain the true and original last will and testament (4)

2. of (5)

    of   deceased

    formerly of (6)

    who died on the   day of   19   domiciled in England and Wales (7) aged (8).

3. No minority or life interest arises in the estate (9).

4. To the best of [my] [our] knowledge, information and belief there was [no] land vested in the deceased which was settled previously to the death [and not by the will (10)   ] of the deceased and which remained settled land notwithstanding such death. (11)

5. Mrs A ...., the sole executrix and residuary legatee and devisee named in the said will survived the said deceased but has since died without having taken upon herself probate of the said will.

6. We are the executors of the will of the said Mrs A .... deceased, probate having been granted to us at the   District Probate Registry on the   day of   19   .

7. [I] [We] will
    (a) collect, get in and administer according to the law the real and personal estate(14)   of the above-named deceased;
    (b) when required to do so by the court exhibit in the court a full inventory of the said estate of the deceased and render an account thereof to the court; and
    (c) when required to do so by the High Court, deliver up to that court the grant of letters of administration (with will annexed).

8. To the best of [my] [our] knowledge information and belief the gross value of the estate(14)(15)   passing under the grant [does not exceed] [amounts to] (16) £   and that the net value of the estate (14)(15)

255

[does not exceed] [amounts to] (13) £   [and that this is not a case in which an Inland Revenue Account is required to be delivered].

Sworn etc.

Notes

(1)   Insert full name(s), address(es) and occupation(s) or description(s) of administrator(s) applying.

(2)   If affirmation made, substitute 'do solemnly and sincerely affirm'.

(3)   Each testamentary document must be signed by each deponent and the person administering the oath.

(4)   Insert 'and codicil[s]' and number thereof.

(5)   Insert full name, address and occupation or description of deceased.

(6)   Insert any previous address(es).

(7)   If deceased died domiciled outside England and Wales, delete 'England and Wales' and insert the state, province or country within whose jurisdiction the deceased died domiciled.

(8)   Insert the deceased's age in years. If the exact age is not known, state the approximate age, e.g. 'over 65'.

(9)   If a life or minority interest does arise, delete the word 'no' and insert 'A'; there must be at least two applicants for the grant.

(10)   Insert 'and codicil[s]' if any.

(11)   Where land remains settled and these applicants are also entitled to the grant in respect of such land the grant will issue 'including settled land'. Where these applicants are not so entitled the grant will issue 'save and except settled land'; a separate grant will be necessary to administer such land.

(12)   Insert the names and capacity to take the grant of persons with a prior right to the grant and the manner in which they have been cleared off.

(13)   Insert capacity of administrator(s) (see page 32).

(14)   Insert 'save and except settled land' if appropriate.

(15)   Where the deceased died domiciled outside England and Wales, insert after 'estate' 'in England and Wales'.

(16)   Where an Inland Revenue Account is required the actual gross and net values of the estate must be inserted; where an account is not required, insert the gross and net values the estate does not exceed, e.g. gross value £145,000 where the death occurred on or after 6 April 1995 (see page 88). The net value should be stated as 'does not exceed £10,000, £25,000, £40,000, £70,000 or £100,000' as appropriate (see scale of Probate Court Fees).

9. Oath for administrator(s) (with will annexed): Bank Trust Company renounced; application by the residuary legatee and devisee

Extracted by
of   Solicitors
DX:

IN THE HIGH COURT OF JUSTICE
Family Division
[Principal] [....District] Probate Registry
In the estate of...Deceased
[I] [We] (1)
make oath and say (2) as follows:

1. [I] [We] believe the paper writing now produced to and marked (3) by [me] [us] to contain the true and original last will and testament (4)

2. of (5)
   of   deceased
   formerly of (6)
   who died on the   day of   19   domiciled in England and Wales (7) aged (8)

3. No minority or life interest arises in the estate (9).

4. To the best of [my] [our] knowledge, information and belief there was [no] land vested in the deceased which was settled previously to the death [and not by the will (10)   ] of the deceased and which remained settled land notwithstanding such death.(11)

5. That a bank trust company the sole executor [and residuary legatee and devisee in trust] named in the said will has renounced probate thereof [and letters of administration (with the will annexed) of the estate of the said deceased].

6. I am the residuary legatee (and devisee) named in the said will.

7. [I] [We] will
   (a) collect, get in and administer according to the law the real and personal estate(12)   of the above-named deceased;
   (b) when required to do so by the court exhibit in the court a full inventory of the said estate of the deceased and render an account thereof to the court; and
   (c) when required to do so by the High Court, deliver up to that court the grant of letters of administration (with Will annexed).

8. To the best of [my] [our] knowledge, information and belief the gross value of the estate (12)(13)   passing under the grant [does not exceed][[amounts to] (14) £   and that the net value of the estate (12)(13)
   [does not exceed] [amounts to] (14) £   [and that this is not

a case in which an Inland Revenue Account is required to be delivered].

Sworn etc.

Notes

(1)   Insert full name(s), address(es) and occupation(s) or description(s) of administrator(s) applying.

(2)   If affirmation made, substitute 'do solemnly and sincerely affirm'.

(3)   Each testamentary document must be signed by each deponent and the person administering the oath.

(4)   Insert 'and codicil[s]' and number thereof.

(5)   Insert full name, address and occupation or description of deceased.

(6)   Insert any previous address(es).

(7)   If deceased died domiciled outside England and Wales, delete 'England and Wales' and insert the state, province or country within whose jurisdiction the deceased died domiciled.

(8)   Insert the deceased's age in years. If the exact age is not known, state the approximate age, e.g. 'over 65'.

(9)   If a life or minority interest does arise, delete the word 'no' and insert 'A'; there must be at least two applicants for the grant.

(10)   Insert 'and codicil[s]' if any.

(11)   Where land remains settled and these applicants are also entitled to the grant in respect of such land the grant will issue 'including settled land'. Where these applicants are not so entitled the grant will issue 'save and except settled land'; a separate grant will be necessary to administer such land.

(12)   Insert 'save and except settled land' if appropriate.

(13)   Where the deceased died domiciled outside England and Wales, insert after 'estate' 'in England and Wales'.

(14)   Where an Inland Revenue Account is required the actual gross and net values of the estate must be inserted; where an account is not required, insert the gross and net values the estate does not exceed, e.g. gross value £145,000 where the death occurred on or after 6 April 1995 (see page 88). The net value should be stated as 'does not exceed £10,000, £25,000, £40,000, £70,000 or £100,000' as appropriate (see scale of Probate Court Fees).

10. Oath for administrators (with the will) to the residuary legatee and devisee

IN THE HIGH COURT OF JUSTICE
Family Division
[Principal] [....District] Probate Registry
In the estate of (deceased's names) Deceased

I, (names and address of administrator) make oath and say that I believe the paper writing now produced to and marked by me to contain the true and original last will and testament of (deceased's names and address) deceased who died on the   day of   19 , aged   years, domiciled in England and Wales.

That the sole executor (name) named in the said will died in the said deceased's lifetime (or has renounced Probate thereof).

That no life or minority interest arises in the estate of the said deceased.

That there was no land vested in the said deceased previously to his death which remained settled land notwithstanding his death.

That I am the residuary legatee and devisee named in the said will.

That I will:

   (i)   collect, get in and administer according to law the real and personal estate of the said deceased;

  (ii)   when required to do so by the court, exhibit in the court a full inventory of the said estate and render an account thereof to the court; and

 (iii)   when required to do so by the High Court, deliver up to that court the grant of letters of administration.

To the best of my knowledge, information and belief the gross estate passing under the grant (does not exceed) (amounts to) £   and that the net estate (does not exceed) (amounts to) £   (and that this is not a case in which an Inland Revenue Account is required to be delivered).

Sworn by the above named deponent

at

this   day of   19

Before me,

a commissioner for oaths/a solicitor.

11. Oath for administrator(s)

Extracted by
of   Solicitors
DX:

IN THE HIGH COURT OF JUSTICE
Family Division
[Principal] [....District] Probate Registry
In the estate of...Deceased
[I] [We](1)
make oath and say (2) as follows:

1. (3)

   of   deceased
   died on the   day of   19   domiciled in England
   and Wales (4)
   aged (5)   intestate (6)

   or any other person entitled in priority to share in the estate by
   virtue of any enactment (7).

2. No minority or life interest arises in the estate (8).

3. To the best of [my] [our] knowledge information and belief there
   was [no] land vested in the deceased which was settled previously
   to the death of the deceased and which remained settled land
   notwithstanding such death (9).

4. [I am] [We are] (10) 'the only person entitled to the estate' or '(one)
   (two) (or as the case may be) of the persons entitled to share in the
   estate'.

5. [I] [We] will

   (a) collect, get in and administer according to the law the real and
       personal estate (11)   of the above-named deceased;
       (12)

   (b) when required to do so by the court exhibit in the court a full
       inventory of the said estate of the deceased and render an
       account thereof to the court; and

   (c) when required to do so by the High Court, deliver up to that
       court the grant of letters of administration.

6. To the best of [my] [our] knowledge information and belief the gross
   value of the estate (13)(14)   passing under the grant
   [does not exceed] [amounts to] £   and that the net value of
   the estate (13)(14)   [does not exceed] [amounts
   to] (15) £   [and that this is not a case in which an Inland
   Revenue Account is required to be delivered].

   Sworn etc.

Notes

(1)   Insert full name(s), address(es) and occupation(s) or description(s) of administrator(s)
      applying.

(2)   If affirmation made, substitute 'do solemnly and sincerely affirm'.

(3)   Insert full name, address and occupation or description of deceased.

(4)   If deceased died domiciled outside England and Wales, delete 'England and Wales' and insert the state, province or country within whose jurisdiction the deceased died domiciled.

(5)   Insert the deceased's age in years. If the exact age is not known, state the approximate age, e.g. 'over 65'.

(6)   Clear any prior rights to the grant by rotation, e.g. by adding 'a widow without issue', 'a bachelor' etc. (see page 50).

(7)   If the deceased died prior to 1 January 1970 or application is made by a spouse and/or a child, delete the words from 'or' to 'enactment'.

(8)   If a life or minority interest does arise, delete the word 'no' and insert 'A'; there must usually be at least two applicants for the grant, but a district judge or registrar has power to dispense with this requirement in exceptional circumstances (his prior agreement should be obtained before the oath is sworn).

(9)   Where land remains settled and these applicants are also entitled to the grant in respect of such land the grant will issue 'including settled land'. Where these applicants are not so entitled the grant will issue 'save and except settled land'; a separate grant will be necessary to administer such land.

(10)   Insert capacity of administrator(s) (see page 32).

(11)   Insert 'save and except settled land' if appropriate.

(12)   If the person(s) beneficially entitled to the estate are minors, or the grant is applied for through an attorney, add 'for the use and benefit of ....'.

(13)   Where the deceased died domiciled outside England and Wales, insert after 'estate' 'in England and Wales'.

(14)   Where an Inland Revenue Account is required the actual gross and net values of the estate must be inserted; where an account is not required, insert the gross and net values the estate does not exceed, e.g. gross value £145,000 where the death occurred on or after 6 April 1995. The net value should be stated as 'does not exceed £10,000, £25,000, £40,000, £70,000 or £100,000' as appropriate (see scale of Probate Court Fees).

12. Oath for attorney of administrator

Extracted by

of   Solicitors

DX:

Family Division

[Principal] [....District] Probate Registry

In the estate of..Deceased

[I] [We] (1)

of

and

of

respectively make oath and say as follows:

1. That (2)

   of

   died on   day of   19   aged   domiciled in
   England and Wales

   intestate (3)

   [or any other person entitled in priority to share in the estate of the
   said deceased by virtue of any enactment] (4) leaving (5)

   [his] [her] (6)

   and only person[s] [now] entitled to [his] [her] estate.

2. That [no] [a] minority [or] [but a] life interest arises under the intestacy (7).

3. That there was no land vested in the deceased which was settled
   previously to [his] [her] death and which remained settled land
   notwithstanding [his] [her] death.

4. That [I am] [we are] the lawful attorney[s] of the said(5)

5. That [I] [we] will:

   (a) collect, get in and administer according to law the real and personal estate of the said deceased for the use and benefit of the
   said (5)

   and until further representation be granted;

   (b) when required to do so by the court, exhibit in the court a full
   inventory of the said estate and render an account thereof to the
   court; and

   (c) when required to do so by the High Court, deliver up to that
   court the letters of administration.

6. To the best of [my] [our] knowledge, information and belief the
   gross estate passing under the grant [does not exceed] [amounts to]
   £   and the net estate [does not exceed] [amounts to]
   £   [and that this is not a case in which an Inland Revenue
   Account is required to be delivered] (8).

Sworn etc.

262

Notes

(1)   Insert full name(s) and address(es) of applicant(s).

(2)   Insert full name of deceased and last permanent address.

(3)   Insert 'a widow without issue'; 'a single man without parent'; or as the case may be.

(4)   Delete as appropriate.

(5)   Insert name(s) of person(s) entitled to the estate.

(6)   Insert relationship to the deceased and any other necessary clearing of persons entitled in priority.

(7)   Where a minority or life interest arises the application should be made by two applicants.

(8)   Where an Inland Revenue Account is required the actual gross and net values of the estate must be inserted; where an account is not required, insert the gross and net values the estate does not exceed, e.g. gross value £145,000 where the death occurred on or after 6 April 1995. The net value should be stated as 'does not exceed £10,000, £25,000, £40,000, £70,000 or £100,000' as appropriate (see scale of Probate Court Fees).

13. Oath for administrators *de bonis non*

Extracted by
of   Solicitors
DX:

Family Division
[Principal] [....District] Probate Registry
In the estate of...Deceased
[I] [We] (1)
of
and
of
make oath and say as follows:

1. That (2)
   of
   died on the   day of   19   aged   domiciled in
   England and Wales, intestate, leaving (3)
   [his] [her] lawful (4)
   [the only] [one of the] person[s] entitled to [his] [her] estate.

2. That on the   day of   19   letters of administration
   of the estate of the said deceased were granted at the [Principal]
            District Probate] Registry to the said (5)   that the
   said (6)   [survived his co-administrator and] died on the
   day of   19   leaving part of the said estate unadministered.

3. That no life or minority interest arises in the estate of the deceased.

4. That there was no land vested in the deceased previous to [his]
   [her] death which remained settled land notwithstanding [his] [her]
   death.

5. That [I am] [we are] the (4)
   of the deceased [the only] [one of the] person[s] entitled to share in
   the estate of the said deceased.

6. That [I] [we] will:

   (a) collect, get in and administer according to law the unadminis-
       tered real and personal estate of the said deceased;

   (b) when required to do so by the court, exhibit in the court a full
       inventory of the said estate and render an account thereof to the
       court; and

   (c) when required to do so by the High Court, deliver up to that
       court the letters of administration.

7. That to the best of [my] [our] knowledge, information and belief the
   gross value of the unadministered estate [does not exceed] [amounts
   to] £   and the net estate [does not exceed] [amounts to]
   £   [and that this is not a case in which an Inland Revenue
   Account is required to be delivered](8)

Sworn by the above named

at
on the

Before me,

a commissioner for oaths/solicitor

Notes

(1)   Insert full name(s) and address(es) and descriptions of the applicant(s).

(2)   Insert full name and last permanent address of the deceased.

(3)   Insert name and relationship of the person(s) who were entitled to the deceased's estate.

(4)   Clear the prior interests (if any) of the person(s) who took out the original grant e.g. 'a widow without issue or parent'.

(5)   Name(s) of the original grantee(s).

(6)   Name and date of death of the last administrator to die.

(7)   Insert relationship of applicant(s) to the deceased.

(8)   An Inland Revenue Account is required on Form A5, this being an application for a second or subsequent grant unless the first grant issued as an excepted case and the value of the unadministered estate does not now exceed the threshold appropriate to the case.

Note: If the applicant is applying as personal representative of a deceased person entitled to the estate his actual capacity and the date and place of the grant should be entered in place of the relationship e.g. 'I am the executor of the will of   probate thereof having been granted to me on the   day of   19   at   District Probate Registry'. All other persons entitled to share who are living must renounce their right to the grant.

14. Oath for administrators: person entitled to apply mentally incapable: no-one authorised by Court of Protection: two persons appointed to apply by a registrar

Extracted by

of   Solicitors

DX:

IN THE HIGH COURT OF JUSTICE
Family Division
[Principal] [....District] Probate Registry
In the estate of...Deceased
[I] [We](1)
make oath and say as follows:

1.   of

deceased formerly of

died on the   day of   19   domiciled in England and Wales
aged   intestate

or any other person entitled in priority to share in the estate by virtue of any enactment. That AB the lawful mother of the said deceased and the only person entitled to his estate is mentally incapable of managing her affairs and that no person has been authorised by the Court of Protection to apply for a grant in the deceased's estate, and no person has been appointed attorney of the said AB under a registered enduring power of attorney.

2. No minority or life interest arises in the estate (8).

3. To the best of [my] [our] knowledge, information and belief there was [no] land vested in the deceased which was settled previously to the death of the deceased and which remained settled land notwithstanding such death (9).

4. That we are the persons appointed to apply for letters of administration of the estate of the deceased by order of Mr District Probate Registrar [District Judge]   dated the   day of   19   for the use and benefit of the said AB and until further representation be granted.

5. [I] [We] will

   (a) collect, get in and administer according to the law the real and personal estate (11)   of the above-named deceased;
   (12)

   (b) when required to do so by the court exhibit in the court a full inventory of the said estate of the deceased and render an account thereof to the court; and

   (c) when required to do so by the High Court, deliver up to that court the grant of letters of administration.

6. To the best of [my] [our] knowledge, information and belief the

gross value of the estate (13)(14)   passing under the grant
[does not exceed] [amounts to] (15) £   and that the net value of
the estate (13)(14)

[does not exceed] [amounts to] £   [and that this is not a case
in which an Inland Revenue Account is required to be delivered].

Sworn etc.

Notes

(1)   Insert full name(s), address(es) and occupation(s) or description(s) of administrator(s) applying.

(2)   If affirmation made, substitute 'do solemnly and sincerely affirm'.

(3)   Insert full name, address and occupation or description of deceased.

(4)   If deceased died domiciled outside England and Wales, delete 'England and Wales' and insert the state, province or country within whose jurisdiction the deceased died domiciled.

(5)   Insert the deceased's age in years. If the exact age is not known, state the approximate age, e.g. 'over 65'.

(6)   Clear any prior rights to the grant by rotation, e.g. by adding 'a widow without issue', 'a bachelor', etc. (see page 50).

(7)   If the deceased died prior to 1 January 1970 or application is made by a spouse and/or a child, delete the words from 'or' to 'enactment'.

(8)   If a life or minority interest does arise, delete the word 'no' and insert 'A'; there must usually be at least two applicants for the grant, but a district judge or registrar has power to dispense with this requirement in exceptional circumstances (his prior agreement should be obtained before the oath is sworn).

(9)   Where land remains settled and these applicants are also entitled to the grant in respect of such land the grant will issue 'including settled land'. Where these applicants are not so entitled the grant will issue 'save and except settled land'; a separate grant will be necessary to administer such land.

(10)   Insert capacity of administrator(s) (see page 32).

(11)   Insert 'save and except settled land' if appropriate.

(12)   If the person(s) beneficially entitled to the estate are minors, or the grant is applied for through an attorney, add 'for the use and benefit of ....'.

(13)   Where the deceased died domiciled outside England and Wales, insert after 'estate' 'in England and Wales'.

(14)   Where an Inland Revenue Account is required the actual gross and net values of the estate must be inserted; where an account is not required, insert the gross and net values the estate does not exceed, e.g. gross value £145,000 where the death occurred on or after 6 April 1995). The net value should be stated as 'does not exceed £10,000, £25,000, £40,000, £70,000 or £100,000' as appropriate (see scale of Probate Court Fees).

15. Oath for administrator(s): person entitled to apply mentally incapable: application by person appointed by Court of Protection

Extracted by

of   Solicitors

DX:

IN THE HIGH COURT OF JUSTICE

Family Division

[Principal] [....District] Probate Registry

In the estate of...Deceased

[I] ₍₁₎

make oath and say ₍₂₎ as follows:

1.   of

    deceased formerly of

    died on the   day of   19   domiciled in England and Wales aged   intestate

    or any other person entitled in priority to share in the estate by virtue of any enactment. That AB the lawful mother of the said deceased and the only person entitled to his estate is mentally incapable of managing her affairs.

2. No minority or life interest arises in the estate ₍₈₎.

3. To the best of [my] [our] knowledge, information and belief there was [no] land vested in the deceased which was settled previously to the death of the deceased and which remained settled land notwithstanding such death ₍₉₎.

4. I am the person authorised by an order of the Court of Protection dated the   day of   19   to apply for letters of administration of the estate for the use and benefit of the said AB and until further representation be granted.

5. [I] [We] will

    (a) collect, get in and administer according to the law the real and personal estate ₍₁₁₎   of the above-named deceased; ₍₁₂₎

    (b) when required to do so by the court exhibit in the court a full inventory of the said estate of the deceased and render an account thereof to the court; and

    (c) when required to do so by the High Court, deliver up to that court the grant of letters of administration.

6. To the best of [my] [our] knowledge, information and belief the gross value of the estate ₍₁₃₎₍₁₄₎   passing under the grant [does not exceed] [amounts to] ₍₁₅₎ £   and that the net value of the estate ₍₁₃₎₍₁₄₎   [does not exceed] [amounts to]₍₁₅₎ £   [and that this is not a case in which an Inland Revenue Account is required to be delivered].

Sworn etc.

Notes

(1)   Insert full name, address and occupation or description of administrator applying.

(2)   If affirmation made, substitute 'do solemnly and sincerely affirm'.

(3)   Insert full name, address and occupation or description of deceased.

(4)   If deceased died domiciled outside England and Wales, delete 'England and Wales' and insert the state, province or country within whose jurisdiction the deceased died domiciled.

(5)   Insert the deceased's age in years. If the exact age is not known, state the approximate age, e.g. 'over 65'.

(6)   Clear any prior rights to the grant by rotation, e.g. by adding 'a widow without issue', 'a bachelor' etc. (see page 50).

(7)   If the deceased died prior to 1 January 1970 or application is made by a spouse and/or a child, delete the words from 'or' to 'enactment'.

(8)   If a life or minority interest does arise, delete the word 'no' and insert 'A'; there must usually be at least two applicants for the grant, but a district judge or registrar has power to dispense with this requirement in exceptional circumstances (his prior agreement should be obtained before the oath is sworn).

(9)   Where land remains settled and these applicants are also entitled to the grant in respect of such land the grant will issue 'including settled land'. Where these applicants are not so entitled the grant will issue 'save and except settled land'; a separate grant will be necessary to administer such land.

(10)   Insert capacity of administrator(s) (see page 32).

(11)   Insert 'save and except settled land' if appropriate.

(12)   If the person(s) beneficially entitled to the estate are minors, or the grant is applied for through an attorney, add 'for the use and benefit of ....'.

(13)   Where the deceased died domiciled outside England and Wales, insert after 'estate' 'in England and Wales'.

(14)   Where an Inland Revenue Account is required the actual gross and net values of the estate must be inserted; where an account is not required, insert the gross and net values the estate does not exceed, e.g. gross value £145,000 where the death occurred on or after 6 April 1995. The net value should be stated as 'does not exceed £10,000, £25,000, £40,000, £70,000 or £100,000' as appropriate (see scale of Probate Court Fees).

16. Administration oath – Cousin german

IN THE HIGH COURT OF JUSTICE
Family Division
[Principal] [....District] Probate Registry
In the estate of (deceased's names) Deceased

I, (names and address of deponent) make oath and say that (names and address of the deceased) deceased, died on the   day of 199 , aged   years, domiciled in England and Wales, intestate a widow, without issue, parent, brother or sister of the whole or half blood or their issue, grandparent or any other person entitled in priority to share in the estate by virtue of any enactment,

1. That no minority or life interest arises under the intestacy, and that there was no land vested in the deceased which was settled previously to her death and which remained settled land notwithstanding her death.

2. That I am the cousin german of the whole blood and the only person entitled to the estate of the said intestate, being the daughter of (names of deponents parent) the sister of the whole blood of the said intestate who died in the intestate's lifetime.

3. That I will:

    (a) collect, get in and administer according to law the real and personal estate of the said deceased,

    (b) when required to do so by the court exhibit in the court a full inventory of the said estate and render an account thereof to the court; and

    (c) when required to do so by the High Court, deliver up to that court the grant of letters of administration.

4. To the best of my knowledge, information and belief the gross estate passing under the grant (does not exceed) (amounts to) £   , and that the net estate (does not exceed) (amounts to) £   (and that this is not a case in which an Inland Revenue Account is required to be delivered)

Sworn by the above named deponent
at
this   day of   199 ,
Before me,

a commissioner for oaths/a solicitor.

17. Oath for administrator – Deceased divorced

IN THE HIGH COURT OF JUSTICE
Family Division
[Principal] [....District] Probate Registry
In the estate of (deceased's names) Deceased

I, (names and address of administrator) make oath and say that (names and address of deceased) died on the   day of   199 , aged   years, domiciled in England and Wales, intestate, a single man (add any other clearings i.e. without issue etc.).

1. That the deceased's marriage with (ex-wife's names) was dissolved by a final decree of the (High Court or name of County Court) on the   day of   199 , and the deceased did not remarry.

2. That no minority or life interest arises in the estate and that there was no land vested in the deceased which was settled previously to his death and which remained settled land notwithstanding his death.

3. That I am the son and the only person entitled to the estate of the said deceased.

4. That I will:

   (a) collect, get in and administer according to law the real and personal estate of the said deceased,

   (b) when required to do so by the court, exhibit in the court a full inventory of the estate, and render an account thereof to the court, and

   (c) when required to do so by the High Court, deliver up to that court the grant of letters of administration.

5. To the best of my knowledge, information and belief the gross estate passing under the grant (does not exceed) (amounts to) £   and that the net estate (does not exceed) (amounts to) £   (and that this is not a case in which an Inland Revenue Account is required to be delivered).

Sworn by the above named deponent
at
this   day of   199 ,
Before me,

a commissioner for oaths/solicitor.

18. Oath for administrators pursuant to an order under s 116 Supreme Court Act 1981

Extracted by

of   Solicitors

DX:

Family Division

[Principal] [....District] Probate Registry

In the estate of...Deceased

I, (names and address of proposed administrator)
make oath and say as follows:

1. That (full names and last permanent address of deceased) formerly
   of   deceased, died on the   day of   19   aged
   years domiciled in England and Wales intestate.

2. That no minority or life interest arises under the intestacy.

3. That to the best of my knowledge information and belief no land
   was vested in the deceased which was settled previously to his death
   and which remained settled land notwithstanding his death.

4. That on the   day of   199 it was ordered by Mr (District Registrar) that letters of administration of the estate of the
   deceased be granted to me under and by virtue of section 116 of
   the Supreme Court Act 1981 (recite any limitation shown in the
   order).

5. That I will:

   (a) collect, get in and administer according to law the real and per-
       sonal estate of the said deceased; (limited as aforesaid)

   (b) when required to do so by the court, exhibit in the court a full
       inventory of the said estate and render an account thereof to the
       court, and

   (c) when required to do so by the High Court, deliver up to that
       court the grant of letters of administration.

6. That to the best of my knowledge, information and belief the gross
   value of the estate passing under the grant [does not exceed]
   [amounts to] £   and the net estate [does not exceed] [amounts
   to] £   , [and that this is not a case in which an Inland Revenue
   Account is required to be delivered).

Sworn by the above-named at
on the
Before me,

a commissioner for oaths/solicitor.

19. Oath for administrators to persons appointed under rule 32(2) to act on behalf of minors

IN THE HIGH COURT OF JUSTICE
Family Division
[Principal] [....District] Probate Registry
In the estate of (full names and alias of deceased) Deceased
We,   and (full names and addresses of applicants)
respectively make oath and say as follows:

1. That (full names and address of deceased) deceased, died on the
        day of   19   aged   years domiciled in England
   and Wales intestate a widow leaving (full names of surviving children) her children the only persons now entitled to share in her
   estate who are minors aged   years and   years respectively.

2. That there is no person with parental responsibility for the said
   minors and that we are the lawful (relationship, if any, to the children) of the said minors and have been appointed administrators to
   act on behalf of the said minors by order of Mr [District] Registrar
          dated the   day of   19   for the purpose of tak-
   ing letters of administration of the estate of the said deceased for
   their use and benefit until one of them shall attain the age of 18
   years.

3. That a minority interest but no life interest arises under the intestacy.

4. That there was no land vested in the deceased previously to her
   death which remained settled land notwithstanding her death.

5. That we will:
   (a) collect, get in and administer according to law the real and per-
       sonal estate of the said deceased limited as aforesaid;
   (b) when required to do so by the court, exhibit in the court a full
       inventory of the said estate and render an account thereof to the
       court, and
   (c) when required to do so by the High Court, deliver up to that
       court the grant of letters of administration.

6. That to the best of our knowledge, information and belief the gross
   estate passing under the grant [does not exceed] [amounts to]
   £   and the net estate [does not exceed] [amounts to] £   ,
   [and that this is not a case in which an Inland Revenue Account is
   required to be delivered].

Sworn by the above-named
at
on the
Before me,

a commissioner for oaths/solicitor.

20. Oath for administrators to person with parental responsibility and a nominee

IN THE HIGH COURT OF JUSTICE
Family Division
[Principal] [....District] Probate Registry
In the estate of...Deceased
We (full name and address of parent of the minor)
and (full name and address of nominated administrator)
respectively, make oath and say as follows:

1. That (full name and last address of deceased) died on the   day
   of   19   aged   domiciled in England and Wales a single
   man/woman leaving (names of deceased's surviving children) his
   (sons and daughters) and the only persons entitled to his estate who
   are now minors of the ages of   years and   years respectively.

2. That the marriage of the said deceased with the above named (full
   name of parent) was dissolved by final decree of the (name of the
   court) dated the   day of   19   and the said deceased did
   not remarry.

3. That the said (name of parent) is the lawful surviving parent and
   the person with parental responsibility for the said minors.

4. That the said (full name of parent) has nominated by a nomination
   dated the   day of   19   the said (name of nominated
   administrator) to be his/her co-administrator.

5. That a minority but no life interest arises under the intestacy.

6. That there was no land vested in the said deceased previously to her
   death which remained settled land notwithstanding her death.

(If the parent applying is the father insert the following paragraph 7)

7. That I the said (full name of parent) was married to the deceased
   at the dates of birth of the minors.

8. That we will:

   (a) collect, get in and administer according to law the real and personal estate of the said deceased for the use and benefit of the
   said minors until one of them attains the age of 18 years;

   (b) when required to do so by the court, exhibit in the court a full
   inventory of the said estate and render an account thereof to the
   court, and

   (c) when required to do so by the High Court, deliver up to that
   court the grant of letters of administration.

9. That to the best of our knowledge, information and belief the gross
   estate passing under the grant [does not exceed] [amounts to]
   £   and the net estate [does not exceed] [amounts to] £   [and
   that this is not a case in which an Inland Revenue Account is
   required to be delivered].

Sworn by the above-named
at
on the
Before me,

a commissioner for oaths/solicitor.

21. Oath for administrators (*ad colligenda bona*)

IN THE HIGH COURT OF JUSTICE
Family Division
[Principal] [....District] Probate Registry
In the estate of (deceased's full names and alias) Deceased
I (We)
(full names, description, and full address of the proposed administrators)
make oath and say as follows:

1. That (full name and address of deceased) died on the   day of 199 , aged   years, domiciled in England and Wales.

2. That (a) (no) life interest or (a) (but no) minority interest arises under the intestacy.

3. That by order of Mr (District) Registrar   dated the day of   199 , it was ordered that letters of administration of the estate of the said deceased be granted to me (us) limited to (limitations imposed by the order).

4. That I (we) will:

    (a) collect, get in and administer according to law the real and personal estate of the said deceased as limited by the said Registrar's order and until further representation be granted;

    (b) when required to do so by the court exhibit in the court a full inventory of the said estate and render an account thereof to the court; and

    (c) when required to do so by the High Court deliver up to that court the grant of letters of administration.

5. To the best of my knowledge, information and belief the gross estate passing under the grant (does not exceed) (amounts to) £   and that the net estate (does not exceed) (amounts to) £   (and this is not a case in which an Inland Revenue Account is required to be delivered).

Sworn by the above named
(FULL NAMES)
this
day of
Before me,

a solicitor/a commissioner for oaths.

22. Oath for administrator(s): Grant of administration to a creditor (person entitled having renounced)

Extracted by
of   Solicitors
                                                         DX:

IN THE HIGH COURT OF JUSTICE
Family Division
[Principal] [....District] Probate Registry
In the estate of...Deceased
I (1)
make oath and say(2) as follows:

1.   of

   deceased(3)

   died on the   day of   19   domiciled in England and
   Wales(4) aged(5)   intestate a widow without issue(6) or any other
   person entitled in priority to share in the estate by virtue of any
   enactment(7) leaving AB her lawful father the only person entitled to
   her estate who has renounced letters of administration of her estate.

2. No minority or life interest arises in the estate (8).

3. To the best of [my] [our] knowledge information and belief there
   was [no] land vested in the deceased which was settled previously
   to the death of the deceased and which remained settled land
   notwithstanding such death (9).

4. I am a creditor of the said deceased.

5. [I] [We] will

   (a) collect, get in and administer according to the law the real and
       personal estate (11)   of the above-named deceased;
       (12)

   (b) when required to do so by the court exhibit in the court a full
       inventory of the said estate of the deceased and render an
       account thereof to the court; and

   (c) when required to do so by the High Court, deliver up to that
       court the grant of letters of administration.

6. To the best of [my] [our] knowledge, information and belief the
   gross value of the estate (13)(14)   passing under the grant
   [does not exceed] [amounts to] £   and that the net value of the
   estate (13)(14)

   [does not exceed] [amounts to] £   [and that this is not a case in
   which an Inland Revenue Account is required to be delivered].

Sworn etc.

Notes

(1)   Insert full name, address and occupation or description of administrator applying.

(2)   If affirmation made, substitute 'do solemnly and sincerely affirm'.

(3)   Insert full name, address and occupation or description of deceased.

(4)   If deceased died domiciled outside England and Wales, delete 'England and Wales' and insert the state, province or country within whose jurisdiction the deceased died domiciled.

(5)   Insert the deceased's age in years. If the exact age is not known, state the approximate age, e.g. 'over 65'.

(6)   Clear any prior rights to the grant by rotation, e.g. by adding 'a widow without issue', 'a bachelor' etc. (see page 50).

(7)   If the deceased died prior to 1 January 1970 or application is made by a spouse and/or a child, delete the words from 'or' to 'enactment'.

(8)   If a life or minority interest does arise, delete the word 'no' and insert 'A'; there must usually be at least two applicants for the grant, but a district judge or registrar has power to dispense with this requirement in exceptional circumstances (his prior agreement should be obtained before the oath is sworn).

(9)   Where land remains settled and these applicants are also entitled to the grant in respect of such land the grant will issue 'including settled land'. Where these applicants are not so entitled the grant will issue 'save and except settled land'; a separate grant will be necessary to administer such land.

(10)   Insert capacity of administrator(s) (see page 32).

(11)   Insert 'save and except settled land' if appropriate.

(12)   If the person(s) beneficially entitled to the estate are minors, or the grant is applied for through an attorney, add 'for the use and benefit of ....'.

(13)   Where the deceased died domiciled outside England and Wales, insert after 'estate' 'in England and Wales'.

(14)   Where an Inland Revenue Account is required the actual gross and net values of the estate must be inserted; where an account is not required, insert the gross and net values the estate does not exceed, e.g. gross value £145,000 where the death occurred on or after 6 April 1995. The net value should be stated as 'does not exceed £10,000, £25,000, £40,000, £70,000 or £100,000' as appropriate (see scale of Probate Court Fees).

23. Grants to creditors and passing over orders

When the deceased dies testate:

clear off (by renunciation or citation) all persons who have a right to a grant, or who have a beneficial interest.

When the deceased dies intestate:

ascertain and clear off (by renunciation or citation) all persons who have a right to a grant or who have a beneficial interest under the Administration of Estates Act.

Where it is believed that there may be a beneficial interest, but it cannot be firmly established, the Treasury Solicitor cannot become involved, and consideration should be given to obtaining a passing over order under s 116 Supreme Courts Act 1981.

Where there is no-one entitled to a grant, and where no beneficial interest can be established, the Treasury Solicitor will administer the estate *in bona vacantia*.

1 Creditor (individual)

1(a) An affidavit should be prepared to lead to a passing over order and should show:

 (i)   the date of death;

 (ii) the deceased's age;

 (iii) whether the deceased died testate or intestate. If this cannot be established, the probable position must be shown together with a resume of the action which has been taken to establish the position;

 (iv) the assets;

 (v)   the liabilities.

1(b) A resume of the action taken:

 (i)   to ascertain the whereabouts of any persons having a beneficial interest;

 (ii) to clear off those interests;

 (iii) confirmation that the Treasury Solicitor does not wish to be concerned with the estate;

 (iv) the amount owed to the creditor;

 (v)   explanation of who the creditor is;

 (vi) any additional information required by the Registrar;

 (vii) a request for the order to be made.

2 Creditor (company)

Where a corporate body (which is not a trust corporation) is the creditor, it cannot apply for a grant in its own name (rule 36 NCPR 1987).

However, such a body can appoint a nominee (by way of a sealed resolution or sealed power of attorney) and that nominee can apply for a grant for use and benefit of that body, limited until further representation be granted.

2(a) In these circumstances, the affidavit leading to the passing over order would also include the following:

(i) that the corporate body was not a trust corporation;

(ii) details of the nominee, and the authority for his nomination;

(iii) details of the creditor;

(iv) if a company is in receivership or liquidation, the receivers or liquidators have the right to appoint a nominee or attorney.

Under the Insolvency Act 1986 a receiver has the power to take possession of all of the company's property. In these circumstances, the affidavit would include the following additional information:

(A) that the company is in receivership;

(B) details of the receivers;

(C) details of the person appointed by the receivers and the power under which they have appointed him.

3 Recommended procedure

(i) Have the draft affidavit settled by the Registrar before it is sworn.

(ii) Agree with the Registrar the exhibits he requires.

(iii) A statutory notice for creditors should be placed to protect the administrator. Such a notice cannot be placed until the administrator has been appointed by the grant of letters of administration.

4 Oaths

(i) Where a passing over order has been granted, the oath does not have to recite all of the material facts. The oath should merely recite that power has been granted by virtue of the passing over order.

(ii) In circumstances where a passing over order is not necessary, and the creditor is a corporate body, the oath must recite the details, as paragraphs 2(a) and 2(a)(A).

24. Aliases

In the appropriate form of oath, where the name of the deceased is to be included, the alias must also be given e.g.:

'In the Estate of Thomas William Jones, otherwise Thomas Jones deceased'

Add an additional paragraph of explanation, e.g.:

'That the true name of the deceased was Thomas William Jones but that he had a bank account with   Bank plc in the name of Thomas Jones'.

25. Clearings

The appropriate clearing off should be included in the form of oath (see page 50) *Example:*

1.   of
   deceased formerly of
   died on the   day of   19   domiciled in England and Wales aged   intestate a spinster without issue or parent or brothers or sisters of the whole or half blood or their issue or grandparents or uncles or aunts of the whole blood or any other person entitled in priority to share in the estate by virtue of any enactment.

4. I am the cousin german of the whole blood being the son of .... the uncle of the whole blood of the said intestate who died in the intestate's lifetime and I am the only person entitled to the estate of the said intestate.

26. Application to prove copy of lost will

(a) Application to prove copy

IN THE HIGH COURT OF JUSTICE
Family Division
[Principal] [....District] Probate Registry
In the estate of...Deceased
We   of
and   of
make oath and say:
                                    of
died on the   day of   19   domiciled in England and Wales
having made and duly executed her last will and testament that we believe
the paper writings now produced to and marked by us to contain the last
will and testament as contained in a [photocopy] [made up draft] [recon-
struction] of   of   , deceased, who died on the
day of   19   , aged   years, domiciled in England and Wales
and that to the best of our knowledge, information, and belief there was
no land vested in the said deceased which was settled previously to her
death and not by her will, and which remain settled and not withstanding
her death.

And we further make oath and say that we are the Executors named in the
said will, that by an order dated the   day of   19   , it was
ordered by Mr   Registrar of this District that the said will be
admitted to proof as contained in the said [photocopy] [made up draft]
[reconstruction] thereof, and that we will (i) collect, get in and administer according to law the real and personal estate of the said deceased, limited until the original will or a more authentic copy thereof be proved; and
(ii) when required to do so by the court, exhibit on oath in the court a
full inventory of the said estate and when so required render an account
of the administration of the estate to the court; and (iii) when required to
do so by the High Court, deliver up the grant of probate to that court;
and that to the best of our knowledge, information and belief the gross
estate passing under the grant (amounts to) (does not exceed) £   and
the net estate (amounts to) (does not exceed) £   (1)

(and this is not a case in which an Inland Revenue Account is required to
be delivered).
Sworn by

Note

(1)   £145,000 where the death occurred on or after 6 April 1995. The net value should
       be stated as 'does not exceed £10,000, £25,000, £40,000, £70,000 or £100,000' as
       appropriate (see scale of Probate Court Fees).

(b) Affidavit by subscribing witness

IN THE HIGH COURT OF JUSTICE
Family Division
[Principal] [....District] Probate Registry
In the estate of...Deceased
I   of
make oath and say as follows:

1. I am one of the subscribing witnesses to the last will and testament of
   of
   deceased the [photocopy] [made up draft] [reconstruction] of the said will bearing date the   day of   19   being now produced to me and marked '......'.
2. The said testatrix executed the original of the said will on the   day of 19   by signing her name on the foot or end thereof in the presence of me and of   the other subscribed witness thereto both of us being present at the same time and we thereupon (to wit after the testatrix had so signed) attested and subscribed the said will in the presence of the said testatrix.

Sworn by the above-named
at   before me

(c) Affidavit by solicitors

IN THE HIGH COURT OF JUSTICE
Family Division
[Principal] [....District] Probate Registry
In the estate of...Deceased
I,   of   , solicitor make oath and say as follows:

1. I am one of the partners in the firm of
   solicitors of   which said firm was on 19   instructed by   to prepare her last will and testament which said will was then signed and witnessed on the   day of   19   .
2. It is the normal practice of   (firm's name) to file original wills in the strongroom and to file draft wills and correspondence appertaining thereto separate from the original documents (but in the same strongroom). In the event of the original will being handed to the client a receipt is attached to the draft and correspondence (which is then transferred to the strongroom). In this case no receipt was found with the draft and the said draft and correspondence had not been so transferred.
3. That in a copy letter dated the   day of   19   and being now produced and marked '......' it is stated that the will has been retained for safe-keeping.

4. On the   day of   19   (firm's name) were
   instructed by   one of the executors named in the said will
   that   (deceased) died on the   day of
   19   . It was then discovered that the original will was missing and
   although a very careful and thorough search has been made throughout these offices the original document cannot be found although
   the draft and correspondence were found in the office.

5. That I believe the [photocopy] [made up draft] [reconstruction] will
   now produced and marked '......' to be a true and authentic copy of
   the original now lost.

   I therefore request the court to make an order under rule 54 of the
   Non-Contentious Probate Rules 1987 admitting the said [photocopy]
   [made up draft] [reconstruction] will to Probate, the said grant to
   be limited until the original or a more authentic copy be proved.

Sworn etc.

27. Renunciation of probate or of letters of administration (with will annexed)

IN THE HIGH COURT OF JUSTICE
Family Division
[Principal] [....District] Probate Registry
In the estate of..Deceased
WHEREAS (1)
of (2)
died on the   day of   19   having made and duly executed [his] [her] last will and testament [and   (3) codicil[s] thereto] (4)
bearing date the   day of   19   [and the
           day of   19 respectively] (5) and thereof appointed (6)
executor
Now I, the said (6)
do hereby declare that I have not intermeddled in the estate of the said
deceased and will not hereafter intermeddle therein with intent to defraud
creditors and I hereby renounce all my right and title to the probate and
execution of the said will [and   (3)   codicil[s]] [and as the
(7)   named in the said will hereby renounce all my right and title
to letters of administration (with the will and (3) codicils) of the estate of
the said deceased](4).

Signed by the said
this   day of   19
in the presence of
Signature of witness (8)
Address

Notes
(1)   Insert name of deceased.
(2)   Insert last address of deceased.
(3)   Insert number of codicil(s) (if any) or delete.
(4)   Delete as appropriate.
(5)   Insert date(s) of codicil(s).
(6)   Insert name of executor.
(7)   Insert capacity in which executor is also entitled in a lower capacity.
(8)   The renunciation must be signed in the presence of one disinterested witness who
        must also sign and state his address and occupation.

28. Renunciation of administrator(s)

IN THE HIGH COURT OF JUSTICE
Family Division
[Principal] [....District] Probate Registry
In the estate of..Deceased
Whereas (1)   of
deceased, died on the   day of   19
intestate (2)
leaving (3)
[his] [her] (4)
[one of] the [only] person[s] [now] entitled to [his] [her] estate.

Now [I] [we] the said (5)
do hereby renounce all [my] [our] right and title to letters of administration to the estate of the said deceased.

Signed by the said (5)
on the   day of   19
in the presence of (6)

Notes

(1)   Insert full name and last permanent address of the deceased.
(2)   Insert status of deceased and clear any prior interests, e.g. 'a widow without issue'.
(3)   Insert full name of persons entitled.
(4)   Insert relationship to the deceased of person(s) entitled.
(5)   Insert name(s) of those persons entitled now renouncing.
(6)   The renunciant's signature(s) must be witnessed by a disinterested witness who must give his/her full name, occupation and address.

29. Retraction of renunciation

IN THE HIGH COURT OF JUSTICE
Family Division
[Principal] [....District] Probate Registry
In the estate of...Deceased
Whereas   of
deceased, died on the   day of   19   having made and
duly executed his last will and testament bearing date the   day of
        19   and therein appointed me, (1)

[his sole executor (2)] or [intestate leaving me, (1)

the residuary legatee and devisee in trust (2)   ]

And whereas I renounced [probate and execution] [letters of administration (with will annexed)] [letters of administration] of the estate of the said
deceased and whereas a grant of [probate] [letters of administration (with
will annexed)] [letters of administration] was made at the
Registry to (3)

and whereas the said (3)

died on the   day of   19   leaving part of the said estate
unadministered.

Now I the said (1)   of

do hereby declare that I retract my said renunciation of [probate] [letters
of administration (with will annexed)] [letters of administration] of the
estate of the said deceased.

Signed by the said
Dated the   day of   19

Notes

(1)   Name of executor who has renounced.
(2)   Or as the case may be.
(3)   Name of grantee.

NB. Leave to retract may only be given by order of a district judge or a District Probate
Registrar.

30. Notice under s 47A Administration of Estates Act 1925 of election to redeem life interest

IN THE HIGH COURT OF JUSTICE
Family Division
[Principal] [....District] Probate Registry
In the estate of...Deceased
Whereas (1)   of
died on the   day of   19   [wholly] [partially] intestate
leaving [his] [her] lawful [wife] [husband] and (2)
issue of the said deceased. And whereas [probate] [letters of administration] of the estate of the said deceased [was] granted to me (3)   and
to (4)   at the   Probate Registry on the   day of
         19
And whereas the said (4)
has ceased to be a personal representative because (5)
and I am [now] the sole personal representative
Now I, the said (3)
hereby give notice in accordance with section 47A of the Administration of Estates Act 1925 that I elect to redeem the life interest to which I am entitled in the estate of the late   by retaining £   its capital value, and £   the costs of the transaction.
Dated the   day of   19
Signed
To the Senior District Judge of the Family Division.

Notes

(1)   Name and address of deceased.
(2)   Names of children.
(3)   Name of surviving spouse.
(4)   Name of second grantee.
(5)   Set out the reason(s).

31. Application to dispense with giving notice to non-acting executors under rule 27 (3)

IN THE HIGH COURT OF JUSTICE
Family Division
In the estate of...Deceased
The district judge or registrar is asked to dispense with the giving of notice pursuant to Rule 27(3) of the Non-Contentious Probate Rules 1987 to the executor(s) (enter names of executors)
(to whom power is to be reserved) by reason of the following circumstances:
It is submitted that for the above reason(s) the giving of notice of the application to the said
is impracticable/would result in unreasonable delay or expense.
Signed:
(Extracting solicitor)
Date:

Rule 27 provides:

(1)   Subject to paragraphs (1A) (2) and (3) below, where, on an application for probate, power to apply for a like grant is to be reserved to such other of the executors as have not renounced probate, notice of the application shall be given to the executor or executors to whom power is to be reserved, and unless the district judge or registrar otherwise directs the oath shall state that such notice has been given.

(1A)   Where power is to be reserved to executors who are appointed by reference to their being partners in a firm and not by their names notice need not be given to them under para (1) above if probate is applied for by another partner in that firm.

(2)   Where power is to be reserved to partners of a firm, notice for the purposes of para (1) above may be given to the partners by sending it to the firm at its principal or last known place of business.

(3)   A district judge or registrar may dispense with giving of notice under para (1) above if he is satisfied that the giving of such a notice is impracticable or would result in unreasonable delay or expense.

(4)   A grant of administration may be made to any person entitled thereto without notice to other persons entitled in the same degree.

(5)   Unless a district judge or a registrar otherwise directs, administration shall be granted to a person of full age entitled thereto in preference to a guardian of a minor, and to a living person entitled thereto in preference to the personal representative of a deceased person.

(6)   A dispute between persons entitled to a grant in the same degree shall be brought by summons before a district judge or a registrar.

(7)   The issue of a summons under this rule in the Principal Registry or in a district probate registry shall be notified forthwith to the registry in which the index of pending grant applications is maintained.

(8)   If the issue of a summons under this rule is known to the district judge or registrar, he shall not allow any grant to be sealed until such summons is finally disposed of.

Note: The application must be made before applying for the grant. The oath will not be accepted unless the above rule is complied with.

32. Nomination of second administrator (with will); mental incapacity and minority or life interest

IN THE HIGH COURT OF JUSTICE
Family Division
[Principal] [....District] Probate Registry
In the estate of...Deceased
AB of   deceased, died on the
day of   19
domiciled in England and Wales having made and duly executed his last
will and testament bearing date the
day of   19 ;
CD the sole executor and residuary legatee and devisee named in the said
will is by reason of mental incapacity incapable of managing his affairs;

I, EF, am the person authorised by the Court of Protection to apply for a
grant of representation of the estate of the said deceased for the use and
benefit of the said CD;

A life [or a minority] interest arises under the said will:

I, the said EF, hereby nominate GH of
          to be my co-administrator in the estate of the said, deceased,
she being a fit and proper person to act in that capacity.

Dated this   day of   199

Signed by the said EF
in the presence of:
[name and address of witness].

33. Nomination of second administrator

IN THE HIGH COURT OF JUSTICE
Family Division
[Principal] [....District] Probate Registry
In the estate of...Deceased
Whereas (full names and last permanent address of deceased)
deceased, died on the   day of   19   aged   years,
intestate (deceased's status e.g. widower, married man etc.)
leaving (full names of person first entitled to share in the estate) and
(names of others entitled to share in the estate) his (relationship to
deceased of those persons entitled) the only person[s] entitled to share in
his estate
And whereas the said
(is) (are) now minors aged   and   [respectively]
And whereas I, the said (first person entitled to share) am the (relationship to others entitled to above) and (the person who has parental responsibility) OR (the person who has been appointed as guardian) of the said
minors,
And whereas there is no testamentary or other lawfully appointed guardian
of the said minor(s)

Now I, the said (first person entitled to share)
do hereby nominate and appoint (full names of appointee)
to be my co-administrator in the estate of the said intestate, he being a fit
and proper person to act in that capacity
Dated this   day of   199
Signed by the said (first person entitled)
in the presence of (names, address and occupation of a disinterested witness).

34. Affidavit of plight and condition

IN THE HIGH COURT OF JUSTICE
Family Division
[Principal] [....District] Probate Registry
In the estate of..Deceased
I, (1)
of
make oath and say:

1. That I am [the sole executor] [the sole surviving executor] [one of the executors] (2)
   named in the last will and testament of (3)
   deceased, the said will bearing date the   day of
   19   being now produced to me and marked '......' and having perused the said will and in particular observed (4)

2. That the said will is now, in all respects, in the same plight and condition as when found by me as aforesaid (5).

Sworn etc.

Notes

(1)   Insert full name and address of deponent and his occupation or description.

(2)   If the deponent is not an executor, the title under which he claims to prove the will should be given.

(3)   Insert full name and address of the deceased.

(4)   Set out the alterations, interlineations erasures etc. present. Pinholes, staple holes or other matter (e.g. torn edge or corner) should be explained. An explanation of the finding of the will in its present condition together with, where possible, details of its whereabouts between execution and finding, should also be included.

(5)   If there was any other document attached which was removed by the deponent, the explanation should be set out in (1) above. Should this be the case, the words 'save and except as set out above' should be added to this paragraph.

35. Affidavit of handwriting

IN THE HIGH COURT OF JUSTICE
Family Division
[Principal] [....District] Probate Registry
In the estate of..Deceased
I (1)
of
make oath and say that:

1. [I am (2)

   of (3)   deceased]

   [I have known the deceased for many years]

   [I have worked with the deceased for many years] (4)

   and have frequently, during the period I have known him, received correspondence from him and have seen him sign his name to documents so that I am well acquainted with his handwriting and signature.

2. I have examined the paper now produced to me and marked '......' which purports to contain the last will and testament of the said deceased bearing date the   day of   19   and being subscribed thus (4)

3. I believe [the whole of the said will together with] the signature of (6) to be the true and proper handwriting of the said deceased.

Sworn etc.

Notes

(1)   Insert full name, address and occupation or description of the deponent.
(2)   'the brother' or as may be, stating the relationship (if any).
(3)   Insert full name, address and occupation or description of the deceased.
(4)   Or as the case may be.
(5)   Insert details of the deceased's signature, e.g. 'J Doe', 'John Doe'.
(6)   Insert name of deceased.

36. Affidavit as to executor's identity

IN THE HIGH COURT OF JUSTICE
Family Division
[Principal] [....District] Probate Registry
In the estate of...Deceased
I (1)
of
make oath and say that:

1. (2)   of
   deceased, died on the   day of   19   having made
   and duly executed [his] [her] last will and testament bearing date
   the   day of   19   wherein [he] [she] appointed (3)
   of
   as [[his] [her] sole executor] [one of [his] [her] executors].

2. I was at the date of the execution of the said will living at the address
   stated as mine and following my name in the will and that there was
   no other such person bearing such name living there.

3. The deceased told me [he] [she] had appointed me as [his] [her]
   executor and that [the deceased always referred to me] [I am sometimes known] as (3).

4. That there was no other person known to or referred to by the
   deceased to whom the appointment in the will can refer. That I am
   a [nephew] of the deceased but the deceased had no other [nephew]
   named(4).

Sworn etc.

Notes

(1)   Insert full true name and address and occupation or description of the executor.
(2)   Insert full name address and occupation or description of the deceased.
(3)   Insert name of executor as it appears in the will.
(4)   Complete if the executor was also referred to by relationship.

37. Affidavit of due execution

Family Division

[Principal] [....District] Probate Registry

In the estate of...Deceased

I (1)

of

make oath and say that:

1. I am one of the subscribing witnesses to the last will and testament of (2)   of

2. The said will being now produced to me and marked '......' and bearing the date the   day of   19 , that the said testator executed the said will [on the date stated therein] [(3) on the   day of   19] by [signing [his] [her] name] [making [his] [her] mark] at the foot or end thereof as the same now appears thereon [in the presence of me [and (4) the other subscribed witness thereto] both of us being present at the same time and that we then both attested the said will in the presence of the said testator after he had so subscribed]

   [in the presence of (5)   who are both now dead]

   [in the presence of (5)

   whose whereabouts, despite enquiries, cannot be traced]

[3. That previous to the execution of the said will by the testator the same was read over to [him] [her] and at the time [he] [she] seemed perfectly to understand the same and its contents]

   OR

[3. The said (6)   died a (7)   and that I am (8) being one of the persons entitled to the deceased's estate if [he] [she] had died intestate and that (9)

   are all *sui juris* and have consented to the admission of the said will to proof without further proof of execution as appears from the consents now produced to and marked by me '......']

   OR

[3. That the said testator executed the said will on the date stated thereon by signing [his] [her] name at the foot or end thereof as the same now appears in the presence of me and (4)

   both of us being present at the same time and that after the deceased had signed we attested and subscribed the said will in the presence of the said testator but that I and (4)

   signed our names above that of the testator because there was insufficient space for us to sign below the testator's signature]

   OR

[3. That the said deceased executed [his] [her] said will on the date stated thereon by acknowledging [his] [her] signature as the same now appears thereon to be [his] [her] signature in the presence of me and (4) both of us being present at the same time by indicating [his] [her] signature on the said will and asking us to witness [his] [her] signature and we then attested and subscribed the said will in the presence of the testator]. (10)

Sworn etc.

Notes

(1)   Insert full name, address and occupation or description of the deponent.

(2)   Insert full name, address and occupation or description of the deceased. Where the address is different from that appearing in the will, add 'formerly of' and state the previous address. Any variations or differences in the deceased's actual names and the names appearing in the will must be explained. Where the deponent is not a subscribing witness this paragraph should state 'I was present at the execution of ......' or as the case may be enabling the deponent to give evidence as to execution. An explanation of why a subscribing witness is not making the affidavit (e.g. his death) must be included.

(3)   Adopt this alternative where the will was dated in error.

(4)   Insert names of other subscribing witness.

(5)   Insert names of subscribing witnesses.

(6)   Insert name of deceased.

(7)   Insert status, e.g. widower without issue, parent, brother, sister, or any other person entitled in priority to share in the estate by virtue of any enactment.

(8)   Insert relationship to the deceased.

(9)   Insert names of other persons entitled to share.

(10)   Or as the case may be.

38. Affidavit of search for will

IN THE HIGH COURT OF JUSTICE
Family Division
[Principal] [....District] Probate Registry
In the estate of..Deceased
I (1)
of
make oath and say that:

1. I am [the sole executor] [one of the executors] named in the last
    will and testament of (2)
    deceased, the said will [bearing date the   day of
    19   ] [being undated] [being incompletely dated] (3)
    being now produced to me and marked '......'

2. That I have made all possible searches and enquiries for any other
    will including a search of the deceased's home and of all places
    where it is likely [he] [she] kept [his] [her] important papers or valu-
    able personal belongings.

3. That I have been unable to discover any testamentary document
    other than the said will.

4. That I have made enquiries of (4)
    in an effort to trace any other testamentary document without suc-
    cess.

5. That I believe the deceased died without having left any will or other
    testamentary document other than the said will referred to above.

Sworn etc.

Notes

(1)   Insert full name, address and occupation or description of deponent.
(2)   Insert full name, address and occupation or description of the deceased.
(3)   Or as the case may be.
(4)   Set out details of persons to whom enquiries have been made, e.g. the deceased's
        solicitor, bank manager, close friend or relative with whom a further testamentary
        document might have been left for safe-keeping.

39. Affidavit for a summons to exhibit an inventory and account

IN THE HIGH COURT OF JUSTICE
Family Division
[Principal] [....District] Probate Registry
In the estate of...Deceased
I, (full names, address and description) make oath and say as follows:
1. (Full names and address of deceased) deceased, died on the
           day of   199   intestate, a widower, domiciled in
   England and Wales, leaving CD his son.
2. That I am the grandson of the deceased and one of the persons entitled to share in the estate being the son of EF the daughter of the
   within deceased who died in his lifetime.
3. That a grant of letters of administration of the estate of the said
   (deceased) were granted to the said CD at the (   ) District
   Probate Registry on the   day of   199 .
4. That the value of the estate sworn by the said CD is less than the
   true value thereof.
5. That part of the deceased's estate consisted of antique furniture
   which has not been valued.
6. In the circumstances, I apply for an order calling on the said CD
   to exhibit upon oath a true and perfect inventory of the estate of the
   within deceased.

Sworn by the above named
at
this   day of   199
Before me,

a commissioner for oaths/solicitor.

40. Affidavit–citation–intermeddling executor to obtain a grant

IN THE HIGH COURT OF JUSTICE
Family Division
[Principal] [....District] Probate Registry
In the estate of..Deceased
I, AB of   builder, make oath and say as follows:

1. CD of   deceased made and duly executed her last will and testament bearing date the   day of   199 , and thereof appointed EF to be the sole executor.

2. That I am the sole residuary legatee and devisee.

3. The said CD died on the   day of   199 , domiciled in England and Wales.

4. That there are no proceedings pending concerning the will's validity.

5. That six months have elapsed since the death of the deceased.

6. That the said EF has failed to prove the said will.

7. That the said EF has intermeddled in the estate by (state how EF has intermeddled).

8. That I wish to compel the said EF to take out probate of the said will.

Sworn by the above named
at,
this   day of   199
Before me,

a commissioner for oaths/solicitor.

41. Affidavit to lead amendment to save and except settled land

IN THE HIGH COURT OF JUSTICE
Family Division
[Principal] [....District] Probate Registry
In the estate of..Deceased
We, AB of   and CD of   make oath and say:

1. That EF of   died on the   day of   19   having appointed us executors in his last will and testament.

2. On the   day of   19   probate of the said will was granted to us at the Principal (or   District) Probate Registry.

3. There was land vested in the deceased immediately before his death which was settled previously thereto (and not by his will) and remained settled land notwithstanding his death, namely under the will of   which was proved at the (Principal or ......District) Probate Registry on the   day of   19   of which the present trustees for the purposes of the Settled Land Act 1925 are LM and NO.

4. The value of the said settled land was [or was not] included in the said grant (and is in addition to the value of the estate in the said grant).

5. We apply for an order that the said grant be amended by the addition thereto of the limitation 'save and except settled land'.

Sworn by the above named
at
this
day of   199
before me,

a commissioner for oaths/solicitor.

42. Affidavit as to alias (administration)

IN THE HIGH COURT OF JUSTICE
Family Division
[Principal] [....District] Probate Registry
In the estate of Peter Henry White, otherwise Peter White deceased.
I, Michael White, of   make oath and say as follows:
That I am the lawful son of Peter Henry White, otherwise Peter White,
of   deceased, who died on the   day of
19   intestate.

That the true name of the deceased was Peter Henry White.

That at the time of his death the said deceased held a savings account in
the National Savings Bank in the name of Peter White. That in order to
deal with the said property, it is desired that the grant should be issued
in the names of Peter Henry White, otherwise Peter White.
Sworn by the above named deponent
at
on the
before me,

a commissioner for oaths/solicitor.

43. Affidavit as to foreign law

IN THE HIGH COURT OF JUSTICE
Family Division
[Principal] [....District] Probate Registry
I, CD, of   (An advocate)) (If not an advocate the deponent's full
names and full qualifications must be stated and he must be fully con-
versant with the laws of the country) make oath and say as follows:

I am conversant with the laws and constitution of and have practised for
     years as an advocate in the courts of that country.

I have referred to the (official/notarial copy) of the last will and testament
of AB of   deceased, bearing date the   day of   199 and
now produced to me and marked 'A' and I say that the said will was made
in conformity with and is valid by the aforesaid laws and constitutions.

The aforesaid copy will is acceptable in the courts of (country) as evidence of the contents of the original will.

I am informed and verily believe (set out the facts leading to deponent's
conclusions).

In the aforesaid circumstances I say that EF and GH are according to the
aforesaid laws and constitutions the persons jointly and severally entitled
to administer the estate of the said deceased.

Sworn by the above named
at
before me,

a commissioner for oaths/solicitor.

44. Affidavit as to the insertion of advertisements for kin

IN THE HIGH COURT OF JUSTICE
Family Division
[Principal] [....District] Probate Registry
In the estate of...Deceased
I, (full names), of   make oath and say, that I am the solicitor for
(full names of administrator) who is applying for letters of administration
of the estate of (deceased's names and address) deceased:

And I further make oath and say that, acting on behalf of the said (administrator), I caused an advertisement requesting the relations (if any) of the
said deceased to apply to me. The advertisement was inserted once in
(morning, evening, or weekly and name of the newspaper and date of
advertisements) as appear in the copies of those newspapers lodged with
this application. That no application in answer to or in consequence of the
advertisements has been made to me. I have been unable to obtain any
information concerning relations (if any) of the said deceased.

Sworn by the above named
at
on the   day of   19 .
Before me,

a commissioner for oaths/solicitor.

45. Affidavit for leave to swear death

IN THE HIGH COURT OF JUSTICE
Family Division
[Principal] [....District] Probate Registry
In the estate of...Deceased
I, (full names, address and description of person applying for the grant) make oath and say that:

1. (full names, address, description, date of birth and age of person presumed to be dead) was last seen alive on the   day of 19   (1).

2. The presumed deceased died testate/intestate (2).

3. The presumed deceased had (3).

4. The presumed deceased had accounts with;

   (A Bank plc)

   (B Building Society)

   and that these accounts have not been used since the disappearance of the presumed deceased.

5. I believe the presumed deceased is dead and request that an order be made giving leave to swear that the deceased died on or since the   day of   19 .

Sworn by the above-named
at
on the
Before me,

a commissioner for oaths/solicitor.

Notes

(1)   Details of when, where, and by whom the presumed deceased was last seen his reason for being there, what were his intentions. Full details of enquiries made, and the result of those enquiries.

(2)   If testate the will should be lodged. If intestate, names, relationship and ages of those persons entitled.

(3)   Details of life insurances, and if insurance companies have accepted that he is dead, or the position they have taken.

46. Consent to trust corporation applying for a grant

IN THE HIGH COURT OF JUSTICE
Family Division
[Principal] [....District] Probate Registry
In the estate of...Deceased
Whereas (deceased's full names and address)

deceased, died on the　　　　day of　　　　19　(having made and
duly executed his last will and testament bearing date the (with codicils)
thereto wherein he appointed (names of executors) his executors and (residuary legatee and devisee) or intestate, a (insert clearings 'widow', 'bachelor' etc.) leaving [the only person entitled to his estate] (one of the persons entitled to his estate)

And whereas the said executors have renounced probate of the said will
[and codicils] and to letters of administration (with will annexed)

I (name of person consenting) the said
of
do hereby consent to letters of administration (with will annexed) of the
estate of the said deceased being granted to (name of trust company)

Dated this　　　　day of　　　　19
Signed by the said
this　　　　day of
in the presence of (disinterested witness's name, address and occupation).

47. Consent to prove a will or codicil as contained in a draft, reconstruction or copy

IN THE HIGH COURT OF JUSTICE
Family Division
[Principal] [....District] Probate Registry
In the estate of..Deceased
Whereas AB of   died on the
day of   19   leaving his last will and testament dated the
day of   19   wherein he named EF as sole executor.

And whereas the said will has been lost (or other details of the reasons why it is desired to prove a copy of the will)

And whereas I, CD of   (address and occupation) am [one of] the person[s] who would be prejudiced by the proving of the said will as contained in the [draft] [reconstruction] [copy].

Now I the said CD do hereby consent to probate of the said will as contained in the [draft] [reconstruction] [copy] being granted to the said EF.
Signed by the within-named CD
in the presence of

48. Citation to accept or refuse grant

IN THE HIGH COURT OF JUSTICE
Family Division

Elizabeth the Second, by the grace of God, of the United Kingdom of Great Britain and Northern Ireland and of our other realms and territories, Queen, head of the Commonwealth, Defender of the Faith:
To (1)   of
Whereas it appears by the affidavit of (2)
sworn on the   day of   19   that (3)
of   died on the   day of   19
[having made and duly executed his last will and testament dated the
day of   19   [now remaining in the Principal Registry of the Family Division] and [thereof appointed you the sole executor] [wherein he did not appoint an executor] [wherein he named you the sole residuary legatee and devisee for life]] (4)
[and that the deceased died intestate a [widower] [widow] (5) or any other person entitled by virtue of any enactment]
leaving (6)   the lawful (7)
NOW THIS IS TO COMMAND YOU (6)
that within eight days of service hereof upon you, inclusive of the day of such service, you do cause an appearance to be entered for you in the Principal Registry of the Family Division of Our High Court of Justice at Somerset House, Strand, London WC2R 1LP (*or* in the District Probate Registry at   ) and accept or refuse [a grant of probate of the said will] [letters of administration (with will annexed)] [letters of administration] of all the estate which by law devolves to and vests in the personal representative of the said deceased or show cause why a grant should not be granted to [you] (8).
AND TAKE NOTICE that in default of your appearing and accepting and extracting [probate of the said will (4)] as aforesaid our said court will proceed to grant [letters of administration (with will annexed)] [letters of administration] to the said (9)
notwithstanding your absence.

Dated at   this   day of   19
Extracted by
of   Solicitor
Signed   District
          Judge/Registrar

Notes

(1)   Full name(s) and address(es) of each person being cited.
(2)   Full names of citor.
(3)   Full name and address of the deceased.
(4)   Or as the case may be.
(5)   Insert any further clearing.
(6)   Name of citee.
(7)   Relationship of citee to deceased.
(8)   Name of other person entitled if appropriate.
(9)   Name of citor or other person entitled as appropriate.

49. Citation to propound paper writing

IN THE HIGH COURT OF JUSTICE
Family Division
[Principal] [....District] Probate Registry
Elizabeth the Second, by the grace of God, of the United Kingdom and Northern Ireland and of our other realms and territories Queen, Head of the Commonwealth, Defender of the Faith:

To EF of   in the county of
Whereas it appears by the affidavit of CD sworn on the   day of
        19   , that AB of   died on the   day of
        19   , a widow, leaving the said CD, her son and and the only person entitled to her estate: and whereas it appears by the said affidavit that the said deceased left a certain paper writing purporting to be a will whereby she appointed you the said EF sole executor and residuary legatee and devisee.

Now this is to command you the said EF that within eight days after service hereof on you inclusive of the day of such service you do cause an appearance to be entered in the Principal Registry of the Family Division of the High Court of Justice (or the District Probate Registry) at and propound the said paper writing should you think it for your interest so to do, or show cause why letters of administration of all the estate which by law devolves to and vests in the personal representative of the said deceased should not be granted to the said CD. And take notice that in default of your so appearing and doing as aforesaid our said court will proceed to grant letters of administration of the said estate to the said CD your absence notwithstanding.

Dated at London this   day of   19   , and in the year of our reign.

Extracted by
of   (Signed)
solicitor   registrar

50. Citation to take probate against an executor who has intermeddled

IN THE HIGH COURT OF JUSTICE
Family Division
[Principal] [....District] Probate Registry
Elizabeth the Second, by the grace of God, of the United Kingdom and Northern Ireland and of our other realms and territories Queen, Head of the Commonwealth, Defender of the Faith:

To EF of   in the county of   .

Whereas it appears by the affidavit of CD sworn the   day of 19   that AB   of   died   on   the   day   of 19   as aforesaid, having made and duly executed his last will and testament bearing date the   day of   19   now remaining in the Principal Registry of the Family Division of the High Court of Justice) or (District Probate Registry), and thereof appointed you the said EF sole executor, and that the said CD is interested in the estate of the said deceased under the said will.

And whereas it is alleged in the said affidavit that you the said EF have intermeddled in the estate of the said deceased:

Now this is to command you the said EF that within eight days after service hereof on you, inclusive of the day of such service, you do cause an appearance to be entered in the Principal Registry of the Family Division or (District Probate Registry)

and show cause why you should not be ordered to take probate of the said will.

Dated at London this   day of   19   and in the year of our reign.

Extracted by
of
solicitor.

51. Power of attorney to take administration (with will annexed)

IN THE HIGH COURT OF JUSTICE
Family Division
[Principal] [....District] Probate Registry
In the estate of..Deceased

1. Whereas (full names and address of deceased) Deceased, died on the   day of   19   domiciled in England and Wales having made and duly executed his last will and testament bearing date the   day of   19   and in the said will appointed (full names of executor donating this power) the sole executor thereof.

2. I, the said (the executor) presently residing at (full address) do hereby nominate, constitute and appoint (name, address and occupation of attorney) to be my lawful attorney for the purpose of obtaining letters of administration (with will annexed) of the estate of the said deceased to be granted to him for my use and benefit until I shall apply for and obtain probate of the said will and I hereby promise to ratify and confirm whatever my said attorney shall lawfully do or cause to be done in the premises.

In witness whereof I have hereunto set my hand this day of 19 .

Signed by the said   .
In the presence of   .

52. Power of attorney to take administration

IN THE HIGH COURT OF JUSTICE
Family Division
[Principal] [....District] Probate Registry
In the estate of...Deceased

1. Whereas (full names, address and occupation of deceased) deceased, died on the   day of   19 , domiciled in England and Wales, intestate, leaving (names and entitlement of person donating the power).

2. I, the said (full names of person giving power)   presently residing at (   ) do hereby nominate, constitute and appoint (full names, address and occupation of attorney) to be my lawful attorney for the purpose of obtaining letters of administration of the estate of the said deceased to be granted to him for my use and benefit until further representation be granted and I hereby promise to ratify and confirm whatever my said attorney shall lawfully do or cause to be done in the premises.

In witness whereof I have hereunto set my hand
this   day of   19 .
Signed by the said   .
In the presence of   .

53. Power of attorney for probate in Jersey

TO ALL OF WHOM these presents shall come, I, ... (executor) of .... in the County of ...., England, SEND
GREETING:

WHEREAS .... (deceased) of .... in the County of
................, England, died on the .... day of ....
19 .... at ...., domiciled in England and Wales:

WHEREAS on the .... day of .... 19.... administration of all
the estate which by law devolves to and vests in the personal representatives of the deceased was granted to me by the High Court of Justice
[............ Registry], as the sole executor named in the will of the
deceased;

AND WHEREAS certain of the assets which belonged to the deceased are
situate in the Island of Jersey and for the purpose of taking possession of
and dealing with the same it is necessary for me, as Executor as aforesaid, to take out probate of the Estate of the said deceased in the said
Island of Jersey;

NOW THEREFORE I, the said .... (executor) do hereby name,
constitute and appoint ...., solicitor, of .... in the
Island of Jersey, to be my true and lawful attorney in the said Island of
Jersey with full power and authority to and for my said attorney in my
name and on my behalf, as executor as aforesaid, to make application to
the Royal Court (Probate Division) of the said Island of Jersey for a grant
of probate for the purpose of dealing with the said personal estate of the
deceased in the said Island of Jersey and to take the customary oath of
office of executor as my lawfully constituted attorney:

ALSO to do all acts that may be necessary or requisite in order to enable
my said attorney to claim and take possession on my behalf, as executor
aforesaid, of the personal estate of the deceased situate in Jersey aforesaid
and to do all acts, deeds, matters and things that may be necessary or
requisite in connection therewith.

AND I agree to ratify and confirm all and whatsoever my said attorney
shall lawfully do or cause to be done by virtue of these presents.

IN WITNESS WHEREOF I have hereunto set my hand in the presence of
the undersigned witness:

Signed by the said ....
on the .... day of ....
One thousand nine hundred and ninety .... in the presence of:

54. Inventory and accounts

IN THE HIGH COURT OF JUSTICE
Family Division
[Principal] [....District] Probate Registry
In the estate of...Deceased

I, (personal representative's names and address) make oath and say that the following is a true and complete inventory of the assets of the estate of   deceased which have come to my hands:

(here list all of the assets and their values)

I further make oath and say that no other estate of the said deceased has come to my hands or knowledge since the date of death.

Sworn by the above named deponent
at
this   day of 19
Before me,

a commissioner for oaths/solicitor.

55. Deed of disclaimer

THIS DISCLAIMER made the   day of   one thousand
nine hundred and ninety   by Mrs   (hereinafter called
'Mrs   ') WITNESSES that Mrs   HEREBY DISCLAIMS ALL
THAT interest in the estate of   ('the testator') devolving upon Mrs
         by virtue of the will dated the   day of   19   of
the testator who died on the   day of   19   AND
Mrs   DECLARES that she has not in any way entered into possession of the said interest and that she has not done any act or thing that
might be or amount to an acceptance of the said interest.

Executed and Delivered as a Deed on the date of this document

Signed by Mrs
Witnessed by:
Signature
Name
Address
Occupation   .

56. Application for a standing search for a grant

IN THE HIGH COURT OF JUSTICE
Family Division
[Principal] [....District] Probate Registry
I/We apply for the entry of a standing search so that there shall be sent to me/us an office copy of every grant of representation in England and Wales in the estate of:
Full name of deceased:
Full address:
Alternative or alias names:
Exact date of death:
which either has issued not more than twelve months before the entry of this application or issues within six months thereafter
Signed:
Name in block letters:
Full address:
Reference No. (if any)

57. Caveat

IN THE HIGH COURT OF JUSTICE

Family Division

The ....District Probate Registry

Let no grant be sealed in the estate of (full name and address) deceased, who died on the   day of   19   at   without notice to (name of party by whom or on whose behalf the caveat is entered).

Dated this   day of   19

Signed (to be signed by the caveator's solicitor or by the caveator if acting in person)

whose address for service is:

Solicitor for the said

(If the caveator is acting in person, substitute 'In person').

Cost for entering caveat (and for an extension): £4.00.

Duration six months.

58. Warning to caveator

IN THE HIGH COURT OF JUSTICE
Family Division
The Leeds District Probate Registry

To   of   a party who has entered a caveat in the estate of   deceased.

You have eight days (starting with the day on which this warning was served on you):

(i) to enter an appearance either in person or by your solicitor, at the Leeds District Probate Registry setting out what interest you have in the estate of the above-named   of   deceased, contrary to that of the party at whose instance this warning is issued;

or

(ii) if you have no contrary interest but wish to show cause against the sealing of a grant to such party, to issue and serve a summons for directions by a district judge of the Principal Registry or a registrar of a District Probate Registry.

If you fail to do either of these, the court may proceed to issue a grant of probate or administration in the said estate notwithstanding your caveat.

Dated the   day of   19

Issued at the instance of

(name of person warning the caveat)
(date of the will) if any
(details of the interest of the person warning)
(the solicitor's name and the address for service)   Registrar
Lodge either personally or by post.

59. Affidavit of service of warning and of non-receipt of summons for direction

IN THE HIGH COURT OF JUSTICE
Family Division
The Leeds District Probate Registry

I, CD of (description), make oath and say, that on the day of 19 I duly served Messrs of (solicitors for) with a true copy of the warning now produced to me and marked A, by delivering to and leaving the said copy with a member of the firm of the said Messrs at their office aforesaid before the hour of 4 in the afternoon (12 noon on Saturdays) [or by sending the same by prepaid registered post or recorded delivery to their office aforesaid].

I further say that no summons for directions under paragraph (10) of Non-Contentious Probate Rule 44 has been received by my said firm.

60. Appearance to a warning

IN THE HIGH COURT OF JUSTICE
Family Division
The Leeds District Probate Registry
In the estate of ....Deceased
Caveat No.   dated the   day of   19
Full name and address of deceased:
Full name and address of person warning (1)
Full name and address of caveator
(2)
ENTER AN APPEARANCE for the above-named caveator in this matter.
Dated the   day of   19
Signed
Solicitors for
whose address for service is

Notes

(1)   Insert the interest as set out in the warning.
(2)   Insert the interest in the estate of the caveator and the date of the will, if any, under
         which the interest arises.

61. Authority to solicitors to open building society account

Re...Deceased

I/we the personal representative[s] of ...... deceased hereby authorise and request Messrs ...... solicitors to deposit all money received into this estate into building society accounts until such time as the administration of the estate is completed. I/we understand that the interest received into the accounts will be distributed among the beneficiaries according to their entitlement.

....Signed (the personal representative).

62. Specimen advertisement for the London Gazette

The Office of the London Gazette
Atlantic House (Room B82)
Holborn Viaduct
London EC1P 1BN
Dear Sirs

....Deceased

Please insert the following advertisement in the next issue of the London Gazette under 'Notices Pursuant to the Trustee Act (notices for claims)' and forward to us a copy of the insertion. Our cheque for £...... is enclosed:

(i) 'SMITH, Albert Basil / (ii) 1 King Road, Smithtown, Westshire, retired
engineer,
1 January 1986 / (iii) Joe Bloggs, 12 Hewers Lane, Smithtown (Joe Bloggs). (iv) 1 July 1986'.

Yours faithfully

Notes: Before writing, you should telephone the London Gazette and ask the price of the advertisement because payment must be submitted before the advertisement is printed.

The request for the advertisement must be signed by a solicitor.

The sequence of details to be inserted is as follows: (i) name of deceased (surname first); (ii) address, description and date of death; (iii) names addresses and descriptions of persons to whom notices of claims are to be given and names (in parenthesis) of personal representatives; (iv) date before which notices of claims are to be given.

(The current fee at 1 March 1995 is £32.00 plus VAT plus £1.45 for a copy gazette).

63. Specimen advertisement for local newspaper

....Deceased

NOTICE is hereby given PURSUANT TO SECTION 27 OF THE TRUSTEE ACT 1925 that any person having a claim against or an interest in the estate of .... deceased, late of .... (address) and who died on .... (date) and whose will was proved on ....(date) is hereby required to send particulars in writing of his or her claim or interest to the undersigned and to send such particulars not later than (date, which must be at least two months after the date the advertisement is to be published) after which date the personal representatives will distribute the estate among the persons entitled thereto having regard only to the claims and interests of which they have had notice and will not, as respects the property so distributed, be liable to any person of whose claim they shall not then have had notice.

Dated......................

Signed .... (name)(address)

Personal Representative.

64. Letter of request

LETTER OF REQUEST

Please complete in typewriting or in block capitals

above this line for Registrar's use only

REQUEST BY EXECUTORS OR ADMINISTRATORS OF A DECEASED HOLDER TO BE PLACED ON THE REGISTER AS HOLDERS IN THEIR OWN RIGHT.

Full name and address of undertaking	TO THE DIRECTORS OF

*Full description of security

Number or amount of shares, stock or other security and, in figures column only, number and denomination of units if any	WORDS	FIGURES
		(units of)

Full name of deceased ....Deceased

late of ....

I/We, the undersigned, being the personal representative(s) of the above-named deceased, hereby request you to register me/us in the books of the Company as the holder(s) of the above-mentioned Stock/Shares now registered in the name of the said deceased.

Dated this ....day of ....19........

Signature(s) of Personal Representative(s)

....,..................

....

....

Full name(s) and full postal address(es) (including post code(s) of the personal representative(s)) in the order in which they are to be registered

Please state title, if any, or whether Mr, Mrs or Miss

IF AN ACCOUNT ALREADY EXISTS IN THE ABOVE NAME(S) IN THE SAME ORDER THE ABOVE-MENTIONED HOLDING WILL BE ADDED TO THAT ACCOUNT, UNLESS INSTRUCTIONS ARE GIVEN TO THE CONTRARY.

The Certificate(s) in the name of the deceased if not already with the Company's Registrars must accompany this form	Stamp or name and address of person lodging this form.

No stamp duty is payable on this form in the case of a company registered in England; in the case of a company registered in Scotland stamp duty may be payable

A separate Letter of Request should be used for each class of security.

This form must be returned to: The Registrar

....(Name of Company)

....(Address)

....

....

Request by executors or administrators to be placed on register

Form F156
© Fourmat Publishing
27 & 28 St Albans Place
London N1 0NX
August 1984

This form is approved by the Institute of Chartered Secretaries and Administrators.

65. Stock transfer form

STOCK TRANSFER FORM

(Above this line for Registrars only)

Certificate lodged with Registrar

Consideration Money £ ....

(for completion by the Registrar/Stock Exchange)

Name of Undertaking

Description of Security

Number or amount of Shares, Stock or other security and, in figures column only, number and denomination of units, if any

Words | Figures

(units of   )

Name(s) of registered Holder(s) should be given in full: the address should be given where there is only one holder

If the transfer is not made by the registered holder(s) insert also the name(s) and capacity (e.g., Executor(s)) of the person(s) making the transfer.

In the name(s) of

I/We hereby transfer the above security out of the name(s) aforesaid to the person(s) named below.

Signature(s) of transferor(s)

Stamp of Selling Broker(s) or, for transactions which are not stock exchange transactions, of Agent(s), if any, acting for the Transferor(s)

1. ....
2. ....
3. ....
4. ....

Bodies corporate should execute under their common seal

Date..

Full name(s) and full postal address(es) (including County or, if applicable, Postal District number) of the person(s) to whom the security is transferred.

Please state title, if any, or whether Mr., Mrs., or Miss.

Please complete in typewriting or in BLOCK CAPITALS.

I/We request that such entries be made in the register as are necessary to give effect to this transfer.

Stamp of Buying Broker(s) (if any)

Stamp or name and address of person lodging this form (if other than the Buying Broker(s)

Form F151 (Formerly S1)

Meredith Fournat

Tel: 0161-745 8222

Reverse side of stock transfer form

FORM OF CERTIFICATE REQUIRED WHERE TRANSFER IS EXEMPT FROM STAMP DUTY

Instruments executed on or after 1st May 1987 effecting transactions within the following categories are exempt from stamp duty:–

A. The vesting of property subject to a trust in the trustees of the trust on the appointment of a new trustee, or in the continuing trustees on the retirement of a trustee.

B. The conveyance or transfer of propety the subject of a specific devise or legacy to the beneficiary named in the will (or his nominee). Transfers in satisfaction of a general legacy of money should not be included in this category (see category D below).

C. The conveyance or transfer of property which forms part of an intestate's estate to the person entitled on intestacy (or his nominee). Transfers in satisfaction of the transferee's entitlement to cash in the estate of an intestate, where the total value of the residuary estate exceeds that sum, should not be included in this category (see category D below).

D. The appropriation of property within section 84(4) of the Finance Act 1985 (death: appropriation in satisfaction of a general legacy of money) or section 84(5) or (7) of that Act (death: appropriation in satisfaction of any interest of surviving spouse and in Scotland also of any interest of issue.

E. The conveyance and transfer of property which forms part of the residuary estate of a testator to a beneficiary (or his nominee) entitled solely by virtue of his entitlement under the will.

F. The conveyance and transfer of property out of a settlement in or towards satisfaction of a beneficiary's interest, not being an interest aquired for money or money's worth, being a conveyance or transfer constituting a distribution of property in accordance with the provisions of the settlement.

G. The conveyance and transfer of property on and in consideration only of marriage to a party to the marriage (or his nominee) or to trustees to be held on the terms of a settlement made in consideration only of the marriage. A transfer to a spouse after the date of marriage is not within this category, unless made pusuant to an ante-nuptial contract.

H. The conveyance or transfer of property within section 83(1) of the Finance Act 1985 (transfers in connection with divorce etc.).

I. The conveyance or transfer by the liquidator of property which formed part of the assets of the company in liquidation to a shareholder of that company (or his nominee) in or towards satisfaction of the shareholder's rights on a winding-up.

J. The grant in fee simple of an easement in or over land for no consideration in money or money's worth.

K. The grant of a servitude for no consideration in money or money's worth.

L. The conveyance or transfer of property operating as a voluntary disposition inter vivos for no consideration in money or money's worth nor any consideration referred to in section 57 of the Stamp Act 1891 (conveyance in consideration of a debt etc.).

M. The conveyance or transfer of property by an instrument within section 84(1) of the Finance Act 1985 (death: varying disposition).

(1) Delete as appropriate. (2) Insert "(A)","(B)" or appropriate category. (3) Delete second sentence if the certificate is given by the transferor or his solicitor.	(1) I/We hereby certify that the transaction in respect of which this transfer is made is one which falls within the category(2) .... above. (1)I/We confirm that (1)I/We have been duly authorised by the transferor to sign this certificate and that the facts of the transaction are within (1)my/our knowledge (3)

Signature(s)   *Description ("Transferor", "Solicitor", etc.)*

....

....

....

....

Date .... *19*..........   ....

NOTES

(1) If the above certificate has been completed, this transfer does not need to be submitted to the Controller of Stamps but should be sent directly to the Company or its Registrars.

(2) If the above certificate is not completed, this transfer must be submitted to the Controller of Stamps and duly stamped . (See below).

FORM OF CERTIFICATE REQUIRED WHERE TRANSFER IS NOT EXEMPT BUT IS NOT LIABLE TO *AD VALOREM* STAMP DUTY

Instruments of transfer, other than those in respect of which the above certificate has been completed, are liable to a fixed duty of 50p when the transaction falls within one of the following categories:–

(a) Transfer by way of security for a loan or re-transfer to the original transferor on repayment of a loan.

(b) Transfer, not on sale and not arising under any contract of sale and where no beneficial interest in the property passes: (i) to a person who is a mere nominee of, and is nominated only by, the tranferor; (ii) from a mere nominee who has at all times held the property on behalf of the transferee; (iii) from one nominee to another nominee of the same beneficial owner where the first nominee has at all times held the property on behalf of that beneficial owner (NOTE:–This category does not include a transfer made in any of the following circumstances: (i) by a holder of stock, etc., following the grant of an option to purchase the stock, to the person entitled to the option or his nominee; (ii) to a nominee in contemplation of a contract for the sale of stock, etc., then about to be entered into; (iii) from the nominee of a vendor, who has instructed the nominee orally or by some unstamped writing to hold stock, etc., in trust for a purchaser, to such purchaser.)

(1) Delete as appropriate (2) Insert "(a)" or "(b)" (3) Here set out concisely the facts explaining the transaction Adjudication may be required	(1) I/We hereby certify that the transaction in respect of which this transfer is made is one which falls within the category(2) .... above. (3) ....

....

....

....

Date .... *19*..........   Signature ....

                                   Description ....

....

....

Transferors Transferees

NOTE–The above certificate should be signed either by all the transferors and transferees, or a member of a Stock Exchange or a Solicitor acting for one or the other of the parties, or an accredited representative of a bank. In other cases the certificate should be signed by a Solicitor or other person (e.g. a bank acting as trustee or executor) having full knowledge of the facts.

Appendix 6

Part A

District Probate Registries and Sub-Registries: telephone and address list

BIRMINGHAM
The Priory Courts
33 Bull St, Birmingham B4 6DU
DX: 701990 Birmingham 7
Tel (0121) 681 3400
(0121) 681 3414.
Fax (0121) 681 3404.

Registrar: C F Marsh
Chief Clerk: Miss P Walbeoff

Probate Offices
Coventry
Northampton
Kidderminster
Wolverhampton
Lichfield

Stoke on Trent
Combined Court Centre
Bethesda St, Hanley
Stoke on Trent ST1 3BP
DX: 20736 Hanley
Tel (01782) 213736.
Fax (01782) 201944.

Chief Clerk: Mrs H Bateman
(acting)

Probate Offices
Crewe
Stafford
Shrewsbury

BRIGHTON
William Street
Brighton BN2 2LG
DX: 98073 Brighton (3)
Tel (01273) 684071.
Fax (01273) 688281.

Registrar: M N Emery
Chief Clerk: P R Ellwood

Probate Offices
Chichester
Hastings
Crawley

Maidstone
The Law Courts, Barker Road
Maidstone ME18 8EW
DX: 51972 Maidstone 2
Tel (01622) 754966, Ext 234/235.

Chief Clerk: Mrs B Phillips

Probate Offices
Canterbury
Folkestone
Chatham
Tunbridge Wells

BRISTOL
Ground Floor
The Crescent Centre, Temple Back
Bristol BS1 6EP
DX: 94400 Bristol 5
Tel (0117) 273915
   (0117) 264619.
Fax (0117) 259377.

Registrar: R Joyce
Chief Clerk: P F Curran

Probate Offices
Bath
Weston-Super-Mare

Bodmin
Market Street, Bodmin
Cornwall PL31 2JW
DX: 81858 Bodmin
Tel (01208) 72279.

Chief Clerk: R T Longshaw

Probate Offices
Plymouth
Truro
Penzance

Exeter
Eastgate House, High Street
Exeter, Devon EX4 3JZ
DX: 8380 Exeter
Tel (01392) 74515.

Chief Clerk:

Probate Offices
Barnstaple
Yeovil
Newton Abbott
Taunton

CARDIFF
Probate Registry of Wales
PO Box 474
2 Park St, Cardiff CF1 1ET
Tel (01222) 376467.
Fax (01222) 376479.

Registrar: R F Yeldman
Chief Clerk: J L Walker

Probate Offices
Bridgend
Pontypridd
Newport

Bangor
1st Floor Bron Castell
High Street, Bangor
Gwynedd LL57 1YS
Tel (01248) 362410.

Chief Clerk: R Perry

Carmarthen
14 King Street Carmarthen
Dyfed SA31 1BL
DX: 51420 Carmarthen
Tel (01267) 236238.

Chief Clerk: B M Lee

Probate Offices
Aberystwyth
Swansea
Haverfordwest

IPSWICH
Level 3, Haven House
17 Lower Brook Street
Ipswich, Suffolk IP4 1DN
DX: 3279 Ipswich
Tel (01473) 253724
(01473) 259261.
Fax (01473) 280889.

Registrar: E R Alexander
Chief Clerk: D N Mee

Probate Offices
Chelmsford
Colchester

Norwich
Combined Court Building
The Law Courts, Bishopgate
Norwich NR3 1UR
DX: 5202 Norwich
Tel (01603) 761776.

Chief Clerk: H R Oates

Probate Office
Lowestoft

Peterborough
1st Floor, Crown Buildings
Rivergate PE1 1EJ
DX: 12327 Peterborough 1
Tel (01733) 62802.

Chief Clerk: Mrs P Pinnington

Probate Offices
Cambridge
King's Lynn

LEEDS
3rd Floor Coronet House
Queen Street
Leeds LS1 2BA
DX: 26451 Leeds (Park Square)
Tel (0113) 431505.
Fax (0113) 448145.

Registrar: A P Dawson
Chief Clerk: Mrs J Hardman

Probate Offices
Bradford
Wakefield
Harrogate
Huddersfield

Lincoln
Mill House, Brayford Side North
Lincoln LN1 1YW
DX: 11048 Lincoln 1
Tel (01522) 523648.

Chief Clerk: Mrs E Moorfoot

Probate Office
Grimsby

Sheffield
The Court House, Castle Street
Sheffield S3 8LW
DX: 26054 Sheffield 2
Tel (0114) 29920.

Chief Clerk: Mrs S L Holding

Probate Offices
Chesterfield
Doncaster

LIVERPOOL
Queen Elizabeth II Law Courts
Derby Square, Liverpool
L2 1XA
DX: 14246 Liverpool
Tel (0151) 236 8264.
Fax (0151) 236 5575.

Registrar: B J Thomas
Chief Clerk: C W Fox

Probate Offices
St Helens
Southport
Wallasey

Chester
5th Floor Hamilton House
Hamilton Place, Chester
CH1 2DA
DX: 22162 Chester Northgate
Tel (01244) 345082.

Chief Clerk: Mrs W M Bevan

Probate Offices
Rhyl
Wrexham

Lancaster
Mitre House, Church Street
Lancaster
LA1 1HE
DX: 63509 Lancaster
Tel (01524) 36625.
Chief Clerk: Mrs N A Willis

Probate Offices
Barrow
Blackpool
Preston

MANCHESTER
9th Floor Astley House
23 Quay Street, Manchester
M3 4AT
DX: 14387 Manchester 1
Tel (0161) 834 4319.
Fax (0161) 834 5651.

Registrar: M A Moran
Chief Clerk: P A Burch

Probate Offices
Bolton
Wigan
Nelson
Stockport
Oldham
Warrington

Nottingham
Upper Ground Floor
Lambert House
Talbot Street, Nottingham
NG1 5NR
DX: 10055 Nottingham
Tel (0115) 414288.
Fax (0115) 243374.

Chief Clerk: J Hill

Probate Offices
Derby
Mansfield

NEWCASTLE
2nd Floor Plummer House
Croft Street
Newcastle Upon Tyne NE1 6NP
DX: 61081 Newcastle Upon Tyne
Tel (0191) 261 8383.
Fax (0191) 233 0868.

Registrar: P Sanderson
Chief Clerk: Mrs M C Riley

Probate Office
Morpeth

Carlisle
Courts of Justice, Earl Street
Carlisle CA1 1DJ
DX: 63034 Carlisle
Tel (01228) 21751.

(For Chief Clerk see Newcastle
DPR)

Probate Office
Workington

Middlesbrough
Teeside Combined Court Centre
Russell Street, Middlesbrough
Cleveland TS1 2AE
DX: 60536 Middlesbrough
Tel (016212) 340001
Fax (016212) 232947.

Chief Clerk: Miss F M Kelly

Probate Offices
Darlington
Sunderland
Durham

York
Duncombe Place, York
YO1 2EA
DX: 61543 York
Tel (01904) 624210.
Fax (01904) 624210.

Chief Clerk: R Tunnicliffe

Probate Offices
Hull
Scarborough

OXFORD
10a New Road, Oxford
OX1 1LY
DX: 4337 Oxford
Tel (01865) 241163.
Fax (01865) 204402.

Registrar: R R D'Costa
Chief Clerk: P L Gannaway

Probate Offices
Aylesbury
Swindon
Slough
Reading
High Wycombe

Gloucester
2nd Fl. Combined Court Building
Kimbrose Way, Gloucester
GL1 2DG
DX: 7537 Gloucester
Tel (01452) 522585.

Chief Clerk: Miss R C Meats

Probate Offices
Cheltenham
Worcester
Hereford

Leicester
Leicester House, 5th Floor
Lee Circle, Leicester
LE1 3RE
DX: 13655 Leicester 4
Tel (0116) 538558.

Chief Clerk: J T Shaw

Probate Offices
Bedford
Kettering

WINCHESTER
4th Floor Cromwell House
Andover Road, Winchester
Hant SO23 7EW
DX: 96900 Winchester 2
Tel (01962) 853046
    (01962) 863771.
Fax (01962) 877371.

Registrar: A K Biggs
Chief Clerk: Mrs S Halligan

Probate Offices
Basingstoke
Newport IOW
Bournemouth
Portsmouth
Dorchester
Salisbury
Guildford
Southampton

Part B
General addresses

Bonds and Stock Office
Blackpool
Lancs
FY3 9YP

Chartered Accountants (if name or
address changed)
The Institute of Chartered
Accountants
Gloucester House
399 Silbury Boulevard
Central Milton Keynes
MK9 2HL
Tel (0171) 920 8100.

The Principal
Court Funds Office
22 Kingsway
London WC2B 6LE.

CTO addresses
Inland Revenue
Capital Taxes Office
Ferrers House
PO Box 38
Castle Meadow Road
Nottingham
NG2 1BB
DX: 701201 Nottingham 4
(pre grant – DX: 701202
Nottingham 4)
Tel IHT General Enquiries
(0115) 974 2400
Customer Service
(0115) 974 2424.

Shares Valuation Division
Inland Revenue
Shares Valuation Division
Fitz Roy House
PO Box 46

Castle Meadow Road
Nottingham
NG2 1BD
DX: 701203 Nottingham 4
Tel (0115) 974 2222.

Northern Ireland
Level 3
Dorchester House
52–58 Great Victoria Street
Belfast
BT2 7QL
Tel (01232) 236633.

Scotland
Mulberry House
16 Picardy Place
Edinburgh EH1 3NB
DX: ED 305
Tel (0131) 556 8511.

The National Association of
Prepaid Funeral Plans
618 Warwick Road
Solihull
West Midlands
B91 1AA.

The Funeral Standards Council
30 North Road
Cardiff
CF1 3DY.

Investment Management
Regulatory Organisation
(IMRO)
Imro Ltd
Centre Point
103 New Oxford Street
London WC1A 1PT.

The Insurance Brokers Registration
Council
15 St Helens Place
London
EC3A 6DS
Tel (0171) 588 4387.

The Association of British Insurers
51 Gresham Street
London
EC2V 7HQ
Tel (0171) 600 3333.

The Registrar of Friendly Societies
15 Great Marlborough Street
London
W1V 2LL
Tel (0171) 437 9992.

The Insurance Ombudsman Bureau
City Gate 1
135 Park Street
London
SE1 9EA.

Life Assurance and Regulatory
Organisation (Lautro)
Lautro Ltd
Centre Point
103 New Oxford Street
London WC1A 1QH.

National Savings Bank
Glasgow
G58 1SB.

OPCS
Office of Population Censuses and
Surveys
General Register Office
Smedley Hydro
Trafalgar Road
Birkdale
Southport
Merseyside

PR8 2HH
Tel (0151) 471 4200 or (01704)
569 824.

Post-war credits

HMIT
PWC Centre
Ty Glas
Llanishen
Cardiff
CF4 5TX
Request: repayment of PWC form
DC 351 (new).

Savings Certificate and SAYE
Office
Durham
DH99 1NS.

St Catherines House (Registrar
births, marriages and deaths)
Smedley Hydro
Trafalgar Road
Birkdale
Southport
Merseyside
PR8 2HH
Tel (0151) 471 4200.

The Supreme Court Taxing Office
(Court of Protection Branch)
Room 271
Royal Courts of Justice
The Strand
London WC2A 2LL.

T.V. Licensing
Bristol
BS98 1TL

The Unit Trust Association
65 Kingsway
London
WC2B 6TD
Tel (0171) 831 0898.

War Pensions Directorate
Norcross
Blackpool
FY5 3TA
Tel (01253) 858 858.

Index